MW00906345

# DIVORCE

## A GUIDED TOUR

# Suzanne Hillier

Suzanne L. Hillier
32 Stanford Drive,
Rancho Mirage, CA. 92270
E-mail: szhillier@gmail.com

The anecdotes set forth in this book are based on actual incidents. They all occurred in the Canadian Courts. Federal and State Laws may vary in your locale. Be sure to check all pertinent laws in your area with your attorney All names, some of the professions and a few of the locations mentioned have been deliberately changed to protect the privacy of the individuals involved. This Summary is only meant as a guide to point the way. Hopefully, your attorney will fill in the specific details relating to your case.

Library of Congress Cataloging in Publication
Hillier, Suzanne L.
Divorce/A Guided Tour
Printed in the United States
Divorce ~ A Guided Tour/ by Suzanne L. Hillier

NON FICTION/How To/Legal

ISBN: - 10: 1466219831
ISBN: - 13:978-1466219830

PUBLISHING

Palm Desert, CA 92211

# Praise for Divorce ~ A Guided Tour

*"A must read for anyone involved in divorce proceedings."*
**~ Thomas Smotrich, Attorney"**

*"Valuable advice on how to to avoid unnecessary legal fees."*
**~ Ron Sharrow, Attorney & Novelist**

*"A tour of the unintended consequences when divorce mistakes are made. Don't do it that way!"*
**~ Dr. Judi Hollis, Arthur, Licensed Family & Marriage Counselor**.

# Dedication

For Garth Macdonald

# Table of Contents

# Prologue

Marriage vows include the phrase,
*"...until death do us part."*
Probably because death is so much cheaper and emotionally
less draining than divorce!

*~Anonymous*

# Introduction

This book is not for attorneys. It is not a *law book* even though it concerns a smattering of law. It is a book for you, if you are faced with the prospect of ending a marriage, or are at the beginning, or in the middle, of that sometimes earth shattering trauma of life known as divorce.

For over thirty years, I have represented, comforted, supported — and yes, also lectured and berated — some ten thousand clients who have come to me for help while in the process of dissolving their marriages.

A portion of them have literally breezed through the entire process and have emerged stronger and happier than before the separation. Most often, these were individuals for whom separation meant a happy relief from a miserable union. They had independent careers, were childless, or had children who were already independent, and, more importantly, had a significant other already in the wings or often in the nest.

For others, divorce meant misery, financial and emotional insecurity, resentment, vindictiveness and ongoing frustration. So eager were some clients to get revenge on the spouse who initiated the separation, that they ruined their unfaithful mate's career, ignoring the fact that in the process, they undermined their own financial security.

Some were rendered so irate by their spouse's wish to end the marriage, that, instead of considering an early, guilt-inspired, handsome offer of settlement, they insisted on pursuing revenge through the courts, ending up with so much less.

Still others spent thousands of dollars in legal fees, pursuing phantom money. Others refused to sell joint assets, sabotaging the marketing of properties so that they, as well as the despised spouse, ultimately ended up the losers.

Then there were those despicable individuals, who, indifferent or ignorant of their children's mental health, mounted crusades to alienate them from the estranged spouse. They succeeded, only to end up with broken children, whose battered self-esteem forever undermined their scholastic and emotional futures.

People do stupid and harmful things when they are upset. They ruin themselves financially and they ruin their children emotionally. They spend needless thousands in legal fees merely because they refuse to grant the label *joint custody* to the other parent. On occasion, they permit themselves to be exploited by unscrupulous attorneys who take advantage of their ignorance and *keep the meter running* to their own financial advantage.

For the last thirty years, I have witnessed women so angry with their husbands that they did things that would render them certifiable under any other circumstances. I have seen fathers frustrated and depressed beyond belief when they were denied access to their much loved children for weeks or even months. As a consequence, they were forced to spend thousands of dollars in legal fees just so they could exercise their prerogative of being a dad.

I have seen physically abused spouses, male and female, and clients who *lost it* and paid dearly as a result.

This guide attempts to pinpoint and address, in a practical way, many of the issues of law which trouble the ordinary individual going through a divorce.

You may not always agree with my recommendations. For example, I do not advise confessing infidelity. Nor do I advise severing a relationship because of a single sexual lapse or even a brief affair, provided it is no longer ongoing. But I do advise taking advantage of guilt and timing. I take a practical approach based on my own past observations. You'll find that it works and in the long run it will save you considerable money and maybe even considerable heartache.

I do not gloss over the facts. There are bad attorneys and judges as well as excellent attorneys and judges; judges so astute and sensitive it is an honor to appear before them.

There are men who would cheat, hide assets and lie regarding their worth rather than give their wives their rightful share of Community or Net Family Property. There are women who are capable of the vilest acts to get even in the payback lottery. Then there are those significant others who make it a career to prevent the wife and kids from the first marriage from having sufficient funds to lead a decent life.

And then, there are the *crazies*, quite a few of them, from whom you can only protect yourself by a solid pre-nup — or flight.

To illustrate all of this, and more, I have used examples from actual incidents I have encountered in my practice. I have changed names, at times businesses, professions, places, and physical descriptions. I have no wish to embarrass any of my former clients, many of whom still phone me on occasion and for whom I have the fondest of memories.

This book focuses on issues rather than the intricacies of law, which are best left to the legal profession. As such, it can be of use to those in both Canada and the United States who are involved or will be involved in divorce proceedings.

The law, when referred to, is the law of the Province of Ontario, Canada, where all provinces have an approximately similar property regime. The Divorce Act, a federal statute, is uniform throughout Canada. The laws of the *Community Property* States, Alaska, Arizona, California, Idaho, New Mexico, Texas, Washington and Wisconsin are similar to the property laws of Canada. All of these Provinces and States have provisions to equally share property and debts accumulated during the marriage. They exclude inherited property and deduct the value of property owned before marriage.

The other States have what are known as Equitable

Distribution Laws, in which property acquired during marriage belongs to the spouse who earned it; but property must be distributed in a *fair and equitable manner.*

In these States there are no set rules and the courts look at a variety of factors. As these vary with each State, although there are many similarities between States, the reader had best rely on the advice of an attorney who can consider their unique circumstances and place of residence.

I cannot stress enough the importance of competent attornies to prepare prenuptial and separation agreements, and pre-trial motions, which are uniform throughout North America. Their experience and knowledge will be of great benefit to an individual facing divorce, regardless of their place of residence.

I want to share my experiences with you. It is my belief that despite the well known adage that ignorance is bliss, it is not bliss at all, but a looming disaster. By being aware of the mistakes made by others, you can avoid making your own. By learning from the good choices made by others, you can decide to emulate them. You can and will have a successful divorce!

This is your guided tour.

# Chapter 1
## Dishing the Dirt

He was a sturdy, red-haired, detective sergeant with a square jaw, who could put down the Hulk in an arm wrestle.

"The problem started on our wedding night. He came out of the bathroom in a long black wig, full makeup, including false eyelashes, painted fingernails and a long pink nightgown with a plunging neckline that showed a red hairy chest with no cleavage," she told me.

"I almost died," she murmured.

"I would think so," I replied, picturing the burly police officer I had seen occasionally giving evidence at court when I did criminal work.

"No previous indication of this?" I asked.

"None," she replied with conviction.

"It was," she explained, "the only way he could get himself really excited. He got off on all sorts of 'stuff'."

As if to prove it to me, she handed me a huge bag of *utensils*, for lack of a better description, including various wigs, huge women's undergarments, suspender belts and webbed stockings. There were large wooden rings — suitable for a large wooden organ — and at least six pairs of handcuffs. She asked that I keep them — in case we needed to use them as exhibits.

"Lord," I mused. "He must really get a kick out of making arrests."

She was a nice Jewish girl who had been an office manager for ten years before they met during his investigation of a real estate fraud.

"What was the attraction?" I asked.

"My last boyfriend had come out of the closet and the sergeant seemed so masculine — so really straight."

She laughed, shaking her head, and I joined her.

I thought that anyone who could keep a sense of humor under these circumstances deserved a medal — or at least, a divorce.

Although she had gone along with it, her tolerance had started to wear thin. For their last dinner date, he had worn scarlet nail polish, female underwear beneath the sports jacket and slacks and had insisted on handcuffing her on the way to the restaurant.

"It's become a real drag," she complained — which of course it was!

"When I told him I was coming here, he said, 'let's keep some things between us. You've been a party to this remember?' Then he told me that he wanted to share the kids but he didn't want to pay child support. We'd split the house money equally but his pension wasn't to be considered."

"He's being a real bastard, especially when I gave fifty thousand from my grandmother's inheritance to pay down the mortgage on our home. I just want what I'm entitled to, that's all. I've been out of the work force since the birth of my oldest child and I've got to get some re-training. All I want is a leg-up for a couple of years."

I suspected she had met someone else, but didn't ask. It always made things easier when a party had a significant other, especially if the significant other had funds. I gave her the news.

"The fifty thousand you paid toward the mortgage from your inheritance is gone. You were kind enough to reduce the debt on a joint asset and any judge will tell you that you intended to benefit your spouse. Just forget about it.

Unless he wants to give you a bit extra, you're not going to get it."[1]

I continued to explain, "We can get his pension evaluated; you can get one-half of its increase since the marriage. With his shift work and irregular hours, we can't do this one-week on, one week off, two-step that's become a joint custody trend. By necessity, you'll have to work around his schedule, which means you must stay on friendly terms. But there's no real point in not doing that anyway, is there?"

I sent a letter setting out proposed covenants for a separation agreement and suggesting that the sergeant see an attorney. A week later, a reply came back from an attorney whose practice was limited to criminal work. The sergeant was unwilling to agree to any of the reasonable demands and wished to work toward reconciliation.

My client became annoyed, "That is simply out of the question," she said.

He retained a criminal attorney, because he had, most probably, worked with him in a trial and the lawyer might be doing it for him free — *pro bono.* His attorney was obviously unaware of current family law. His refusal to even consider any of our reasonable proposals was a clear indication that he shouldn't have involved himself in a matrimonial dispute.

I sent another letter citing the applicable law supporting each of the previous demands and politely suggesting in the last paragraph that he might consider referring his client to an attorney more acquainted with matrimonial law.

The sergeant advised my client that I had really insulted his attorney.

My client was justifiably irritated. It had been two months since she had first consulted me and nothing was happening. Conditions at home were becoming increasingly strained and the kids were feeling it.

"I want you to use everything I told you," she

---

[1] This is similar to the law in most States and Provinces where inherited property is exempted only if kept separate.

instructed me. "If his buddies at the precinct found out he was into pink nightgowns, wigs and handcuffs, he'd have to quit. And he loves being a police officer — and he's a good one. I don't believe his behavior at home has affected his being a good police officer. But, I need some short-term support and the kids need ongoing support. I don't want to do anything to put his job in jeopardy, but get this thing settled!"

Even though it was all irrelevant, I drafted a divorce petition including every detail of my client's sex life with the sergeant, commencing with the pink nightgown on the honeymoon. Conduct, unless it is financial misconduct, or at least has financial implications, is simply not taken into consideration in Canada or in many of the United States, except when there is a custody dispute. Some courts in the United States, however, do consider conduct even if it appears to have no financial impact. [2]

What really matters is the equal division of family property and the amount of spousal and child support. This was also a problem, because as with all police officers and teachers, the take home amount was never as impressive as one would expect when considering the gross, because of the large deductions for pensions and income tax.

Just after the kids went to bed and the sergeant had consumed his second Molson-lite, my client presented him with the draft petition.

The Sergeant left a message the next morning. He instructed that under no circumstances was the divorce petition to be issued in its present form nor was it to be sent to his attorney. He requested a settlement conference.

I informed him that we would not meet with him without his attorney but agreed not to make reference to the proposed divorce petition. We demanded financial disclosure in regard to the pension, which would be evaluated by an agreed upon appraiser.

The meeting went well. He withdrew his demand to

---

[2] At that time there were no Child Support Guidelines or Spousal Advisory Guidelines in Canada, so the amount was subject to negotiation.

4

buy out her interest in the matrimonial home and agreed to place it on the market.

Her share of his pension was to come out of his one-half equity in the home together with a small lump sum, which was, in reality, compensation for the fifty thousand which had been applied to reduce the mortgage.

There would be a designation of joint custody, which is a big deal for daddies, even though it may not always make any difference in actual time spent with the kids. In an ideal world, it should mean actual sharing. From a practical standpoint it means you can tell friends and family that you have joint custody. This is helpful when you wish to speak to the pediatrician or your kids' teachers.

In this case, because of the sergeant's erratic hours, a flexible access timetable was necessary and my client was glad to cooperate. I still suspected there may have been someone else in her life, but she was a reasonable woman and the boys adored their father. None of the embarrassing details of his sexual proclivities were ever released and the divorce went ahead in due course based on the grounds of the parties having been living separate and apart for more than one year.[3]

Several months after the divorce, I received a telephone call from the sergeant. He was buying several properties and wondered if my firm could represent him. In other words, he was ensuring my future silence. There is a strict rule of confidentiality between a lawyer and client, and as a result all information relating to the client is privileged. As I had always known, the sergeant was not a stupid man — just kinky.

The satisfactory ending to this potentially destructive situation could have been very different. Had the interesting scenario of the sergeant's personal life been exposed, his job may have been jeopardized or certainly his relationship with his fellow police officers. The animosity created would have prevented the mutually satisfactory and inexpensive separation agreement that was negotiated.

---

[3] In the various states grounds differ, for example in California, a divorce can be finalized 6 months after the filing of the Petition for Summary Dissolution.

Don't destroy the source of your future financial well being.

On the other hand, sometimes a little nudge, as in this case, is just what is needed to get things on track.

He was a mechanic and I felt that even submerging himself in a tub of suds for a week would never remove the dirt from his fingernails and his other extremities. He had with him a tattered divorce petition which, no doubt, he had been carrying around in a greasy pocket for way beyond the period allocated for a reply. Luckily for him, there had been no interim motion and pleadings had not been noted as closed.

She worked as a dietician in a hospital and, I was sure, was much more hygienic than my client. Besides a sale of the home, she sought a non-harassment order, because she claimed he had been stalking her. Two of their adult children, who were in their twenties, were living in the home with their father. One had a serious drug problem.

"I love my wife and want her back," he told me.

After reading the petition, I told him that I believed the possibility was remote.

"What's she doin' bringin' up somethin' that happened twenty-five years ago?" he complained.

What indeed — except to lend color to the petition, it was not relevant. But it would hardly endear him to any judge or anyone else who became privy to the information.

At a stag party the night before his wedding, his buddies had procured the services of a hooker-dancer to provide the evening's entertainment. To show his friends his appreciation, he became a participant in the performance. As a result, both he and his pregnant new wife contacted gonorrhea. Both of them were extremely distressed and the marriage hardly got off to a rollicking start.

"But why bring it up now," he grumbled. "It didn't hurt the baby and she forgave me back then."

I had to agree with him. There was absolutely no financial reason to bring this up twenty-five years later, especially when he had supported her while she completed her university degree in order to become a dietician.

"I never cheated on her again. In fact, I wouldn't call it cheating what I did. We weren't even married yet. It was just that the guys had hired this broad and I was drunk out of my mind."

I assured him if we were to proceed, I would move to have the stag episode "struck" or removed from the pleadings as being irrelevant.

He suffered from severe arthritis and made much less from his employment than his wife. The drug-addicted son, whose problem had worsened since his mother's exodus, could almost be categorized as a dependent child as he did not work and was totally dependant on his father for his support. These issues were an important consideration.

There was no settlement. He kept insisting on a reconciliation which was clearly out of the question. Believing there was merit to his demand for spousal support as well as support for the son, the wife did not go ahead with a court motion asking for a sale of the home.

He did not want to pay more legal fees to move the matter to a conclusion, so it simply languished unresolved. In retrospect, this was exactly what my client wanted but surely not his wife.

A lesson to be learned: Do not have your attorney clutter up your petition with irrelevant and embarrassing incidents that have nothing to do with the validity of your claim. This can only cause unnecessary animosity and distraction. Had this matter proceeded, the offending paragraphs would have been deleted with resulting costs against the wife. Why put yourself in that position?

I know what you think about insurance brokers. You think about dignified men in pinstriped suits who carry large briefcases full of important material and whose idea of diversion is a quiet Saturday night bridge game and a Sunday afternoon of golf. You may be right. I'm sure many insurance men wear pinstripe suits, carry large briefcases and indulge in conservative diversions.

When I think of insurance guys, however, I think of Mr. Rideout with his big fat bottom high in the air while his wife powders his butt and then fixes his diaper after giving his bits and pieces a nice soapy wash. And yes, this was always followed by a warm bottle with a free flowing nipple — half milk and half rum.

Mrs. Rideout, accommodating lady that she was, diligently powdered, creamed, and diapered Mr. Rideout's privates for eight years until she decided that not only did it not stimulate her, but that there were more enjoyable ways to promote sexual activity. In fact, all the creaming, diapering and powdering had made her, as she put it, "a nervous wreck."

She was so distraught, that she was incapable of ever working again. She wanted Mr. Rideout to compensate her fully for those tortured years by giving her generous ongoing support and a greater division of property than the Family Law Act would otherwise allow.

"You will not get an unequal division of net family property because you catered to your husband's sexual peccadilloes," I warned Mrs. Rideout. "Nor will it affect your quantum of spousal support. Of course your inability to work is relevant, preferably evidenced by a psychiatric report. And of prime importance is your husband's ability to pay. Hopefully, we can settle the matter."

But Mrs. Rideout was not listening. "He will be embarrassed and he will settle," she assured me.

He was her third husband. She had walked away from the other two with very little. In fact, from her last marriage, nothing at all. It was different, however, with Mr. Rideout. He had bought out his partner and his insurance company was worth a substantial amount. This was based to a large degree on his affable personality, which added to his popularity with his clients in the small city where he and Mrs. Rideout resided.

"His clients would just die if they knew," she told me.

She had not sought psychiatric help for her emotional state nor had she been placed on medication by her general practitioner. She just went merrily on powdering and diapering Mr. Rideout until she felt she could bear the marriage no longer. Her feelings were no doubt heightened by her hiring a recently divorced personal trainer, who was teaching her how to keep in splendid shape with Pilates.

Mrs. Rideout wanted full details of the diapering and powdering to be included in a divorce petition. I cautioned her that it was not a good idea. Besides, it was clearly irrelevant to financial issues.

She had no evidence to show that she had been adversely affected emotionally by acquiescing to Mr. Rideout's regression to an infantile state as a prelude to sexual arousal. In fact, Mrs. Rideout had been living an active life throughout the eight years of marriage, exercising, horseback riding and changing her hair color at least once a month.

Although she did not provide details, I was suspicious that the personal trainer was supplying her with a lot more than a toned body. This also was irrelevant, and, if true, Mr. Rideout was unaware of her extra-curricular activities.[4]

Our best bet, I advised Mrs. Rideout, was to emphasize that as a result of the eight-year marriage, she had terminated her employment as a court reporter and, since she had been out of the field for a prolonged period, she was unaware of the substantial changes in technology that had taken place. Besides, she had become accustomed to a somewhat grandiose lifestyle of traveling and shopping. It would be unfair to have her revert to an ordinary lifestyle without a cleaning woman and all the other amenities that Mr. Rideout was able to provide.

Mrs. Rideout, however, insisted on the inclusion of the powdering and diapering part of the marriage. I finally agreed, hoping it would not prevent a decent settlement or incite Mr.

---

[4] Conduct such as adultery is relevant in some states when considering amount of support and division of property.

Rideout to the point where he would fight us all the way to the courtroom.

Unfortunately, it did both. Mr. Rideout was furious, calling Mrs. Rideout a *harlot*, a word I had last heard many years before when studying Chaucer at university.

"It was all lies," he stated, and he would not even commence negotiation until this disgusting material was removed from the divorce petition.

The Rideouts were still under the same roof. Mrs. Rideout had been advised not to leave under any circumstances, as had Mr. Rideout, whose attorney knew that upon his exodus, Mrs. Rideout would be applying to the court for exclusive possession of the luxurious matrimonial home and for ongoing spousal support. This would create a bad precedent and Mr. Rideout's attorney, an experienced and astute adversary, was well aware of it.

So the Rideouts remained miserably together in the matrimonial home with Mr. Rideout going undiapered and unpowdered. Mrs. Rideout, nervous about Mr. Rideout's accusations, forfeited her enjoyable Pilate's sessions, which were one of the things that made her life worthwhile.

It had to end and it did.

After two hours of mutual recriminations during a five-hour meeting, a settlement was reached. Once the parties got down to business, they found mutual grounds for an agreement, with which neither party was happy. Usually that means it was a fair agreement.

Mrs. Rideout received ongoing support but the amount was to be revisited after a five-year period. The home was to be sold and the proceeds divided. Mrs. Rideout was to get additional money from Mr. Rideout's share to compensate her for the increase in value of Mr. Rideout's insurance brokerage since the date of marriage. The business had obviously been much more successful than the Rideout marriage.

There were other concessions but these were the most important to Mrs. Rideout. The divorce petition, with its noxious description of Mr. Rideout's propensities toward infantile pleasuring was to be withdrawn and the allegations were never to be reinstated in any future petition.

Did the use of these allegations advance the settlement efforts and actually enhance the results for Mrs. Rideout? To an extent they probably did, but only at the price of considerable animosity and caustic negotiation even though the matter never did get past the initial serving of the petition. One thing is certain; any hope of even remote civility between the parties was forever eradicated. Luckily, no children were involved.

Was dishing the dirt a good idea in this particular case? I did not think so and believed that the matter would have settled in any event. But Mrs. Rideout would not be convinced. Her goal was to embarrass and then collect as a result, ignoring the fact that for eight years she had been a willing participant in the sexual conduct she finally found so repelling.

A waste of time, I suggest, that initiated the most antagonistic feelings from Mr. Rideout.

**M**y second insurance wife was not nearly as attractive as Mrs. Rideout, who, although in her early forties, could pass for someone in her late twenties, and who still caused a commotion every time she passed a construction site.

Mrs. Perry, on the other hand, was over fifty and looked every year of it. Her hair, much too golden, and cupid mouth, much too red, seemed inappropriate for this slightly plump, post menopausal female, whose only interesting feature were black boots with very high heels. It had been a second marriage for both but it had lasted for twenty-five years.

Mr. Perry had left her. She handed me the letter from Mr. Perry's attorney, who was subsequently appointed to the bench and turned out to be one of the most respected judges in the matrimonial field.

The letter was not encouraging. It spoke of Mrs. Perry's

ability to re-establish herself within a limited time period and reminded the reader that Mr. Perry possessed substantial assets prior to the twenty-five year marriage. The letter went on to state that the marriage ended because of the *unhappy differences* resulting from Mrs. Perry's mother moving into the marital home during the previous year.

Mrs. Perry assured me that her only work experience had been behind the men's accessories counter at Eaton's Department Store twenty-five years ago where she had served Mr. Perry. She further added that under no circumstances would she ever be capable of obtaining employment again, because varicose veins made it impossible for her to stand for longer than twenty minutes at a time.

"You'll notice," she said, her scarlet Cupid's bow lips curling with annoyance, "he doesn't say what these *unhappy differences* are. He's just blaming my mother, not because of anything she does...it's just that her presence interferes with some of his pleasures."

"I'm not sure I understand," I replied.

She explained that among his pleasures was a robust sex life that invariably followed a torture session which would put the Marquis de Sade to shame. Mr. Perry, it seems, liked to eat his dinner from a saucer while on all fours wearing a leather dog collar with a leash held by Mrs. Perry. There were spankings galore and whippings with a collection of thirty whips of various sizes and colors. In the basement was a contraption from which Mr. Perry was hung by his wrists and another device which held him motionless except for his protruding buttocks.

Mrs. Perry took an active role in all of this. She insisted she was not an enthusiastic participant, but knew that without these preliminaries there would be no sex life at all. So she complied with all requests, even initiating some of them, knowing it would please Mr. Perry and that what would follow would be pleasing to both of them. All of this occurred before the creation of Viagra or Cialis, although I'm not sure they would have made much difference in this particular case.

I suppose this could have gone on indefinitely until Mr. Perry ran out of testosterone or suffered a stroke as a result of all this sexual excitement, but something occurred that stopped everything in its tracks.

Mrs. Perry lost her father and insisted upon moving her mother into the Perry household. Her presence totally curtailed all of the sexual hi-jinks that were so dear to Mr. Perry's heart. Mrs. Perry refused to descend to their torture chamber in the basement for fear that her mother, who was still mobile and not one to retire early, would stand on the basement stairs and view one of their torture pageants.

Certainly, Mr. Perry could no longer eat his dinner from his dog dish while Mrs. Perry pulled on his leash and spanked him gently with his favorite whip. The romance, if you could call it that, totally died with the entrance of Mrs. Perry's mother into the household and was not likely to return until Mrs. Perry's mother followed her departed husband.

Mrs. Perry assured me that this was the sole cause of Mr. Perry's departure and the subsequent break-up of the marriage.

"It was all so very unfair," she whined, "that after all of the years spent in exciting him, he would cast me aside for God knows who — possibly some paid for dominatrix — just so he could enjoy his twisted sex life."

She conceded she had been a willing partner, but surely not an equal one. In fact, had Mr. Perry not initiated it all, she would have never even have thought of such things. Such behavior had not occurred during her first marriage and the entire fault rested at the doorstep of Mr. Perry because of his nutty demands.

Unlike the Rideout situation, none of Mr. Perry's S & M proclivities ever made it into a divorce petition. The fact was that Mrs. Perry, pudgy and whiney as she was, was a realist at heart. As a willing participant, she knew it would now look ridiculous for her to complain. However, if push came to shove, as a last resort, she would not hesitate to press the issue — it *had*, after all, been a twenty-five year marriage.

Mrs. Perry was not, and never would be, in any shape to re-establish herself.

She quite emphatically informed me she did not want to run up legal fees. Not surprisingly, she had borrowed the retainer from her mother, a fact I found oddly appropriate.

After an exchange of financial statements and a formal appraisal of Mr. Perry's insurance brokerage, a private meeting between Mr. Perry's attorney and me was arranged. Scheduling the meeting turned out to be more difficult than the meeting itself. Every time I visited Mr. Perry's attorney he was inexplicably not there, even though the date and time of the meetings had painstakingly been agreed upon with his secretary.

I had the distinct impression that Mr. Perry's attorney was avoiding me. I finally cornered him after he returned from what I guessed to be a two-martini lunch. We chatted in an amiable fashion and I mentioned Mr. Perry's whip collection, torture chamber and dog collar in passing.

The attorney, a broad-minded chap with a pronounced sense of humor, laughed with me. "One never knows about people," he said shrugging.

The matter was settled shortly thereafter, but not, I believe, as a result of the S & M revelations. It had been a twenty-five year marriage and one only had to speak to Mrs. Perry for a brief period to conclude that there was no way that she would ever again find remunerative employment.

The break-up of the marriage placed her at a substantial financial disadvantage; and Mr. Perry's successful business afforded him the ability to pay. He agreed to pay ongoing support in a reasonable amount and even permitted Mrs. Perry and her mother to remain in the home for a two-year period which was quite generous under the circumstances.

When the house sold, Mrs. Perry was to receive a payment from Mr. Perry's one-half of the proceeds in compensation for his ever-growing insurance business, which did not really grow and prosper until after they were married.

I believe that the matter would have settled regardless of Mrs. Perry's sexual revelations. I also suspect, however, that Mr. Perry, as a community leader and church elder would not wish his sexual peccadillo's to be exposed in a public document — and they never were.

Lesson to be learned: If you've been married for endless years, have never worked or even if you have at only a modest employment and your husband or your husband's company has prospered, then you are going to receive appropriate support — most likely according to the Spousal Guidelines that prevail in your State.[5]

Some states only have guidelines for interim, but not permanent support. This leaves the parties at the mercy of the judge's discretion, which may or may not be a good thing depending upon your unique financial circumstances and the judge's level of generosity on that particular day.

If it's your husband's company, as in this case, then you will benefit from the increase in value. If you do not live in a Community Property State you will still benefit although not as directly. There may be no set rules but the court will look at a variety of guidelines among them relative earnings, length of marriage, and the value of a stay-at-home wife.

This is the law and there is no reason to muddy the waters by descriptions of whips and torture chambers. Mrs. Perry had a satisfactory result and modest legal fees.

I question if she had avidly pursued her S&M revelations, whether the results would have been better — in fact, they may well have been considerably worse!

**W**hip thin, with blonde bangs, blue eyes, and a wide smile, Mary White was one of my very few clients who entered marriage a virgin — and she was twenty-seven at the time.

"I didn't know that there were any left," I commented.

"It was religion and sports," she answered. "I was a good Catholic but when I wasn't praying, I was high jumping.

---

[5] Ten years constitute a long term marriage in California.

In fact, I'm still jumping and attend meets all over the world."

The elementary school where she taught allowed her time off to pursue her successful sports activities. They were so proud of her success that a large picture of her flying through the air was on display outside the school auditorium.

She was one of my most pleasant, wholesome and undemanding clients, who laughed easily, although her situation left little to laugh about.

She doted on her three-year-old son, who had the same tousled blonde hair, blue eyes and wide smile.

When it came to husbands, however, she had really blown it.

It should have been an easy case. The parties had purchased a home in joint tenancy just a few blocks away from her elementary school and her son's preschool. Both regularly walked to school. Her husband worked at a local stock brokerage which was about fifteen minutes away by car. Her family lived close by. They were friendly with their neighbors with whom they shared barbecues, a social life and mutual babysitting. It was an ideal home for her and her son.

There were a few disturbing aspects to the case which made things difficult. Her husband had left Mary for a divorced co-worker, who seemed to have unwarranted hostility toward her. Mary was baffled, considering the circumstances and the fact that they had never met.

Shortly after the marriage, Mary discovered she had contacted genital herpes. This embarrassed her and she instructed me not to mention it under any circumstances. There had only been one outbreak but this had been relatively severe.

"You do realize," I cautioned, "that this could cut down your chance of remarriage. It's a gift that keeps on giving."

She shrugged. She still didn't want it mentioned.

I commented that to have been a virgin and then be infected with herpes by one's husband was jarring, to say the least.

After the split, her brother had offered to lend her the money to purchase the husband's interest in their home. There were no other contentious issues, as her school pension was roughly equivalent to his IRA. He was a successful stockbroker to a large extent because she had encouraged all her friends and fellow teachers to use his services.

It was one of those cases which should have been wrapped up in a couple of weeks by a separation agreement after an exchange of financial disclosure. Unfortunately, it did not work out that way.

She made the child available on weekends but he fussed upon leaving and did not relate well to Daddy's girlfriend. She suggested to the husband, that he might just spend an afternoon with his son by himself.

He refused, became hostile and decided he would not see the child at all. This upset her. He also refused to let her purchase his interest in the home, demanding an immediate sale. He was being counseled by one of the most litigious, highly priced attorneys in the nearby city.

"How in the world can he afford him?" I asked with real curiosity.

"Family money" she answered. "His brother also used him, but he's a lot richer."

After a brief exchange of correspondence, the husband initiated an unexpected divorce petition. Part of the relief asked for an immediate sale of the matrimonial home. Other relief requested was joint custody, consisting of alternate weekends and every Wednesday night from 5 p.m. to 8 p.m. This seemed an unfortunate claim for a three year old who screamed when he left his mother and whose bedtime was seven p.m.

For once, the wide smile had disappeared and Mary's perplexity turned to anger. We counter-applied for child support based on an estimated $100,000.00 a year taxable income. We sought exclusive possession of the home or the right to purchase the husband's equitable interest based upon a value determined by an agreed appraiser or the average value based upon the opinions of three real estate agents.

His negative response was accompanied by a financial statement showing his taxable income to be $137 a month.

"This is preposterous," I told her. "He has claimed deductions on everything but his left foot!"

She agreed. "There is no way he makes that little money. He leases a brand new Lexus and lives in an apartment building where the rent is not one cent less than $3,000.00 a month. There's simply no way."

The Judge agreed with us. He estimated the husband's income at $70,000 a year; still much less than the actual amount, but a far cry from the $137 a month put forward. However, he ordered a sale of the home. Since neither party had prevailed in all of their claims, there was no order as to costs. Considering all the circumstances, my client and I were both annoyed by the outcome.

"Guess what," she informed me, rolling her eyes and shifting uncomfortably in her chair. "Sitting in that courtroom, listening to all that blather from his attorney, really stressed me out. I've developed the worst outbreak of herpes."

Our eyes locked, and before she could protest, I told her what I recommended.

The husband's attorney had asked for an expedited trial, which was ridiculous. Money was flying out the door and there was only so much she could borrow from her brother. Her husband was giving Mary all the consideration usually reserved for a serial killer.

"We should amend the counter petition and ask for $500,000 in damages as a result of his giving you herpes. As I warned, it's a gift that keeps on giving. You told me your doctor would substantiate this. It's going to have a financial impact in restricting your future choice of partners and it's damned uncomfortable. Besides, how much more must you take?"

His attorney accepted service of the amended petition. Usually, his MO was to let opposing counsel wait weeks for the honor of a phone call, but his reply came the very next day. It appeared Mr. White was very upset and wished to settle although, his attorney assured me, he had advised him against it.

So insistent was Mr. White that a meeting was scheduled within a week and Minutes of Settlement were signed. Mary White purchased Mr. White's interest in the matrimonial home courtesy of her brother and the claims for access to the three year old became reasonable. It was conceded that his income was at least $100,000 a year and, as such, child support was also reasonable. The buy-out of the home was reduced to compensate Mary for her legal fees — a very satisfactory conclusion. Mary withdrew her $500,000 claim for damages resulting from being infected with the herpes virus.

Were there any regrets about initiating the damage claim arising from the transmitting of the herpes virus? Hardly — Mary was sorry that she hadn't done it sooner. The man was impossible.

I have never understood the preliminary viciousness unless it was the result of the urging of the hostile girlfriend or the husband's attorney who was known for running up costs.

The story, however, has a happy ending. Every Christmas I receive a card from Mary usually with her son, both wearing wide smiles. Last year, it included a great looking fellow she referred to as her future husband. She had met him at a jumping competition.

Lesson to be learned: There are times when embarrassing issues should be exposed, but only when they are relevant to your financial wellbeing. There was fortunately a happy ending in this particular case, but an early revelation would have saved a lot of grief and legal expense.

**W**hat some people want in their divorce proceedings has always perplexed me. One woman actually produced a picture of her husband's penis, fully erect, but with a decided curve. She had retrieved it from one of those skin magazines her husband was prone to reading, where individuals exchanged photos of various parts of their anatomy. She would, she told me with excitement, know it anywhere.

Surely, I told her, there must be other curved penises. In any event, what was the point of describing it in a divorce petition? Other than proving he was the type of individual who wished to promote his crooked penis, it hardly had any financial relevance.

Since my retirement, I have noticed that divorce petitions are becoming sparser and the format discourages detailed pleadings. Most judges wish to discourage allegations as to non-financial conduct altogether, no doubt becoming jaded from reading descriptions of conduct which lacked relevancy. Sometimes pleadings can be struck on the grounds of being irrelevant, verbose and inflammatory.

Often aspects of a party's conduct are included merely to incite the judge. Many judges have been through their own divorces and are not as easily upset as some clients would wish. In fact, many judges are rightfully annoyed by these deliberate efforts to curry favor by maligning the opposition.

Some instances of questionable conduct, however, are clearly relevant as they go to the financial core of the parties' assets. One wife of a client was a compulsive gambler. She had emptied joint bank accounts, run up half a dozen joint credit cards to their maximum and had emptied her spousal IRA.

My client wondered why he should have to equally divide property with his wife under the circumstances. Why indeed?

Such reckless depletion of property could be termed *unconscionable* which means "grossly unfair," justifying an unequal division of family property. My client therefore claimed an unequal division in his divorce petition. One of the saner attorneys advised the wife against further wasting even more of her husband's money by challenging the husband's claim. My client ended up with both the house and children.

Unfortunately, he was still on the hook for spousal support. His wife had lost her employment because of her gambling habit, but her need of support was not diminished even though she was receiving counseling from an addiction center and was trying to re-establish herself.

"It was all totally unfair," he complained.

Some judges are all for redemption, especially if you're female. I suspect this signifies some sort of reverse discrimination.

The angriest clients I've ever had are those whose husbands are alcoholic. Some are driven literally mad. One very attractive woman informed me that after ninety minutes of intercourse in which her husband was unable to reach a climax, a failure which she attributed to his heavy drinking, she heard a screaming voice and only later realized it was her own. This represents an interesting type of disassociation, surely.

There are also the urinary and bowel accidents, which take place in the matrimonial bed after years of dedicated drinking.

Strangely, many of these men are able to continue working and take exception to their wives' accusations. They state that if they drank that much they would not have their exemplary job attendance record. While one does not question their work record, surely their efficiency must be as impaired as their sexual performances.

These cases are often fraught with problems, especially when the alcoholic partner demands weekend access to the children and the wife worries that they may be in danger.

There was one exceptionally horrible case, which fortunately was not mine, but that of a fellow attorney. The judge did not believe the wife's allegations of alcoholism against the husband and awarded him generous access to their three-year-old. Both husband and child were subsequently burned to death while staying at a summer cabin.

For those who are justifiably concerned, I would suggest not releasing a child to a parent who appears to have been drinking and to obtain a court order that the parent will abstain from alcohol during visitation. The problem is the enforceability of this order, which although readily granted, is not so readily enforced.

I did have a client who telephoned the nearest police precinct after her husband insisted on taking the two children for his access period and she believed he had been drinking. He was subsequently stopped by the police and charged. The whole procedure was distressing for the children but not as distressing as a future accident may have been. On the basis of the charge and subsequent conviction, access was restricted to the presence of a third party, who would monitor the husband's drinking. All of this led to a high degree of animosity between the parties, but still better than endangering the children.

My client Doris had a horrible drinking problem. Efficient and hardworking, she had helped her husband build a portfolio of many acres of farmland located all around the large town where they resided. She managed the abattoir in their cattle operation. She was an outstanding helpmate when she was sober. During her drunken periods she was an irrational hellion. She trashed her teenaged son's antique Thunderbird, which he had spent months remodeling, and was abusive to her daughter, who, in spite of it, headed for university. Her children disliked her. She was an irritant and an embarrassment.

Her husband had previously been elected Mayor, but the resulting social activity had been her undoing. Doris left the matrimonial home and moved in with Louise, a retired government worker and quintessential old maid, who became her confidant. Louise had accompanied her to my office and whispered in Doris' defense, "In the early years he had encouraged her drinking, believing it would loosen her up sexually."

Her husband had grown to detest her uncontrolled drunken aggression and resulting escapades, and eventually, Doris herself. She had been forced to have three fingers amputated after passing out in a field one frosty December night. Forgotten were the years of service and running the farms while he attended to his municipal duties. Not forgotten was her drunken behavior that had angered him so much he allegedly had pushed her down the stairs, together with her friend Louise, before her exodus.

Her husband advised the first of his five subsequent attorneys, "She does not deserve one damn cent."

The matter was eventually settled, but not in the amount which would normally be paid. The husband resented giving Doris anything, but that in itself was not an impediment. The courts will award alcoholic spouses maintenance. The ugly truth was that you could not be sure that Doris would turn up at court should a trial ensue, so there was little choice but to settle.

Should you dish the dirt when it comes to your partner's alcoholism? Absolutely, if it has had a financial impact on the spouse's ability to earn a living, or if it endangers your children.

Although judges are sometimes reluctant to award an unequal division of property, most will believe it to be less than fair and equitable to equally divide family money to certain individuals — individuals who have spent most of their lives in a drunken stupor while their spouses carried the burden of all the expenses. Self induced lack of employment and resulting future inability to pay child support all encourage a lump sum payment of support or an unequal division of property.

Dish the dirt by all means. But, a warning to husbands — you may have to support your alcoholic wife. The judge will take the sophisticated view that alcoholism is an illness and after a long term marriage you may have driven her to drink.

I know that it's unfair. But sometimes life is — isn't it?

# Chapter 2
## Tax and Other Complications

I have come to the conclusion that ninety percent of individuals running a cash business cheat on their income tax. This happens as well when there are joint husband and wife businesses. No one ever dreams of disclosing this welcome source of undisclosed cash until one party starts to cheat on or abuse the other resulting in legal proceedings. Then suddenly, one of the parties decides it should be a matter for the I.R.S.

"Don't do it," I begged, my new client, Pina. "You've benefited from this as much as he did. If an audit is ordered you'll both be the losers."

In this particular case the husband carried on a furniture business with his brothers. It seems that every month they had an auction of items in their inventory, many of which were paid for in cash that never found its way into the books. The amounts were considerable, and if reported would triple the income shown on the husband's income tax return.

"His brothers are scared to death and want to break up the company now that we're breakin' up. It's really shakin' everyone up — and it's all his fault. That's what he gets for screwing around on me with some gum chewin' scumbag who answers the phones at his office," she said smugly, snapping her own gum.

"Hell, even birds don't soil their own nests," she continued. "His brothers knew all about the affair…they could have fired the girl."

Of course, now the girlfriend was leaving, but that didn't help matters.

The husband refused to obtain his own attorney and she begged me to see him. I reluctantly consented on the condition that he would obtain independent legal advice before signing any separation agreement.

Her husband was a heavy, dark haired man with a slight Calabrian accent. He leaned forward in his chair and in a husky concerned voice gave me the straight goods.

"Your client's a crazy broad! She's so crazy that my brothers all want to break up our great cash cow for fear she'll blow the whistle and start a tax audit — and they're pissed with me for starting this. I love my kids and I know this whole thing has been one huge mistake."

But it was too late for any of that and he just wanted to settle things so he could get her and his brothers off his back *and be fair*.

I told him, not unkindly, as he was a likeable enough guy, "Being fair is to pay her and the kids support using your actual income figures and not those you report to the Income Revenue Service."

He eagerly nodded his agreement. Also, I suggested, when obtaining an appraisal of the business it would be necessary to consider the additional income from the monthly auctions, which, of course, was not shown on financial statements. This was more reluctantly agreed upon. He feared his brothers wouldn't like it.

The matter was resolved in a satisfactory manner. The worth of the business had already been appraised for buy-out purposes by the brothers and the appraisal was generous, factoring in, I suspected the extra revenue. His share of the business went against his one-half equity in the home which resulted in Pina emerging as the sole owner. Support was paid for her and the children according to his *actual* income. Custody of the three boys was shared, although Pina received support as if the majority of the children's time was spent with her.

This, incidentally, is always a good thing, as I always told my male clients. If you really want to see a lot of your kids, but your wife fears that that will mean a reduction in child support, simply pay her according to the guidelines just as if she were the main custodial parent. It's stupid to let a little thing like money prevent you from having a great relationship and lots of time with your kids.

But, you might argue, it's not fair. Of course it's not. But it's practical and pays off in the long run. In this case, the wife wanted as a condition of access that the boys would not be associating with the former girlfriend. Since the affair had been discontinued this was not a problem, but had it been ongoing it may well have been. I will deal with this type of nonsense later on.

**T**ogether, they had run a very successful fast food franchise located in a small city surrounded by rapidly growing land developments. Within two years they had purchased the building and then a house in the best part of town. For twenty years she had gotten up at three in the morning to bake the fresh bread and muffins and make assorted pie fillings for the restaurant. At seven o'clock he had been at his post, smiling broadly at his customers, while he served coffee, early breakfast, and wrapped lunches to go.

The franchise was run with great efficiency and no one was more pleasant than Gus, except perhaps Lucy, when she occasionally appeared behind the counter away from her ever-busy kitchen.

"Just a great couple," agreed the hundreds of customers, with enthusiasm. There was nobody like Gus and Lucy.

Behind the scenes, their lives could hardly be described as paradise. Getting up at three in the morning six days a week would drain anyone; so Lucy resorted to the odd nip of vodka to *boost her energy level.*

Gus, on the other hand, had a hair trigger temper and was not hesitant to use his fists when he lost it. In fact, Lucy had once been hospitalized and Gus had been charged, convicted and placed on a peace bond to be of good behavior upon his release. It would have been worse for him, but she had not wished to testify against him.

She was, frankly, afraid of him, and although her daughters encouraged her to pursue the case against him, her son, who was close to his father, persuaded her to back off.

Finally, after one particularly bad thumping that dislocated her jaw, she took advantage of the conditions in his bail release. Those conditions prohibited him from going near the matrimonial home and limited his interaction with her to work. Feeling relatively safe, she commenced legal proceedings.

Of course, he wanted her back. He was always sorry and even after the divorce he kept calling her. She even considered reconciliation and telephoned me for advice.

I talked her out of it.

The problem was, before the divorce there was the question of all that unreported income — up to twenty thousand dollars a week for all those years. She informed me she had seen boxes of cash in the house before he moved out. Not that she had counted it or taken any pictures, but she had seen it. And her daughter had seen it too. But her daughter didn't wish to become involved.

Great looking women with taffy colored hair and light blue eyes — both terrified of the ever-smiling Gus.

Then there were Gus's trips to Athens. Lucy was certain there were bank accounts bursting with money belonging to both of them which he had stashed in Greece. We hired a local attorney there and sent court orders that no money in Gus's name was to be released. We heard nothing. Our Athenian attorney assured us that he had used his connections, but he could locate no accounts belonging to Gus.

Perhaps, she suggested, he had opened accounts under

someone else's name — maybe even their son's. If so, she did not wish to do anything about it. She could not risk her son becoming angry.

She was such a sweet woman, but at times I wondered if all those thumpings hadn't affected her ability to think clearly. Finally, she instructed me to stop looking and she gave up claiming one-half of the money. She would satisfy herself with the one half of the business property, a buy-out of the home, which she was afraid to live in, one-half of the monthly income from the franchise, which had been sold, and a division of a few other disclosed assets.

She was comfortable, but not excessively so. Not comfortable enough financially to make up for twenty years of three in the morning get-ups and the years of hard work. But she had a good relationship with the kids, a fully paid for condominium and even a place in Florida, which she bought when the market collapsed and real estate could be acquired for half price. I hear from her periodically and she's not unhappy.

Lesson to be learned: What can be done to avoid being cheated by a tax evading spouse? The solution is not to report the tax cheat to the tax authorities. A huge percentage of tips to the tax department come from disgruntled spouses who feel this is the best way to obtain revenge for financial or emotional mistreatment. I have always warned my clients that this is stupid.

Let someone else report him or her.

The smaller your partner's share of Family or Community Property, the less owing to you by means of an equal division. Money owed to the tax authorities can be deducted from your partner's share of his or her property and this in turn could mean that your share will be less.

Remember, if you live in any of the Community Property States, the goal of the legislation is for you and your spouse to walk away from your marriage with equal amounts.

If, because of your whispering in the ears of the IRS, a

subsequent audit reveals your husband has considerable taxes owing, his property share may be so reduced that you may end up owing him money. Not your intention, I am sure.

In assessing income, as in Pina`s case, factoring back the unreported cash gave a fair amount upon which to base spousal and child support. Of course, the husband cooperated, and that may not always be the case.

Absconding with unreported cash is another matter. Lucy should have obtained hard evidence of the vast amount of money being stashed by Gus. There should have been photographs, documentation of amounts, all with direct observation by an independent third party. Judges simply will not accept the fact that considerable amounts of money are unaccounted for unless hard evidence is given.

I still have pangs about Lucy, but fear is a great motivator and she was, for good reason, reluctant to move forward. Things should have worked out differently.

# Chapter 3
## Guilt, Jealousy and a Matter of Timing

She was over fifty, with shoulder length apricot hair and a face that had seen too many sleepless nights and too many shots of Vodka. She was only slightly more than a hundred pounds and when she smiled her pearl like dentures quivered unsteadily on her shrunken gums. She informed me proudly, "I can rock a guy's world with my blow job." No doubt her teeth were removed to accomplish that feat.

He was a sixty-year old bachelor whose idea of excitement was flirting with the waitresses in a small coffee shop located in a two-story building on the main street of the small town where they resided. His father and grandfather before him owned the building that housed the coffee shop. He lived on its rather unimpressive rentals, which he refused to increase because of his great relationship with the tenants.

He was well known in the town and his reputation meant everything to him. She, on the other hand, had lived in many places and was just passing through when they met.

Whether it was her oral expertise or the fact that both his parents had died the year before, they married after a very short courtship. Most of their time had been spent traveling to Florida where he played golf each winter. Unsurprisingly, there were problems shortly after they were married and settled down.

As if there weren't enough contention, her unemployed son moved in to further worsen the situation. Then, one night, fueled by vodka, she let loose a tirade because her husband had given a birthday card to one of the waitresses at the coffee shop. One thing led to another and he pushed her out of the way when she tried to block his exodus from the home. The police were called and he was subsequently charged with assault.

As usual, part of the condition of his release was that he not go within five hundred feet of the wife, which effectively gave her exclusive possession of the matrimonial home where she, naturally, wanted to remain. It meant free rent since there was no mortgage and he carried all of the expenses. Periodically, she worked as a caregiver, earning barely enough to pay for, as she put it, "Booze, butts and burgers."

He had owned the home before the marriage, which had lasted less than two years. It was one of those cases where dividing the home equally would be inappropriate. The marriage had lasted much less than the five-year period which is often the criteria used to determine full entitlement.

To get rid of her once and for all, he offered her one-half of the market value of the home, a fair amount considering the shortness of the marriage. She refused, demanding support as well.

"You're not being reasonable...you weren't even married two years," she was warned by her attorney.

The husband became angry and withdrew his offer after changing attorneys. Then, no doubt embarrassed by the fact that he had been excluded from his home, and humiliated in front of his friends, he decided he would give her nothing at all, but would place the situation before the local judge.

I transferred the file to another attorney when I retired. The last I heard was that things were not going well for my former client. Legal fees were mounting and the parties seemed irreversibly headed for trial. She telephoned me once, obviously after drinking and informed me that she should have just taken what was offered and called it a day. I agreed.

This represents a classic case of timing. As it happens in so many divorce cases, there is a crucial point when one party decides they want to settle. If the offer is fair or as often occurs, more than fair, it should be taken advantage of. Individuals do not become more generous as an action progresses. Legal fees mount and significant others become more opinionated.

Be practical, and with the help of your attorney, weigh your options!

**A**nnabelle Brown was not a pretty woman. Her chin was too long and her bright brown eyes too close together. She was, however, fashionably slim. Her crossed legs, the left one of which swung restlessly in my direction, were noteworthy and her slim ankles and high muscled calves were perfectly displayed in her spike-heeled pumps.

The oldest of her three daughters sat with her eyes lowered, her plump, pale, sixteen-year-old hands intertwined on her tight, blue-jeaned lap.

"I want you to take him to the cleaners. I want you to drag him through the courts. I want him to pay for what he's done to us," my new client demanded.

Her voice had an edge that could cut tough steak. She was hoarse, both from anger and the Marlboro cigarettes which she constantly chain-smoked. It was the late 1990's and people were still smoking — even some of the people who wore expensive suits and had their hair professionally styled.

She had not come to her first visit with an attorney unprepared. She had print-outs of both their IRA'S and even a pension statement from the well-known sports franchise of which he was an area manager. She had even contacted a local real estate agent and found out the approximate value of their matrimonial home, which was located in one of the best areas of West Toronto. They had managed their finances well. There was no mortgage and even her two-year-old Cadillac SUV was paid for.

She informed me that she had not worked during the seventeen years since she had become pregnant with their oldest daughter — the one who sat stolidly beside her, studying her running shoes and refusing to look at either me or her mother.

Although she was only forty, she stated that she could never work again. She had been a typist in a manufacturing company and had no computer skills.

She worked out three times a week at the local health club, had lunch with the same three friends every Wednesday, and had her hair and nails done once a week at the local beauty salon. The rest of the time she chauffeured her daughters to various activities, sometimes remaining to watch their performances. She was a social member of her husband's golf club, but had been taking lessons so she could become involved in the game. She had a cleaning woman who came every week.

It had not been a bad life, she admitted, although her husband had been forced to travel several months of the year — until he had gone and ruined everything.

Following his last trip up north, she had unpacked his suitcase and was gathering his shirts to take to the laundry, responsibilities she dutifully assumed. She found two condoms, still intact in their packages, in his shirt pocket

"They sure as hell weren't meant for me. I had my tubes tied after Emily was born. I asked him about them, but he refused to discuss it. I kept after him, because I couldn't sleep. Finally he told me he had an affair with a girl up in Sudbury…a *French* girl who was a manager in one of the stores!"

It was obvious to me that the fact the girl was French had incited even greater anger. I suspected she had conjured up some intense acrobatic lovemaking that she associated with the French.

"Some women will do anything," she commented archly.

The sixteen year old suddenly got up from her chair and left the room.

"Do you think it was wise to bring her?" I asked, nodding toward the door through which her daughter had just disappeared.

"She may as well know what her father is. She's a real Daddy's Girl...always loved her daddy more than me. Now she knows just how much her daddy really thought of her."

"He didn't do it to her," I said mildly. "In fact, he didn't even do it to you. He didn't want you to know about it. Is he still involved with that woman?"

She shrugged, "He says not. Says he told her it was all finished...said it was just one of those things that happen."

"Perhaps you might consider putting this behind you."

"Whose side are you on anyway? No, I won't put it behind me. I could never trust him again and I won't live like that. And I want him to pay for what he's done."

"How is he taking all this?"

"Not well. He feels guilty...really guilty. And he should feel guilty. He says I can have everything — the house, the IRA's and the SUV. All he wants is to keep his pension, which is not that great anyway as he changed companies four years ago and rolled all his severance into the IRA's. He says nothing has to change. He'll keep supporting the kids and me. I can even keep my membership in the golf club, as if I'd want to. Why would I want to run into him in the dining room with some new little bimbo?"

It was a time for rational thought, which apparently had blown out the window like the condoms in his shirt pocket, had they been inflated.

"He's being very generous. He may not remain that way," I advised. "You should take advantage of his offer. There is no way the court will give you the home free and clear, all the IRAs and let you have ongoing spousal support. You're a comparatively young woman. They'd expect you to attempt to re-establish yourself, although the kids will get child support right up to the time they graduate from university.[6]

You'll be expected to start a new life within a certain length of time. If you are really lucky, you might get exclusive possession of the home for a few years, but a judge will order its eventual sale. You should take his offer very seriously. If he seeks legal counsel, the lawyer may talk him out of it."

"I already told him I wouldn't accept it. I want to go to court and tell a judge just what he's done. Anyway, he already has a lawyer. I'm sure you'll be hearing from him."

I watched her from my office window as she trotted toward her shiny SUV, her daughter walking slowly beside her, head down, blonde streaked hair covering her face.

The woman was an idiot, I thought to myself. If anything, the offer her guilt-ridden husband had made was unbelievably generous. It was something that should be reduced to writing, signed and witnessed with all due haste. Any attorney worth anything would try to talk him out of it. If he had come to me and told me his offer, I would have questioned his sanity and attempted to convince him otherwise.

Within a week, I received a letter from the office of a young and inexperienced attorney who had been retained by her husband. The emphasis of the lawyer's practice was in real estate matters. Unbelievably, he had reduced his client's overly generous offer into a formal offer of settlement. It was all there — the house, the IRAs, the support, and the SUV.

The only furniture he kept was a desk, which he had inherited from his father. The support was generous — over half his income and ongoing. Her sole concession would be that they were to have joint custody, which in reality was only a label. The girls were actually to spend most of their time living with their mother in the former matrimonial home and were to spend only every second weekend and summer vacations with their father.

---

[6] In Ontario, Canada, child support is paid until a child completes his or her first university degree, which could be up to age 23. In most of the United States such is not the case, for example, in California, child support stops at age 19.

In addition, if the matter were concluded by means of a separation agreement, he agreed to contribute twenty-five hundred dollars towards his wife's legal fees. A financial statement was attached to the offer as if to convey the sincerity of its contents.

A copy of this phenomenal offer was sent to my client. It was two weeks before she made an appointment. She had no impetus to hurry, as his entire pay check was being deposited into a joint account to which she had access.

Her life was essentially the same, except he had complied with her request to leave the home. He was now renting a furnished apartment near his office in Toronto.

She informed me on her second visit that she had no intention of making things *any easier* for him. She insisted that she wanted *to drag him through the courts and make him pay.*

"Besides, there's no reason he should have joint custody. I won't have my daughters exposed to some little French whore. Anyway, at the present time, they don't want to see their father."

I argued; I explained; I warned; I cajoled. There was no way that she could do better in court: indeed, she could do considerably worse. She was a healthy, relatively young woman, who would be expected to contribute to her own support after a period of re-establishment. She would not be permitted to stay in a five thousand square foot home forever. The children would come around. They had been listening to her too much. With any encouragement, they would see their father and would re-establish their relationship. He had been a great dad and was still one regardless of his affair.

If she insisted on going to court under the circumstances, the legal fees could be considerable. The money would be better spent on her re-establishment and the children's education. I informed her she could use the money *to get on with her life*, a phrase so often used by various judges I couldn't believe I was using it. But it was very appropriate in this particular case.

I could have been speaking to a wall. Her mind was made up. I asked for a much larger than usual retainer, hoping that its size would at least nudge her into a world of reality. There was no hesitation. She pulled a checkbook from her Gucci bag and executed the check from their joint account, signing her name with a flourish.

I made a last effort. "You know, they don't really look at conduct anymore. Although adultery and cruelty are still grounds for divorce, very few attorneys ever use them. You can get a divorce after being separate and apart for one year and that's the way it usually goes."

No fault divorce can be done by mutual consent without grounds in most States, although cruelty, abandonment, and adultery still exist. In California, there are two grounds for a no-fault divorce: irreconcilable differences causing the irremediable breakdown of the marriage or incurable insanity.

To get a no-fault divorce, one spouse must simply state the grounds recognized by the law of that State. All States and Provinces allow divorces regardless of who is at fault.

She had given the matter considerable thought. "I want her named in the Petition and served. I want her served in front of the whole store. I want management to know just what kind of bitches they hire to run their stores. It's against company policy you know—relations between company members. He could get into major trouble for that."

In spite of the sizeable retainer, I was losing patience. "And if he loses his job, then what?" I asked.

She only shrugged.

It lasted for over a year. Luckily, he held on to his employment, but Miss Quebec did not. Sympathy for her predicament apparently brought them together again and the brief affair, which had been terminated before the lubricated condoms had been discovered, was on again with renewed vigor.

After the divorce petition was served, with all its exorbitant demands, the previous offer, which had been produced by the inexperienced young attorney, was formally withdrawn by the astute and experienced lawyer who was now representing the husband.

Things progressed in the usual fashion with court motions, discoveries and an eventual trial. The offer of the home was no longer on the table. The husband wanted it sold so that he could purchase his own home and have his daughters spend extended periods of time with him. In fact, he desired to have a home in the same area so that the girls could come to him directly from school.

He had made arrangements with his employer to travel less and was actually asking for full custody in order to overcome *the alienating tactics* of the mother. Moreover, the now unemployed Miss Quebec had no doubt persuaded him that his former generous offer of spousal support was no longer feasible.

The joint account was closed and the amount awarded by the judge in the motion that followed was considerably less than the previous offer. In fact, His Honor suggested that the wife should commence computer studies in furtherance of future employment.

It was all having a devastating effect on my client, who now complained to me that she needed sleeping pills to sleep and antidepressants to function. She complained that her daughters were turning against her. They blamed her for their newly-reduced circumstances and she felt that their father was "buying them."

A week before the trial, offers were exchanged. Our offer was exactly the same as the one made by the husband at the beginning of this legal circus. But she had gone too far and the husband's offer, although not completely unreasonable, bore little resemblance to the previous one.

The house was to be immediately listed for sale. The proceeds of the sale, IRAs and the husband's pension were to be divided equally. Spousal support was to terminate after a two-year period. Child support was to be in accordance with the guidelines, but he would pay for all extraordinary expenses — ballet classes, figure skating, etc. She was allowed to keep the SUV and he would continue to use the leased vehicle supplied by the company. Each party would pay their own legal fees, which by then were considerable.

She sat slouched in her chair and said, "It's not acceptable. It's all the fault of the French bitch and the new attorney. Surely, a judge will see how unfair he is being."

She now had no choice but to go to court. She was a terrible witness. Too many sleeping pills and antidepressants had taken the edge off her voice and she appeared almost comatose at times. The judge, noted for frugality in his personal life, pursed his lips in disapproval at her list of monthly expenses including her proposed recapping of teeth and beauty salon visits.

He ordered her support to be limited to a two year period. Joint custody of the three daughters was awarded, with the girls effectively going between the two homes, as recommended by the psychologist who had carried out a court assessment.

The girls, in spite of the mother's *alienating tactics*, wished to remain in close touch with their father, who had remained generous to them throughout the proceedings. Each party was to bear his or her own costs, although His Honor insinuated that he was tempted to award the costs to the husband, since his offer was quite close to the actual judgment. However, an award of costs against the wife would "substantially impede her future re-establishment."

The result was seen as a disaster by my client. Coming out of her drug-induced haze, she blamed me, the judge, the husband, Miss Quebec, the husband's attorney and her *treacherous little girls*.

Sometime later I was told that the two older girls had gone to live permanently with their father. The younger child was considering joining them and a motion had been brought to court in furtherance of this change in custody. She refused to pay her final legal fees, stating that the case should never have gone to court. She was completely correct — except that she blamed everyone but herself!

Sharon, my former receptionist, who was considered to be an aficionado of the singles-bar scene in Toronto, told me she had run into Annabelle. In her words, "She looked stoned and was with some dude I wouldn't even look at." Considering Sharon's taste in men, I shudder to think of the *dude*.

This fiasco is a classic example of a client who wouldn't take advantage of early separation guilt and the advice of her attorney. She threw away a very generous offer and ended up with an unsatisfactory result.

Annabelle Brown could have had her palatial home in West Toronto, her social membership in the golf club, her kids to chauffeur and ongoing support, had she simply accepted her husband's guilt induced offer at the very beginning. As it was, not only did she end up with no home, but her kids ended up with her much-maligned spouse, who was much richer and one hell of a lot more pleasant.

The lesson is obvious. Look at that first guilt induced offer carefully. Timing is vital. See your attorney and go over it. Does it exceed the parameters of existing law? Can you live well with it, or at least comfortably? Don't be ridiculous about the joint custody label. It is, after all, just a label. It's the provisions under the label that count. Going to court unnecessarily is an ugly luxury you can't afford, unless, of course, there are hidden assets, and a totally unreasonable and uncooperative attitude from your estranged partner.

**H**e told me, his round ruddy face quivering with conviction and ill repressed anger, "It goes against everything I was ever taught or believed in."

He'd been brought up by his grandparents, church going Baptists, in a small town in Western Ontario. He'd never known his father, a visiting American, who disappeared after spending one seductive night with his librarian mother, who was still living at home at the time.

His mother married three years later, but he remained with his grandparents, who, he assured me, were *great people*. When not attending church and Sunday school he had played hockey. Although he was not drafted to play hockey in North America, he played well enough to be drafted by a professional league in Europe, where he had traveled, competing in the Balkan States.

In Denmark, he had met his wife — a slim, blonde, softly spoken girl who was a perfect foil for his blustering, loud self. She spoke four languages, and although not particularly well educated, obtained an impressive position running a stock account for a group of Danish businessmen, who paid her a six-figure income for her efforts.

She did, in fact, have a much better income than he did, after he put an end to his professional hockey career and returned to Canada. After two failed efforts, he finally obtained a real estate license, marketing less expensive homes in the Greater Toronto Area. His career was not successful and, although an aggressive hockey player, he appeared to lack this initiative in his employment.

"Not the brightest," quipped my legal clerk.

*And bull-headed to boot*, I thought.

His grandparents had died within six months of each other and had left him, due to their Scottish thriftiness, over half a million dollars, which in the late 90's was still a substantial figure. With this money, he had purchased an impressive home, placing the title in joint tenancy with his wife. There was a large backyard where his six and eight-year old sons could practice hockey with him and a hoop above the garage door for basketball. He belonged to the Masons and attended the local church, hoping his affiliations would aid his limping real estate career.

She complained at times of their lack luster life but by and large it was not an unhappy marriage. She was quiet and encouraging to him and placed her large monthly income in their joint account, from which all expenses were paid. She was a fond and affectionate mother to the boys.

In fact, everything was going reasonably well until the most prominent member of the Danish Financial Group came to Canada for a meeting and the wife ended up spending a Saturday morning in his hotel room.

She had, my client informed me, told him she had some "loose ends" to straighten up at work. But she never worked on Saturdays, and he was suspicious, knowing that the group head was arriving. He parked the kids with a neighbor and followed her. Afterwards there was a confrontation, a denial, and then, under a barrage of questions, a confession.

He informed me it was something he could not overlook. He insisted she had proved herself to be an unfit mother and he wanted custody of his sons. He wanted the house, since he had paid for it entirely from the money he inherited from his grandparents, who of all people would not want some adulteress profiting from their years of thrift.

After her reluctant confession, she had told him he could keep the house. And he was holding her to it, he told me.

He also wanted her to pay child support.

I assured him it was very generous of her to offer the home which was, as I recall, worth about six hundred thousand dollars. He had chosen to title the house in both names and as such there was a presumption of gift.

It had been a relatively long marriage of about ten years during which she had contributed the greater amount of the income that she had willingly shared. There were no separate accounts — everything was jointly owned. A judge would assuredly conclude that his intent was to share the home with her when it was titled as a joint tenancy. In any event, it was the matrimonial home, an asset traditionally shared. She was also willing to share a significant IRA and joint custody of the children. She was willing to procure a home in the general area so that the boys could attend school from both homes and both parents could continue to be part of their lives.

I assured him it was a very generous proposal, no doubt motivated by her remorse over his obvious displeasure and outrage upon his discovery of her Saturday morning dalliance.

"Take advantage of this," I advised him. "She has not seen an attorney yet and a lawyer will doubtless try to talk her out of it. Certainly her attorney will attempt to change her mind about walking away from her three hundred thousand share of the matrimonial home, which may well be, after all, the only tax free asset in Canada."[7]

I attempted to give motherly advice. "Things really haven't been that bad between you have they? Are you sure you can't try to overlook this? Time is a great healer and there's no indication that this has happened before or will happen again. People do silly things and then they are sorry."

Apparently she had been dealing with this man for several years over the phone and then, when they finally met face-to-face, things really heated up.

There was no way, he informed me, that he could ever overlook her adultery. She was untrustworthy and he would no longer have any peace of mind. Besides, he owed it to his sons to protect them from this type of woman. He wanted custody and they would be under his supervision.

The concept of joint tenancy eluded him. He attempted to justify his refusal to face the legal implication of property held in both names. "I only put her name on the deed as long as she stayed true to me. There was no deal that she would share in anything if she started to screw around on Saturday mornings with her boss. Besides, any judge would understand my feelings and be disgusted. Her conduct was European...or even worse...*Un-Canadian*."

He produced a wrinkled piece of paper upon which she had written out her agreed forfeiture of her financial interest in the home and her joint custody wishes. He pointed to her signature with an emphatic jab of his finger. *"See, she's even put it in writing!"*

"It doesn't mean much without her obtaining some legal advice," I cautioned. "She could always argue that you bullied her into signing it...I wouldn't count on it."

He ignored me. "I want her to leave. She won't go. She won't leave the kids. She says if anyone leaves, it's got to be me."

---

[7] Unlike the United States, there is no capital gains tax on the sale of a primary residence in Canada. Mortgage payments are not allowed as a tax deductible expense.

I dictated a letter in his presence in which I affirmed the agreement regarding the home and set forth his desires for sole custody, which I suspected would be a deal breaker.

He had informed me that she had retained one of the more conciliatory attorneys in town, so I was somewhat surprised to receive a letter from one of Toronto's top attorneys in reply to the wish list contained in mine. Not surprisingly, he totally rejected the desire for a transfer of the home, stating that if a paper had been signed to this effect, it was entirely due to the coercion of my client who he accused of using *bullying tactics.* The question of even joint custody was out of the question. She had been the party who was most responsible for the children and her hours were regular, unlike my client's who could be called on a house showing at any time. If, indeed, my client persisted with his ridiculous demands, they would be starting legal action.

"This is going to end up in court and you really don't want that. It's best to back off," I warned my client. "You're still under the same roof, so try to placate her. There's nothing wrong with joint custody. You're both good parents. There shouldn't be a problem here."

He had once told me, laughingly, that he had been known as *Meathead* by members of his hockey team. I returned the laugh at the time, but the appropriateness of his nickname became more and more apparent as time went on.

He kept badgering his wife. There were raised voices, banging of doors and accusations. In her affidavit, she said, "His behavior has been disruptive and frightening to the children. It is negatively affecting their schoolwork."

She wanted him to leave the home, but he could not afford to, so he refused.

There was a court motion, complete with a rendering of what could be called euphemistically, a *spirited exchange.* He was consigned to the basement where there was a bedroom and bathroom. He would be permitted to see the children only at allocated times. Now even more incensed, he became surly with the boys.

Moreover, a psychological assessment was ordered by the court to be conducted by a psychologist who was well known and often used by the wife's attorney. When I protested, the judge assured me that there was no way this eminent gentlemen would compromise his integrity by showing bias in favor of a firm which gave him most of their business.

Not surprisingly, the psychologist found her to be the more appropriate parent and criticized my client for his *intemperate and uncontrolled conduct* in front of the children.

The week before the inevitable trial, I went over evidence with my client whose limitations at that point appeared staggering. Whether through nervousness or total stupidity, he was unable to grasp even the basic rudiments of his financial statement.

"We must," I begged him, "make them an offer. Things don't look good and unless you make a reasonable offer you may very well have to pay her costs, which considering the Rambo who has been representing her, could be considerable."

Reluctantly, he agreed to permit the house to be sold with proceeds divided sixty/forty in his favor because of his greater contribution. There would be joint custody with the wife to have care and control of the boys, but with generous allocation of access to the father. The IRAs would be divided equally. Either party could buy out the other's interest in the home at an agreed upon price. The offer went on and on, but was, I warned him, much too aggressive —as no judge would be awarding an unequal division of property under the circumstances.

Not surprisingly, the offer was refused. The wife had paid too much in legal fees to back down now. Remorse had turned to genuine dislike. Although a shy and somewhat self-effacing person in real life, she was a superb witness, no doubt due to the efforts of her silver-tongued counsel.

My client took the stand and pulled a blank. I prefer not to remember most of the evidence, but one line comes back to me with a sickening thud. When asked by Mr. Smooth-talking Counsel why he wanted custody of his children, he replied, "Because my wife does."

At this point, I locked eyes with the Judge, who obviously thought little of my client and I knew the game was over. The wife's counsel had scored the winning goal and after that it was all a waste of time.

The wife, incidentally, purchased the husband's 50% interest in the home where she currently lives with her new boyfriend and the two children. Apparently the children refer to the boyfriend as *Daddy* in spite of his mild objections.

When I last saw my client, he was shopping at a nearby supermarket. He told me he was not doing well and had discontinued his real estate practice despite there having been several years of a buoyant market. He had gone through much of the money he received as his payout for the home. He had been forced to reduce his child support payments, as his new job — selling sports equipment, was not going well either.

His ex did not appear to object or notice the reduction. He assumed she was making so much money that it made no difference to her in any event. Besides, the new boyfriend did well and had apparently co-signed the mortgage, the proceeds of which she used to pay off his interest in the home.

"Life's really unfair," he complained, while we moved along the aisle at Fortino's Supermarket. "It's good that my grandparents are long dead so that they don't know what's happened to their money."

I found the last statement confusing, but then this particular client was not known for clear thinking.

He was right, of course, life is unfair and he should not have lost his inheritance or a great part of it in a divorce settlement. But his wife would doubtless argue that she should not have had to spend a hundred thousand dollars in legal fees for a result that was far inferior for her husband than the offer she had made to him the previous year.

I wished him well and told him I was sorry and genuinely meant it. I did not remind him that all of this could have been avoided if he had been willing to listen to counsel at the very beginning. Why rub it in?

What is to be learned from these two very similar cases? I suggest the following: Think seriously before you let a single lapse of infidelity break up your marriage. Distinguish in your mind between an ongoing affair in which your spouse has made an emotional commitment and a minor dalliance for which your spouse expresses regret and which appears unlikely to reoccur. Better still — don't cross-examine until damaging confessions are made. It's hard to explain away two lubricated condoms in one's shirt pocket, but any pseudo-logical explanation will do — although I can't think of one at the moment. Following one's spouse to a hotel, while tempting, may not achieve the desired result.

If this happens, then it's better to accept the spouse's denial of any impropriety, even though you are suspicious that a three-hour period at a hotel on a Saturday morning may not have been spent going over the group's recent capital gains.

Save face and pretend to accept the explanation even though it's highly unlikely. That is, if you don't want to disrupt your life, your kids, and what was, and could probably again be, a good relationship.

Don't believe those who say you can't break up a happy marriage and a happily married spouse will never screw around. Not true. People screw around for all sorts of reasons and men especially often don't attach as much significance to a frolic on the side as women do. In view of being lambasted by the feminists, if there are still some left, I have found this to be true. Bottom line: Don't embark on the thorny and financially devastating road to litigation unless you feel sincerely there is no turning back, and forgiveness is out of the question.

But if a break-up is inevitable, there is nothing like good old guilt. Play it for all it's worth. If you want to win in the break up lottery, now is your chance and you can do it on the very best terms for both yourself and the kids. If you're female, sob quietly — raucous sobbing can be jarring. Express your feeling of helplessness and hopelessness in a low voice after the children go to bed.

"I wish to keep the house. The children are comfortable in the neighborhood. You don't want them to feel resentful by forcing a sale; it will mean different schools and different friends and it will all be hard enough...God knows."

And by forgiveness, I don't mean that *it* gets paraded the next time you have an argument. Of course, you won't trust him or her again, but trust may be re-established in perhaps twenty or thirty years — just kidding, of course!

Do not hesitate to tell your unfaithful wife that she has devastated you emotionally and you cannot ever foresee another relationship. Never mind the blonde at the water cooler at work who came on to you at the last staff party. You will not under any circumstances call her a bitch, whore, or the *C* word. You will especially not, under any circumstances, admit to the odd frolic of your own. In fact, you have loved her, always loved her, and may always love her.

She has ruined your life, but then perhaps she can make it up to you in other ways: like waiving her rights to your pension, not hitting on you for spousal support, sharing the kids, or even better, perhaps letting you have the kids— who will only interfere with her social life in the long run.

This, I warn you, is a long shot. Most women do not want to hand over their children. Not just for the obvious reasons of motherly love, etc., but because they may be forfeiting a sizable amount of child support. They may also fear that their own family and friends will think less of them.

A mother giving up her children carries a stigma, which is unfortunate, because often some children would be better off with their father. However, this is one of the facts of life, like sharing joint custody with the father, who then feels that he is an integral part of the children's lives, even though the actual situation varies little from a sole custody label.

If, in the first flush of guilt, your erring spouse makes you an unbelievably generous offer, nail it down. If you don't, he or she will quickly see the error of their ways. Encouraged by the new partner in their life, or, by the impossibility of having a decent lifestyle while paying you that promised enormous hunk of spousal support each month, the spouse will awaken to the reality of his or her excessive generosity.

Depending upon the existence and wording of the separation agreement and the laws of your place of residence, the support payments may be tax deductible, but the deduction will hardly lessen the burden of the promises made to ease your guilty conscience.

Remember, when it comes to property, the courts will only give you what you're legally entitled to according to the various statutes governing the law in your particular Province or State. In Ontario, property is equally divided unless doing so would be considered grossly unfair: this is subject to a list of specific criteria.

Similarly, each State has its guidelines upon which to base an unequal division of marital assets. You'd be surprised how very few judges find an equal division of Family or Community Property to be grossly unfair or even inequitable (merely unfair). Instead, most judges run like rabbits from the concept of an *unequal* division, unless you can shock their conscience to such an extent that they try to make things right for the financially mistreated spouse; and by mistreatment I mean actual finagling the finances in bad faith and underhanded financial dealings. Some States, however, do consider abusive non-financial conduct when determining the division of property and the amount of support.

Things like adultery and mental cruelty in which one's self esteem is punctured on a daily basis matter little in Canada other than as grounds for divorce. Believe it or not, some judges commit adultery and belittle their own spouses. Unless you have been financially hoodwinked and blatantly cheated, and have the evidence to back up your claims, then, as Tony Soprano would say, "Fuhgeddaboudit."

Both Annabelle and our hockey player should have walked away from their marriages with homes intact, decent financial settlements and mutually agreeable custodial arrangements.

Most individuals who are relatively young at the time their marriages break up want to have some social life. What better way to have it than to have the kids spend three out of four weekends with the other spouse? And incidentally, if you're a woman who feels she has been unceremoniously dumped by her partner, what better revenge than to relinquish your teenagers to the wanderer and his new girlfriend?

Don't kid yourself; these kids are well aware, without your telling them, who's responsible for the breakup of Mom and Dad's marriage. Nothing breaks up a new union like the intrusion of the kids from the old one.

You can't afford to ignore an offer that's much better than what you'd get under current law — and if it's motivated by guilt, so what? Ongoing support without time limitations, generous and constant, in spite of successful efforts at re-establishment, is a real gift. Getting to keep an asset like a matrimonial home, which may appreciate considerably in future years, is also a real gift. Most judges order an immediate sale of the home so that the parties can *get on with their lives* — as if you can really get on with your life when the kids are angry that they have to change schools, lose friends, and live in an inferior neighborhood.

Believe it or not, kids, especially teenagers, are well aware of these things and have a tendency to place blame on the parent they perceive caused the changes to their lives.

Teenagers, besides being impossible to deal with, are greedy creatures and tend to favor the parent who provides them with designer jeans and state of the art sports equipment, motor bikes and cars.

Exchanging a great lifestyle for a rotten one is as dumb as it gets, especially when it's all forfeited for the dubious motive of dragging your spouse through the courts.

Our hockey hero complained about life being unfair. Whoever said that life was fair anyway? Losing one's kids isn't fair. But then, putting one's personal feelings out in front and railing against a mother whose morals had little to do with the warmth she showed her kids wasn't smart either.

Annabelle's fate should not have been to be stoned at the bar at the Waverley Hotel with some second rate dude and a two bedroom flat on Spadina Avenue as residence, or the hockey player walking alone in the supermarket with a half filled basket of what looked like frozen dinners. They both could have been better off, but they blew it.

They had a choice. They could have overlooked that lack of fidelity, or if not, accepted that great offer that came rolling in drenched with guilt and dripping with unfairness. They could have kept their homes and the kids and had a decent life. Rather than that, they chose to pursue at great legal expense, some mindless act of vengeance through the courts.

My oral sex queen should never have had her spouse arrested. The bad faith that was engendered as a result of his humiliation in a small community resulted in his taking a much more hard-nosed attitude than would otherwise have occurred. Brief marriages, which leave the partners basically the same as when they entered them, are not to be viewed as windfalls by most courts. Getting one half of a home after a two year marriage without having to go to the expense of litigation is an offer that should not be refused.

In all Family Law Acts regardless of whether your State is governed by a Community Property Regime or Equitable Distribution Laws there will be guidelines setting out when there should not be an equal division of property. Your attorney will further clarify this. Unless you come clearly within these guidelines, I suggest you take a conservative path in your road to litigation. If, on the other hand, you are offered a more than equal amount of community property from a guilt-ridden spouse, and it does happen on occasion, then by all means, seize the day!

# Chapter 4
## The Physical Abusers

I was scared," she stated, "scared that he'd kill me." It was one of those horrendous cases of spousal abuse where charges had never been laid. She did, however, produce medical reports that contained diagrams attesting to the extensive bruising.

My client was an overweight, native New Yorker of East European descent. Her husband had come to Canada in his late teens from the same part of Eastern Europe as her parents.

She had a Masters in Education and no doubt would have had an auspicious career except for the physical and emotional abuse which was constant and unrelenting. As a result, she abandoned her teaching career, and became so nervous that she was incapable of even driving a car. The only explanation I can think of as to why she remained in this relationship was that her self-esteem had become so fractured that she could not be proactive. She had sought counseling and was advised to get assertiveness training.

Advances in technology changed my client's life. She made a connection on the Internet, a man who was unfortunately married to an alcoholic. She sent him old pictures of herself in a bikini. She may have lost her self-esteem, but not her sex drive.

Unknown to her, her suspicious husband was having her followed by a private investigator. When she got together with her Internet Lover in the back seat of his ten year old Dodge all was recorded on film. Her husband thoughtfully showed the pictures to their two kids in order to prove that Mommy was *a whore.*

The new relationship was just the impetus she needed to restart her life. I often wondered how she ventured to go as far as she did, but fortunately for her there were still some good urges left.

Both my client and I decided the abuse was totally relevant: except for it, she would have continued teaching and she would have had a substantial pension. Her life had been essentially on hold for several years. She had let herself go physically, but each time she visited my office, I noticed the improvement in her appearance. Her hair was cut and styled; she had lost some weight and, believe it or not, she was smiling. Thank God for the Internet, I thought.

We petitioned for a divorce. He retaliated with an Answer and Counter-Petition charging adultery. His expensive private investigator had done a thorough job and we were served with a ten-page report giving evidence of adultery in minute detail. It was totally irrelevant as far as finances were concerned and, as my client asserted, certainly justified by the years of abuse!

The case, as could be expected, was a total nightmare. Her husband did not want to be bought out of the matrimonial home, but when reminded that her rather poor housekeeping would result in a reduced market value, he consented. Her parents fortunately came up with funds. The parties jointly owned a small condominium building. He insisted that it was worth much less than its actual market value and refused to accept an appraisal stating otherwise — and, of course, refused to place it on the market.

Despite his having used her as a punching bag for many years, he still took great exception to what he kept referring to as her *adulterous conduct* in the Divorce Petition.

Strangely, his female attorney took the whole matter

personally and was obviously not instructing him as to his legal obligations. In fact, when there was a court order requiring a sale of the condominium building, she threatened an appeal and took the position that this jointly owned asset was not divisible, which was blatantly ridiculous. More ridiculous was the fact that he did not see any need to pay child support — since the teenagers were residing with his wife!

Everything eventually settled a few days prior to a scheduled trial, as my client resented the legal fees involved to further fight her obstructive spouse. I believe, however, that she missed not having her day in court where she could have described her years of abuse in great detail.

On the good side, the children adjusted well, although there were ongoing problems obtaining a fair division of university fees. His claim to the money gifted by her parents was finally waived after a year of insistence that they consisted of some hidden slush fund. I was confused as to what he believed to be the source of that money. My client, as he was fully aware, had stopped working and remained separated from her career during the entire marriage.

Her new Internet mate proved to be laid back and non-abusive, although she complained that she was supporting him and that an unfair amount of his salary went to support his alcoholic wife. Their sex life, however, continued to be hot and she was enormously happier. Which goes to show, I suppose, that you can't have it all, but sometimes Internet love does work out and divorce can be a very good thing.

Jim Powers was six feet tall and two hundred pounds, but he looked as if he had gone ten rounds with Mike Tyson on a good day. His five-foot-three-inch, one hundred and twenty pound wife, periodically beat him up.

"Can't you hold her down?" I asked, hardly believing him.

"If I lay a hand on her," he informed me, "she says she'll telephone the police and then there'll be an order that I can't go near our house. I know…it happened to a friend of mine. I don't want to leave the kids and I can't afford to leave the house."

It was a ridiculous situation. In the divorce petition I described in great detail how these assaults would be triggered by so minor a trifle as his delay in putting out the garbage or forgetting to fill her car with gas. The purpose of detailing the assaults was to obtain a restraining order which appeared to be necessary.

The trouble was no one believed my client. The judge hearing the motion and seeing my client, broad shouldered in his sports jacket, actually laughed and refused to grant an order. The matter was eventually settled, but only after an order was issued by a female judge requiring that the home be sold and with a warning to the wife that if the assaults against her husband continued, he would be given exclusive possession of the home pending its sale.

Perhaps it takes a woman to believe what another woman is capable of. At one point, I instructed my client to telephone the police. They had the same reaction as the first judge. In fact, they thought it was hilarious. It makes you wonder where people's heads are, especially at a time when you see some real violence by actresses in widely distributed movies.

Abused wives have other problems. One serious problem is that they have identified with their spouse's poor assessment of them. They believe that they are only worthy of being punching bags and that in some weird way they deserve all those black eyes, pushes and four-letter words.

One woman, who saw me only on one occasion, had cauliflower ears from being pummeled by her husband, an Army Sergeant, who forced the children to drill like recruits at 6:00 a.m. each morning. I begged her to start proceedings and I would attempt to get an order giving her exclusive possession of the home. I also attempted to persuade her to go to a shelter for abused women prior to my issuing and serving a divorce petition and to see a counselor for assertiveness training. Unfortunately, she had never seen a doctor after any of the ongoing assaults, nor had pictures been taken. She had never called the police. There was no evidence of her allegations, other than her cauliflower ears.

In any event, my advice was all for nothing. She never returned and I never found out what happened. So terrified was she of her husband, that she insisted on paying me in cash so that he could never find any proof that she had seen a attorney.

✦ ✦ ✦ ✦ ✦ ✦ ✦

Another client of mine, a short haired elementary school teacher with a firm Irish jaw and turned up nose, had discovered that her spouse had been having an affair with her cousin. She literally went mad. She telephoned her husband's employer, disclosing information unrelated to her husband's adultery and managed to ruin his quite successful career. As well, she telephoned both families, including his mother, and disclosed every juicy detail of his and the cousin's escapades. Unfortunately, the cousin was married and her husband was also enlightened by my client.

The spouse, not surprisingly, took her conduct quite seriously. So seriously, in fact, that he assaulted her, leaving some facial and arm bruising. He was arrested, charged, and released on the undertaking that he would not go near the home or my client. The undertaking, unfortunately, did not preclude the husband telephoning my client every hour on the hour to threaten her life.

Resourceful soul that she was, she taped some of the calls and returned to the local police precinct with the tapes She was equipped with a special bracelet with which she could contact the police if endangered. The husband was charged again.

Threatening death by telephone is a serious offence under the Criminal Code of Canada. The recognizance, signed as a condition of his release several days later, contained provisions that he was not to contact my client in any way or go within a hundred yards of the matrimonial home and the school where she taught.

At this point nothing deterred the spouse. Using his set of house keys, he entered the home a few days later and succeeded in tying my client to the bed. He informed her that he intended to send her to hell in a blaze of glory, courtesy of kerosene and a cigarette lighter.

She was able to use her police bracelet to summon the police. His proposed barbeque was interrupted and he was subsequently charged with attempted murder. This time there was no release.

Still undeterred, her recalcitrant spouse was caught conspiring with a fellow inmate to have my client murdered.

A divorce petition was issued and served on the husband at the detention center where he was residing and awaiting his trial. Why or how he ever got out of jail remains a complete mystery to me, but get out he did, and two years later he accosted my client in a parking lot outside a local supermarket. After she refused to speak to him, he shot her in the abdomen.

She survived and to the best of my knowledge, the husband remains in Kingston Penitentiary. She was placed under the Witness Protection Program, provided with a new name and teaches at an unknown school. She developed a well-founded paranoia and absolutely no one knows her name, address, current place of employment or anything else about her, including her attorney.

I managed to obtain her divorce on the facts alone as she would not appear in the courtroom. This was a complete horror from start to finish and a horrendous example of what can happen when two individuals of vindictive temperaments find themselves betrayed.

Without a doubt, my client overreacted to her husband's infidelity, but her reaction was nothing compared to his lethal overreaction to her response. He was doubtless sentenced to a considerable length of time in the penitentiary and she was sentenced to a lifetime of looking over her shoulder and forging a new life for herself.

It could have been worse — she could have been killed.

✦ ✦ ✦ ✦ ✦ ✦ ✦

**S**he was a relatively new attorney who had only been with my firm for a couple of years. She was enthusiastic, determined, and passionate about her client's rights — and she knew the law. Her client was a slight, dark-haired woman of Italian descent, in her late twenties, with two small children. She had been consistently physically abused by her husband from the first week of marriage.

"Her shins," stated her lawyer, "are permanently blue."

The client had worked as a part-time waitress and was friendly with a waiter at the same establishment. He listened sympathetically to her complaints, and advised her to see an attorney. Upon hearing that she had, her husband threatened her life.

Her lawyer did everything right. She obtained a civil restraining order and contacted the police. The husband was subsequently charged, but released on the condition that he not go near his wife. The condition of his release did not deter him; it only further incensed him.

He sat in his car with his brother in front of her rented apartment. Every time she emerged from or entered it, the brothers both drew their hands across their throats as an apparent threat.

Terrified, the wife wished to take the children, leave town and go into hiding. She had limited funds and her parents, who were from the old country, refused to fund the proposal.

My legal colleague, never deterred, obtained yet another specific restraining order forcing the police, who were less than proactive, to again charge the husband and his brother with threatening.

Unfortunately, the husband was released after being charged. He immediately went to the home, where the two children were present together with the visiting waiter. He kicked down the front door, entered the home and found his wife hiding in the bathroom. After kicking down the bathroom door, he threw her to the floor, put a knife to her head while she helplessly lay there, and kicked it through her temple.

The husband was charged, found guilty of attempted murder and incarcerated. The client remains permanently brain damaged in an east end hospital, where she babbles incoherently. Her parents took the children. The attorney still practices matrimonial law, but with understandable cynicism and vigilance when violence enters the picture.

What is the solution to this sort of tragedy? The police now have a zero tolerance policy towards spousal violence. It is now unlikely that a violent husband will be released, as in the past. If released, his breach of probation will result in additional incarceration. Breach of a civil restraining order obtained by an attorney is now seen as a criminal offence in Canada and in the United States.

Despite this, in all practicality, how do you avoid being murdered by a spouse who appears hell bent upon your demise? Have all guns removed from the home — the police will happily take them. Of course, guns can again be purchased in the United States, but not without a permit or license in Canada. Report every incident of violence directly to your local police precinct and, if you feel threatened — leave. Do not expose yourself to a potentially violent spouse.

I would say get your own gun, with the caveat that intimidated spouses may not be the best gun carriers. Shooting off your own toe helps no one and could be embarrassing. And you hardly wish to be shot with your own revolver.

McArthur drove an oil truck, a job for which he was paid quite well. He had lived with Phyllis for some twenty-eight years—and the last ten had been mutually miserable. They had two sons, one of whom lived with his girlfriend in a basement apartment of the party's home that was in McArthur's name. McArthur was frugal to a fault and was determined that Phyllis would have no claim whatsoever on *his* home or any of *his* property, including *his* pension.

As the years went by Phyllis' antagonism toward McArthur increased. She berated him with enthusiasm in front of their friends and physically attacked him, kicking him down the steps of *his home*. She refused to do any housework, or more seriously, to permit anyone else to do it.

When he came to my office during the coldest winter in years, McArthur was living with his dog in a trailer in the front yard. He professed his fear that she would somehow invade his frosty abode while he slept and finally finish him off. He brought along pictures of their filthy kitchen, which defied description, and informed me that his abusive partner had a physical set-to with his son's girlfriend when she attempted to clean it up. He wanted to be rid of her, which hardly surprised me, but he adamantly took the position that he would not give her one red cent unless ordered to by a judge.

There was no settling this case. Phyllis insisted that she wanted half the home. Since they had never been married, it was not a matrimonial home — so she had no claim. She claimed that she had contributed an extremely small amount from an inheritance from her mother during the time of cohabitation, but there was no evidence to support her claim. She even claimed one-half of McArthur's inherited property, to which, even had they married, she would have no claim. Inherited property is excluded from division by the Family Law Acts of Canada and the United States.

Interestingly, however, had Phyllis lived in Colorado she would have enjoyed all the rights of a married spouse upon a break-up, as do spouses in Saskatchewan, Canada, provided the couple had been together for an uninterrupted period of two years.

Her claims were unrealistic and drove McArthur, in his trailer smoking four packs of unfiltered cigarettes a day, crazy. Surprisingly, when Phyllis was asked during a discovery as to whether she had assaulted her husband, she agreed she had, stating, "He deserved it."

She appeared at motions court for an order for interim support, all five-foot ten of her, with a lantern jaw, short tinted hair swept back and an ample bosom pressing against a short leather jacket. McArthur sat behind me, smelling strongly of

Player's cigarettes and oil.

I related Phyllis' extreme conduct in detail to the judge. I stated that she had taken over the home, while McArthur cowered in his trailer after being physically ejected and argued the relevance of this evidence. I suspect that the judge did consider it, but he quite properly mentioned only the truly relevant factors — the twenty-eight year relationship, the birth of two sons and the fact that Phyllis had worked little during the period of cohabitation, producing only a very modest income, which compared unfavorably with McArthur's trucking income.

At that time, Phyllis was unemployed and the court believed McArthur had the ability to pay. His regular salary was imputed to him, not the reduced amount he produced to the court, complaining that his bad back had worsened since being attacked by Phyllis. The thousand dollars a month awarded to her for support was much less than would have ordinarily been ordered.

Paying Phyllis was like tearing a piece of flesh from McArthur, who promptly gave away most of his savings to his two sons. He earned their gratitude, but rather stupidly impoverished himself. He regarded his own self- impoverishment as a guarantee against future spousal support for Phyllis.

The matter finally settled when Phyllis acquired a another truck driver boyfriend, who she quite obviously did not see the need to physically attack, and McArthur acquired a girlfriend, who assured him that she loved him for himself alone. McArthur was finally convinced to pay a lump sum to rid himself of his monthly support to Phyllis, which was akin to monthly surgery without anesthetic.

These examples are cautionary tales and fortunately not typical. More often the abuser turns out to be nothing but a hollow bully, who, when a divorce petition sets out a series of violent acts, denies them, and acts like a reborn pussycat from then on.

A few of my clients have become so impressed with the new, softly spoken, kindly figure in their lives, that they have reconciled, only to have Mr. Hyde resurface within a few weeks: the second reincarnation proving to be even more challenging than the first. Unfortunately, judges and the police appear to feel that if there has been reconciliation, then perhaps the offending spouse was not so bad after all. As a result, they are less likely to make the requisite orders asked for in the divorce petition. Regardless of counseling, therapy and religious conversions, I am always hesitant to believe violent individuals basically change.

Abused women have become much less tolerant in accepting mistreatment and the police have adopted a zero tolerance position — the alleged abuser gets charged regardless. If you are a woman who fears potential violence, I suggest the following: As previously set out if there are weapons in the house, telephone the police and attempt to have them confiscated. I have found the police very cooperative when this occurs. After you have left, or after you have informed your husband that you are leaving, do not go back to the matrimonial home without a police escort, especially if he has been threatening or was violent in the past.

One of my clients attempted to retrieve personal property from the former matrimonial home and had wisely gone with a police escort. Upon seeing the police, her husband, who had been hiding in the attic with a gun, shot himself. Doubtless had my client been alone, she would have been the first victim.

Another mother of four, who returned home from a domestic violence shelter to get some possessions, was killed by the husband as she was leaving. She was not my client, but her cousin related the details. There was a history of abuse and the children testified against their father at the trial. The husband had attempted violence previously at the shelter. Whatever was she thinking?

Special care must be taken, especially if there has been a history of mental illness. Remember if your spouse is bi-polar, a depressive episode can be triggered by a loss — death, divorce, etc. Often if a separation has been disruptive, medication can be ignored. Do not place yourself in a position where you can be the target of a joint tragedy.

One of my clients, recognizing her husband's propensity towards violence, took the children and left the province immediately upon separation, leaving him with all the family property. I begged her not to go as I believed I could obtain a restraining order and provide protection. She refused to listen. Perhaps she knew her husband better than I did.

One problem relating to abuse is that the victim often refuses to cooperate as a witness at trial. This, of course, means that the charges are withdrawn or dismissed, and the perpetrator of the abuse has another opportunity, which could prove to be even more damaging.

Another problem is that charges are brought on flimsy and inconsequential evidence, taking advantage of the Zero Tolerance Policy. One pleasant and generous client of mine threw a pillow at his wife and was subsequently charged with assault. Needless to say, he became much less generous. A few others were goaded into protecting themselves by holding their wives flailing arms and were subsequently charged.

To give some unfortunate spouse a criminal record for this type of so-called assault is unfair and shortsighted, especially if traveling across the border is part of his employment. The real reason for it, of course, is to get a restraining order so that the so-called abuser is prevented from entering the home and the spouse can use this in a future court motion for exclusive possession of the marital home.

I have warned my male clients to just walk away, regardless of the provocation and if assaulted by their wives, to leave and go immediately to the nearest police precinct to file an incident report. This sometimes makes the police more reluctant to charge on some bogus future happening.

Don't hold your breath waiting for them to charge your wife. Nothing less than an actual bullet or knife attack seems to warrant that. It's a real basic lack of equality when it comes to the sexes. There is a genuine reluctance on the part of the police and, some of the judiciary to conclude that some women are as vicious as some men. In fairness, the majority of assaults are indeed perpetrated by men.

Some mental conditions result in financial abuse, even if not deliberately perpetrated. My client's husband, a chartered accountant, went on a spending spree across Canada. He used jointly owned credit cards and ran the balances up to the maximum. Most of the credit card companies would not accept my client's request to be exonerated as a joint owner. Neither were they agreeable to canceling the card considering the circumstances. Some did agree upon receiving a letter from me warning that if they failed to cancel the card, they would be legally responsible for payment for future purchases.

The garage was packed with dozens of expensive shoes, state-of-the-art tools, and the best designer suits. What did it all indicate — just an extravagant guy wanting to look his best? Not at all. In this particular case, it indicated a bi-polar individual, un-medicated and having a manic episode.

In this case, should a spouse merely suck it up, knowing that the individual was mentally ill at the time of these purchases and that the happening was nothing that a regular dose of Lithium or any of the dozen drugs currently on the market wouldn't cure? In this particular instance, my client refused to be responsible. After long discoveries, motions and a five-day trial in which her husband was funded by his family, who branded her as *completely heartless,* she withdrew from the marriage with her one-half of the home intact.

This did not, however, protect her from the demands of third parties and the credit card companies that pursued her relentlessly, garnishing her government income as soon as they concluded that the well was dry and the husband was unemployed. A sympathetic judge did give her an order against the husband that upon his obtaining employment again she could get some compensation. She told me she was not holding her breath.

With but few exceptions, most people are simply not good at dealing with mental illness. The most successful marriage I encountered involved a psychiatric nurse, whose husband was bi-polar. He would go into a depression each November and remain in bed until April. At that time, he would do a Lazarus, get up full of piss and vinegar and be extremely successful at his own business, which suffered during the six months he was unavailable.

During his good period, in which I suspect he was slightly manic, he was a marvelous father and doting husband. My client advised me that she would not consider ever obtaining a divorce, but she wished to be conservative about running up debt. Upon my advice there were no credit cards, lines of credit or any other credit sources that did not require both signatures. The husband, a splendid fellow during his good period, was well aware of his problem and adored his wife for putting up with him. She was, of course, a psychiatric nurse!

Unfortunately, many of those married to individuals with psychotic problems do not fare as well. As already related, people simply do not understand mental illness. Many believe the individual is merely acting badly.

Quite understandably, children tend to be quite judgmental in this regard, because they feel a deep sense of betrayal and disappointment when a parent acts irrationally. There is also the ever-threatening fear of suicide, which sometimes occurs when a sense of loss triggers a depressive episode. This results in a searing outpouring of guilt and grief that requires professional help for both the remaining parent and children. Children often seem to feel personally responsible for their parents' problems and have to be constantly assured that they are not.

One client's husband mixed his medication with copious amounts of liquor and kept the house in a constant uproar. One week after she obtained an order giving her and the children exclusive possession of the home, he overdosed. He was well insured and all assets were jointly owned. She inherited everything under the power of survivorship. I detected a distinct sense of relief. She confided that the children were much happier, although everyone, especially the teenagers, were questioning their involvement or lack of it in their father's life. The entire family received grief counseling.

**M**y client, Margaret, was not an attractive woman. In fact, she was dead homely and showed little interest in looking otherwise. In spite of this, her psychotic husband insisted she had a stable of lovers in hot pursuit. She was not allowed to leave the home to obtain employment, to mix with her friends or family or to even drive a car, unless accompanied by her older children. He even followed her to the supermarket, which was near the home and where she was allowed to shop once a week. She acknowledged he was sick—and, I added, *hallucinatory and delusional.* She desperately wanted out. He threatened death if she left him. When she did, he carried out his threat: hanging himself in the basement.

She was unabashedly and openly delighted and relieved, especially when the insurance company did not hesitate to make the payout, despite the fact that there was a proviso against suicide in the policy. They accepted that there was mental illness involved. There was no grief counseling, but she mused aloud to me as to whether she could have somehow changed things.

She could not force him to seek psychiatric help and the family doctor had refused to intervene, as did the police, who did not believe that excessive jealously met the criteria for possible harm to others.

I frankly believe that it's sheer madness to permit deeply disturbed psychotics to ruin the lives of others, and ultimately their own, by not forcing them to obtain medication and therapy because of supposed violation of their civil rights.

But then what do I know? I am only an attorney.

# Chapter 5
## Summary of Solutions & Preventive Measures

What, you may ask, do we learn from all of this? I suggest that adding some color to your divorce proceedings is all well and good, provided there is some relevancy to the color. And what, you may ask, is considered to be relevant? As well-known entrepreneur and business expert, Kevin O'Leary, always states, "It's all about the money."

Applying this theory, the washing, powdering and diapering of Mr. Insurance, let alone his rum flavored baby bottles, in reality, made not a whit of difference in the future financial arrangements between him and his wife. In fact, an adept attorney could very well have these paragraphs in a divorce petition "struck" as being outrageous, inflammatory and irrelevant.

Mrs. Insurance concocted the flimsy rationale that this type of foreplay affected her emotionally so that she was unable to carry on employment. This assertion lent a strained, but most probably ineffectual, financial rationale to her position.

Whether Mr. Insurance settled this matter because he feared some embarrassing revelations would be leaked to his substantial group of clients is hard to say. The marriage had been long enough to warrant support and Mr. Insurance was in a much better position financially than his wife. The income of his business had increased throughout the marriage and an agreed upon appraiser showed it to be much more valuable. Besides, there was the matrimonial home, which was to be shared, although the sole contributor had been Mr. Insurance.

The wife, with her eye on her personal trainer, insisted upon a lump sum rather than monthly support, which she feared, might be reduced if she started to cohabit. Mr. Insurance wanted his spousal payments to be tax deductible. Since a lump sum payment would not be deductible he held out for monthly support payments. He did agree to make payments of the same amount for a specific period, regardless of the wife's change in circumstances, a change that I suspected she had fully in mind from the start.

It was a reasonable settlement with each party feeling they were dealt a bad hand. More than likely that would have been the case even if the embarrassing sexual life of the parties had not been revealed by the wife.

Had we gone to court, I do not believe for one moment that most judges would have accepted the fact that the vulnerable Mrs. Insurance had been emotionally scarred by her motherly duties to Mr. Insurance.

In fact, I can almost hear one of our local judges commenting, "I didn't just fall off the back of a turnip truck, Mrs. Hillier."

**O**ur insurance couple with the dog collar, torture chamber in the basement and an assortment of spanking equipment, settled irrespective of the revelation of these little goodies. The wife's revelation of the husband's need for domination and the kinky sex, which the arrival of her mother ended, was absolutely not relevant. It was mentioned to the husband's attorney as merely part of a conversation in passing and his attorney laughed, although I'm sure he passed it on to the husband.

The wife had suffered an economic disadvantage as a result of the termination of the marriage regardless of the reasons for it. In addition, she had not worked after the first few years of this long-term marriage and was now in her middle fifties. She could hardly be expected to re-establish herself, particularly since her employment, even during the early years of the marriage, was only as a low salaried sales girl.

Since the date of the marriage, the insurance brokerage had become more valuable, a fact established by an appraisal. The increase in value could certainly not be attributed to the wife's entertainment of business associates or the occasional weekends when she tidied things up and filed some material for her husband.

She was entitled to one-half of the value of the home, and what is considered in Canadian law as an *equalization payment* representing the increase in value of the brokerage.

In many States this would merely be considered as a division of *Community Property*. The husband also shared his IRA'S and paid ongoing support, which would not be decreased should the wife wish to obtain part-time work as perhaps a receptionist. It was a satisfactory conclusion made easier by the attorney for the husband, who was well aware of the current law and who indeed became a well-known and respected judge in matrimonial law a few years after.

Lesson to be learned — if you have some really titillating stuff, why not just mention it in correspondence or have your attorney mention it at the same time that you are exchanging financial statements? Don't reduce it to writing and place it in the divorce petition, unless it has financial implications. From a practical point of view, the wife wished ongoing support, which was dependent on the husband's doing well at his insurance brokerage.

Why do anything that could jeopardize that?

✦ ✦ ✦ ✦ ✦ ✦ ✦

**O**ur battered spouse, who was well aware of the thousands tucked away in vaults in Athens or buried in accounts under other names in local banks, presented another problem. The courts demand evidence.

*Suspicion* without hard evidence is insufficient to prove the existence of hidden money, or what courts often refer to as a *lack* of *financial disclosure*.

Had Lucy even counted the money she found in a box in the matrimonial home, taken some pictures or even invited a third party to witness its existence, this could have been helpful. If she had diligently searched for documentation which may have been in the husband's possession after his many trips abroad, this also would have helped. Unexplained expenditures could have substantiated the availability of extra money.

Fortunately, well meaning friends tipped her off to a hidden mortgage of two hundred and fifty thousand dollars held by the husband: it was traceable and provable through the Registry Office. There was simply no evidence to prove the existence of the considerable amount of money she alleged was hidden away in Athens.

Sometimes it's necessary to add family members as third-party respondents. In Lucy's case, several houses had been placed in the children's names. My client declined to interfere, although doing so would certainly have been to her financial advantage. She simply did not want to alienate her much loved son. The daughters willingly gave the money from the sales of their houses to their mother.

Cases where assets are hidden by an unscrupulous spouse are notoriously difficult. Suppose for example, it was determined that a husband's mother, who had been a cleaning woman all her life and who was living on sparse survivor's and old age pensions, had five hundred thousand dollars in a bank account. Surely, regardless of how unpalatable it may seem, that would be a case where the mother should be named as a third party defendant.

If you've been in business with your spouse, you've both, no doubt, profited from the cash side of the business. Even if your spouse may have profited much more than you did, an audit by the IRS may very well reduce the value of your husband's net family property, but it will also reduce yours.

I have had many clients, all women, who wanted to go to the IRS and report their husbands. I have always dissuaded them. Regardless of how it turns out, the informant is the one that suffers in the long run. Ruining someone you wish to get money from is not a sound idea. I was told by an auditor friend from the Income Tax Department that a vast number of the tips they receive are from estranged spouses.

My unequivocal advice is: **DO NOT** report your duplicitous spouse to the IRS.

**M**ore often than not *dishing the dirt* over past lapses of decency is not only a waste of time but can undermine your cause of action. My client's squalid little episode with the stripper at his stag party the night before his wedding more than twenty-five years earlier, and as a result of which he transmitted a STD to his pregnant wife had no relevance to his wife's petition for a divorce. It was obviously inserted to inflame a judge as to the character of my client. The wife, I suspect, wrote a story of her marriage and passed it on to her attorney, who inserted every detail in the divorce petition.

Should your attorney be naïve and unaware of the current law regarding non-financial conduct, then you have a good reason to question his or her judgment. In this case, it set the stage for a series of nasty allegations that went back and forth and which eclipsed the one important aspect of conduct which was relevant — that my client had entirely funded his wife through university and a dietician's course, and as a result her earnings far exceeded his quite modest income as a maintenance mechanic for a local golf club.

On the other hand, the amending of a divorce petition to include damages of $500,000 for the transmission of the herpes virus, was, I believe, a relevant and valid claim. My client had been unaware that her spouse was infected with this virus and as such was unable to protect herself. The claim caused her husband serious concern — so serious, in fact, that after a year of court motions and hours of discoveries, the matter was settled within a week. The exposure of having transmitted a venereal disease is no doubt embarrassing and poses a valid claim. My client's obligation to explain to a new mate that she had contacted this lifetime virus could quite conceivably end the relationship, with a resulting financial impact.

**P**hysical abuse by either party must be disclosed. This includes female spousal abuse, even if such claims are all too often not taken seriously enough by judges, police or opposing counsel. Physical abuse may very well escalate and one can end up, as did my client, under the Witness Protection Program, or worse, like the battered waitress, babbling in her hospital bed as a result of a knife being kicked through her temple. Each was an assault carried out by a husband who served much too little time.

If you are being abused and you have not yet started an action, see your doctor the next time there is bruising, or if there are no signs of the abuse, at least obtain a prescription for an anti-anxiety drug. Take pictures. Tell your close friends and show them proof, if possible. Go to the police station and file an incident report or merely have them open a file which states that you have spoken to some of the officers regarding threats made against you.

You do not have to file charges against your mate if you visit the police, but at least, if there are documented incidents, there will be a history of past conduct which can be referenced. If you do have your spouse charged, go through with it. Refusing to proceed can make you much more vulnerable in the future.

My school teacher client, whose husband took a contract out on her while in prison and who eventually shot her in a parking lot, would be dead today had she not gone to the police and had them equip her with an emergency bracelet in case her husband violated his bail provisions and came to the home.

Incidentally, I always wondered why, knowing his propensity towards violence, as surely she must have, she made all those unfortunate telephone calls to his employer and girlfriend's husband. This is not to say that I am in any way condoning this man's behavior which was unforgivable, but provoking the violent is not always advisable.

My client, who had endured so many years of physical abuse that she abandoned her teaching job, had all of the assaults well documented and had seen her doctor, not only for anxiety medication, but also to have a witness to her severe bruising. In the end, she was disinclined to proceed to trial. Luckily, no threats or physical abuse took place after the separation.

I was certain she would have received compensation for the years in which she made no pension contributions nor received any salary as a teacher. She had re-established herself, however, and did not wish to proceed further. It is worthy of note that she had everything fully documented including an actuarial assessment of the money lost by virtue of the abandonment of her career.

Violent behavior to either a spouse or a child is relevant when it comes to obtaining an order for exclusive possession of a matrimonial home. It does, moreover, give the victim a leg up in the litigation process and at least keeps the children in the same environment pending a sale of the home. If the assaults are real and the victim has genuine fear, there should be no hesitation in contacting the police, who have in my municipality, as previously stated, a zero tolerance code of conduct.

It is not a wise idea to fabricate or exaggerate a so-called assault so you can obtain exclusive possession of the home. I have known clients to do this and it ends badly. The targeted spouse is outraged and all too often the matter which could probably have been settled ends in expensive and protracted litigation.

My four-pack-a-day, battered truck driver thought he had his bases covered when he refused to marry his spouse and kept everything in his name. The trouble was that the union however miserable for both parties, lasted twenty-eight years and produced two children. There was no way his partner was going to be denied continuing support, regardless of new boyfriends or deplorable conduct.

On the other hand, to force one's partner to freeze his butt in an un-insulated trailer during a Canadian winter is cruelty in the extreme. The judge did order monthly support, but I do believe the psychological impact of the wife's conduct influenced the meager award. Most other judges would have probably done the same thing.

Cohabitation does not give the other party any rights to property, unless there has been an actual contribution of money or work done on the property in question, which could result in the imposition of a trust. No one seems to know this. Time and again, I have had male clients come to me believing that because their girlfriends have been living with them they now have a rightful claim to one-half of their homes. They don't unless they live in Colorado, a state that gives property rights even to the unmarried.

To claim a division of property under the property laws of your State or Province you must have gone through a marriage ceremony. This applies in Ontario, Canada, even if the ceremony proves to be invalid because of a failure to obtain a State or Provincial license, or if the individual performing the ceremony lacks qualification. You must, however, have good faith and believe in its validity. The law apparently recognizes your good intent.

The Province of Saskatchewan, similar to the State of Colorado, does not require marriage for a property division. In all other States and Provinces if you are not married, you cannot take advantage of the property provisions of the Family Law Acts and Community Property Divisions — it's that simple. You may, however, be liable for the support of your spouse if you've been cohabitating with him or her for over three years in Canada, or for the required time period specified in States where such support is allowed. This, of course, depends upon a proof of need and the financial ability to pay.

Needless to say, you are always obligated to pay child support even if you are not married and haven't been living together. If you have not been living together and the new addition looks strikingly like the new mother's past boyfriend, then do insist on some DNA testing. If you must pay, and indeed you must under the Child Support Guidelines regardless of where your place of residence may be, at least you should have the peace of mind of knowing that the child is your biological offspring.

**I** often wonder how tragedies, like the permanently disabled young wife in palliative care for life, can be prevented. The attorney involved did everything within her power to prevent what happened. A restraining order had been obtained and the husband incarcerated for a period for its breach. Nothing dissuaded him. Perhaps more direct contact with the police would have helped. With each tragedy, the law has become more strict and the police more willing to charge.

Unfortunately, all too often the victims will not testify against their abuser and indeed reconcile with him or her shortly after. This discourages the police, who may in time tend to be less zealous as a result.

I have also found that some cultures appear more tolerant of spousal abuse than others. I had a Jamaican client, who was so badly battered she could hardly sit in a chair in my office. She briefly got together with her abuser after a five-day trial and even signed a mortgage on his behalf against the quite valuable matrimonial home, which I had acquired for her pursuant to the court judgment. Needless to say, he did not make the payments and the home was eventually lost. She had effectively undermined her own case.

If abused, you can always go to a shelter. No one actually enjoys this, but at least a shelter provides a temporary place of safety. There is a risk, however, when the victim leaves the sanctuary even temporarily. As previously shared, in 2002, in Woodbridge, Ontario, a mother of four was shot in the face after returning from a shelter in order to retrieve her belongings. At the subsequent trial for second-degree murder, the children all gave evidence against the father—too late, unfortunately.

I would also caution you, male or female, if you are involved with another partner, let matters de-escalate while you are negotiating with your spouse. In other words, *chill*. Nothing enrages a discarded spouse more than to have the children inform them that they have seen *Uncle* Bill or *Aunt* Betty while on visitation and what fun they had. There is nothing like good old jealousy to prevent settling anything and you can be sure that the children will all have colds next weekend and visitation will be denied. Also, jealous spouses seldom exhibit normal behavior.

For everyone's sake, keep it under wraps.

# Chapter 6
## The Vindictive Spouse

I often wonder why gorgeous women believe that their husbands are immune from having affairs. Your spouse's playing about has nothing to do with your being drop dead gorgeous, or the plainest, plumpest thing around. Men are susceptible to women who make a play for them, regardless of how hot their spouse may be. This, I have often told my female clients, is not to be taken personally. Of course, it always is, but some take it more personally than others. And as a result they do unbelievably stupid and harmful things, which unfortunately turn around and bite them in the butt, as well as ruining their husband's careers and their own financial future.

Take Lisa MacDonald, for example. On her first visit to the office, my receptionist telephoned me to merely say "WOW." Lisa was the most immaculately turned out woman I had ever seen, bar none. Her streaked hair was perfect, worthy of Vogue, and her makeup so expertly applied that it must have taken her a full hour before leaving the house. She was thin, just short of anorexic, but her size C cup was intact and, I suspected, surgically enhanced. Her nails, an interesting maroon color, tapped on my desk as if relaying a conspiratorial sort of Morse Code.

After two minutes I got the message. Her husband, Constable Gerry MacDonald, of the Local Regional Police, had indulged in an affair with "some low-life on social services" — a single mother in subsidized housing who wouldn't know a manicure from a pedicure. It had lasted for some three weeks, until Lisa became suspicious about all his extra duty hours. It stopped the night she cornered him upon his return home, when he made a full confession.

I had seen Jerry a few times before around the criminal courts when he testified. He was a big amiable fellow — always smiling — even when he stopped the occasional driver for going thirty miles over the speed limit. Not a brilliant individual, but well-meaning and exactly the type that would become involved with a single mother in subsidized housing, believing no one would ever know.

"Do I look like a woman whose husband would run around on her?" she demanded.

I assured her that she did not and tried to pacify her by explaining that this temporary lapse probably meant little to Constable MacDonald and that it was a great mistake to take it personally.

I could have been talking to a wall. She wanted to immediately commence divorce proceedings charging him with adultery and have the woman served. She saw no necessity as to why she should wait for a year before getting rid of this "puke".

She worked part time in the cosmetic department at Holt Renfrew which explained the clothes and makeup. But she needed money for her and the kids until she could get a better paying job. Naturally, she would have full custody of the boy and girl, ages six and seven, although he was, she sniffed, "a good dad…if you considered someone who had affairs a good parent."

"One seldom has anything to do with the other," I interjected, but again I was speaking to a wall.

She came in the next week to sign her petition. Things had worsened and she informed me the petition and grounds needed to be amended.

Leaning forward, she informed me in a confidential but even tone, "Do you know he's been sexually abusing the kids?"

I looked at her carefully. One well-plucked eyebrow was lifted and she wore a slight smile.

"In fact," she continued, "I'm going to have him charged. You don't believe me, do you?"

"Not for one moment," I answered.

"Then I'll get someone who does believe me," she answered, her voice with an edge that could cut through anything including her kids' hearts. "Bill me out and I'll take my file right now."

"Some people," I murmured, "will believe anything."

And they did. Gerry MacDonald was duly charged with sexually abusing his two children and was suspended from all duties at his precinct. His access to his children was restricted pursuant to a court order in which the judge was doubtless influenced by the criminal charge. Apparently he had admitted, after hours of questioning, that he had once masturbated in the same room as the children while they slept. How this could constitute sexual abuse of the children I did not know.

The trial did not take place for two years. He was completely exonerated, as I knew he would be. Every cent he had went to pay the well-known criminal attorney he hired, who did his usual meticulous job.

Although the police force offered reinstatement, he voluntarily withdrew. "Too much had gone down," he had told a friend of mine. He obtained a job as a security guard at Walmart paying one-third of his original income. During the two-year period of restricted access, his kids had become estranged and did not wish to see him, which I suspected was due to the urging of his former wife. Rather than distress them, he also withdrew from being a father, which, even she had acknowledged, he was so good at.

Lisa MacDonald got her one-half of the home, plus one-half of his police pension against his equity. The rest of his house money went to pay his attorney. His income was so small that he was unable to aid his spouse in her re-establishment to any extent and his child support payments were also low.

I hope her second spouse is meeting all her needs. No one deserves what happened to Gerry MacDonald.

Why, I wonder, do so many cops fall into affairs and booze? Perhaps it's the shift work and the ongoing stress of policing. A lot of them sit around with their fellow officers and drink after work. Not all of them, of course, but quite a few. Their social life revolves around other police officers. This is understandable for obvious reasons. The older and more mature officers don't fall into this and know enough to withstand the constant come-ons from women that the uniform seems to attract.

When Constable Adam Foote came into my office, I would never have suspected he was a police officer, except for the uniform. Short and slight, with pale blue eyes and an almost girlishly full mouth, he would have looked more at home teaching elementary school or giving piano lessons. Make no mistake, however, Adam Foote loved being a police officer and the last thing he wanted was to lose his job.

"I want you to read this," he said softly, handing me a divorce petition, which looked like it was a hundred years old.

"I have," he explained, "shared it with my buddies."

I looked at it carefully. The allegations set forth in the petition, to justify his wife's claims for support, a restraining order and an order for exclusive possession of the matrimonial home, defied all belief.

His wife, a grade two elementary school teacher, alleged that he forcefully sodomized her in the full view of his neighbors on their lawn in the greater Toronto area.

As if this were not enough, she claimed he had then abducted her and driven to her parent's home in Niagara Falls, where he raped her some dozen times. Following this, she went on accuse him of hiring a moving van and removing every stick of furniture from the home, with the exception of the refrigerator and stove, in order to force a sale.

Not only were these accusations set out in great detail in the divorce petition, but also in an affidavit used in support of a Motion to be heard the next week. The Motion sought to obtain an order prohibiting Constable Foote from coming within five hundred feet of his wife or the school where she taught, and granting her exclusive possession of the home. In addition, the wife telephoned the Officer in Charge at his precinct and the Chief of Police for the Region, informing them of all the crimes committed against her personally and asking that they charge her husband. Needless to say, it would put a swift end to his policing career.

"Is there anything else that I'm missing?" I asked.

"Yeah," he replied. "She went to my girlfriend's and trashed her house."

"And when did this happen?" I asked.

"Just after she found out about us and I was supposed to have sodomized her on our front lawn, raped her in Niagara Falls and cleaned the furniture out of the house.

It was, of course, all utter garbage. Not only did my miserable client not forcibly sodomize his wife on the front lawn, rape her in her parents' home or drive to Niagara Falls, but neighbors informed him they had seen her supervising the removal of furniture from the home. They had even supplied him with the name on the moving van.

"And where does all this leave you?" I inquired.

"I'm doing desk duty. They've taken me off all my cases and they're investigating the allegations. She really wrecked my girlfriend's house, but she's not pressing charges."

Luckily, it was not a case where we had to wait two years for a trial to get rid of the allegations while my client remained on desk duties with a large cloud over his head. The movers were tracked down and swore to an affidavit that they were following the wife's instructions when they moved all the furniture from the home. This was attached to another affidavit, which pointed out the ridiculous nature of the other charges.

The presiding judge, a sensible woman in her forties, was not amused. In fact, such blatant perjury incensed her. Costs of $8,000 which included the out of town trip to the movers were awarded on a substantial indemnity basis. That is the equivalent of an award in the United States of costs and attorney's fees where the losing party is ordered to pay not only the costs of the court proceedings, but the other party's legal fees as well. In addition, the paragraphs in the affidavit containing the offensive material were "struck," as were the paragraphs in the divorce petition.

Mrs. Foote's credibility was in shreds and her embarrassed attorney removed himself from the case shortly thereafter. I frankly do not know what he was thinking. Copies of Her Honor's order, which included a scathing paragraph on the wife's perjury, were immediately sent to the Chief of Police and the Officer in Charge of the precinct. Constable Foote was exonerated and no longer assigned to desk duties.

Mrs. Foote's new attorney was naturally eager to settle. I urged Constable Foote to get all that was coming to him, including having an appraisal of his wife's school pension, which I believed to be superior to his plan. In addition, I demanded that she pay every cent of the costs.

She had, I insisted, caused us both enormous aggravation and, although he had been exonerated and reinstated with the police force, things could have been a lot worse. But I had overlooked good old guilt, which, as described by the Irish, "sits like a bird on yer shoulder." All Constable Foote wanted was to have his wife buy him out of the matrimonial home, at what I considered to be a rather low figure, considering all the circumstances. He was also willing to allow her to keep all the pirated furniture, which had been stashed sixty miles away.

"She was very upset," he explained to me.

"Evidently so," I answered.

And what can be learned from these cautionary tales? Lisa MacDonald ruined her husband's career, cleaned him out of funds and irreparably severed his relationship with his two children. This was all because she wanted to punish him for having an affair, which she interpreted as a personal affront to her, rather than accepting it as a fleeting weakness on the part of her husband. While she did get her vengeance, it cost her a great deal financially, as her child and spousal support were much lower than they would otherwise have been. This is not to mention the harm done to the children as a result of their estrangement from their father.

Mrs. Foote's idiocy similarly almost ruined Constable Foote's career. Had the facts regarding the furniture removal not been brought to light when they were, there could have been years of prolonged agony for the husband and large legal expenses for them both. Lying in an affidavit or at trial, and having your lies exposed, places you in a position where nothing you have said will be believed. The penalty of having costs assessed against you can be substantial.

One of my clients was accused by her husband of giving him an incredible black eye, as evidenced by a color photograph. Evidence at the trial showed that on the date she had supposedly blackened his eye, he had been involved in a serious motor vehicle accident in which he not only injured his eye, but other areas of his body as well. My client, who was no fool, produced an accident report and a medical report, which revealed the real cause of the injury.

It greatly undermined the husband's evidence and the resulting judgment showed that the presiding judge discredited the husband's testimony and listened only to the wife.

I have found that, on occasion, when handling divorces involving police officers, an element of blackmail enters the picture. Minor lapses in conduct admitted to the wife in confidence all of a sudden rear their ugly heads. I had one client who instructed me to prepare a separation agreement and send it to her husband, a police officer, who would go to his own attorney and have it executed.

I was perplexed. "Don't you think we have to negotiate it?"

"I have too much on him," she replied.

She was right. The agreement came back duly executed by the husband.

Another client, a police sergeant, who dearly loved his work on the force, settled his case in the wife's favor, and, against my strong protests, forfeited seeing his son and moved to a precinct two hundred and fifty miles away. I do not know what he had gotten himself into and did not ask, but apparently it was sufficient to have him expelled from the force; and he could not envision a future without being a police officer.

I tried to persuade him not to do this, as he was proud of his five-year-old son and I knew that the child would doubtless feel rejected by his father's absence. It made no difference. He was simply not willing to risk his career.

One of my clients with *interesting connections* was an exemplary father who babysat the children night after night while his wife went to nightclubs, arriving home if not drunk, at least showing signs of having had an interestingly intimate evening. It was a nasty breakup but no allegations of his other *job* were ever mentioned.

"Doesn't she know what you do?" I asked

"No," he answered firmly. "I never told her."

"But you told me," I protested.

"It's okay to tell you, you're my attorney and you can't tell anyone."

He was right. Information given to an attorney by one's client is privileged and cannot be repeated. However, I was impressed by the fact that his wife of six years had no idea of the nature of his employment, which could have directly influenced his wish for joint custody.

This may serve as a lesson to all you fellows on the force,

or in other *interesting* vocations that may not bear scrutiny. Perhaps it would be a good idea not to confide the nature of your work to your wife, especially if your employment involved some *irregularities.*

Sometimes goodness appears in surprising places. That last client, who had been closed mouthed about his criminal sideline, had accepted a child as his own that his wife was pregnant with at the time they were married. It was obviously not his child, as his brother kept pointing out to him in my office. The boy adored him. I witnessed their close relationship when he once brought him to an appointment. I agreed with the brother; it was not his child — and he knew it as well. It was one of those things, however, that he chose to ignore. A class act, I thought, regardless of the way he made his living.

**S**ome people are just so mad with their spouse that they do the craziest, most destructive things— none of which ever turn out well. One of my most attractive clients, a tall redhead who spoke in a modulated voice, and whom I expected to be nothing but refined, actually cleaned out her husband's closet when she found out he was leaving. She placed all of his two thousand dollar suits in plastic bags and scattered lye all over them. When she was finished with the lye, she started with the Clorox.

According to the pleadings, the husband's entire wardrobe had been destroyed and he was demanding fifty thousand dollars in compensation for the willful damage to his property. It was a profoundly stupid thing to do. Had the case gone to trial, I am convinced that she would have had to pay compensation. When I asked her why she had done it, she answered, "It seemed like a good idea at the time."

Actually, it delayed settlement by several months and made her look worse than her husband, who had treated her so badly.

Who says lightening doesn't strike twice? Dr. Blackler abruptly left his new spouse, the one for whom he had left his first wife, when the new Mrs. Blackler threatened him with homicide. Similarly, she withheld all his clothing, forcing him to flee wearing his one remaining dark suit. Refusing to replenish his wardrobe, he wore it for two months, until legal action was commenced. She felt he had taken advantage of her financially and was awarding herself punitive damages. It was a ridiculous case, which took two years and thousands of dollars in legal fees, when it should have been settled within a few months.

**W**orst of all was the husband who refused to list the family farm for sale even though it was not used for his livelihood and he was employed elsewhere. When a court ordered the sale of the home, he was living alone in the house and had dedicated himself to seeing that no one would ever purchase it.

He started by refusing to show the home at convenient times, and when the would-be purchasers finally arrived, toilets which had been recently used, were never flushed and strange greasy substances were found in unexpected places.

The house was finally withdrawn from the market when real estate agent number two brought a prospective purchaser who, for obvious reasons, vomited after entering the downstairs bathroom.

An order was finally issued, ending the husband's exclusive possession of the home and ordering that all clean up costs be deducted from his one-half interest after the house was sold. A sale finally did take place several months later, after the professional cleaners had spent a week on the home.

By that time, the prime selling period had ended and we were heading for December when sales are notoriously slow. My client estimated that the price finally obtained was one-third less than the price which could have been obtained the previous June. In other words, nobody really benefited, except that the husband caused my client considerable aggravation, which was exactly what he meant to do. In the long run, he lost money. But then it wasn't about money, was it?

So what to do if you have an irresistible urge to render havoc on that two-timing bitch or bastard that you were stupid enough to marry, when you were old enough to have known better, or young enough not to. First, talk to your best friend or one of your parents about it. Regard this as necessary venting. You should receive a lecture on the consequences of losing self control and leave the conversation feeling contrite. You should be convinced you will not carry out your threats and understand the long term consequences. If you are not, then seek out someone versed in anger management and beg for an immediate appointment.

Everyone gets these anger itches sooner or later, especially when that grinning black knight of betrayal enters the picture, but get even in court. Don't do something so stupid that it can follow you all through your case and eventually into a courtroom, where the opposing counsel will say, "Mr. or Mrs. Nutbar, is it not true that in a fit of pique, you destroyed your spouse's entire wardrobe or refused to release your husband's clothing for two months when he fled the matrimonial home after you threatened him with the machete that you had sent back to your home from an African Safari?" Or, "Is it not true that when your wife was attempting to sell the matrimonial home, you undermined its sale by refusing to flush toilets after what appeared to be bouts of diarrhea, and deliberately released strange greasy substances in hidden corners prior to an inspection by would-be purchasers?"

All of this, of course, will make you appear an absolute idiot, and certainly can have financial consequences. Evidence of your behavior at the final hearing would bias even the most fair-minded judge. Of course, those who are temporarily deranged are sometimes *too* deranged to seek professional help.

More expensive, but just as effective would be an emergency visit to your attorney, who, I guarantee, will be sufficiently alarmed by your professed intentions, that he or she will talk you out of that rash act you are contemplating.

There are those of you who feel you have to do *something* and you do it, but you do it within the framework of your legal action.

Irma was over fifty and looked every year of it. Short, slightly plump, with sharp features, deep lines around her eyes and clipped grey hair, she was neither a candidate for remarriage or plastic surgery. She had married at age twenty-two. Her husband was an engineer, just getting started in a successful government career, and she was commencing her first year as a French teacher at a local college.

Athletic, with a lust for travel, they spent their generous summer vacations touring Europe and winter vacations skiing in Switzerland or Colorado. It was their plan to exhaust their travel lust, buy a home and then start their family in their early thirties.

Things went according to plan, but at age thirty-two, the husband developed Celiac Disease.

This allergy to gluten consumed his life. He refused to travel or even socialize. He informed my client that he would no longer consider having a family, as he would not wish to pass this problem on to any child. Besides, he had no energy and could not, under the circumstances, put up with having to tolerate young children.

Enthusiastic and energetic soul that she was, Irma built her entire life around him, catering to his Celiac disease. She became head of the Celiac Society and home cooked gluten-free bread, rolls and other goodies. She forfeited all her thoughts of a family. There was no more social life, or traveling, because he wished to retire early, complaining that the disease was sapping him of energy.

Apparently this went on for years, but finally in his mid-forties, he saw some improvement and again started to pursue athletics. They started walking, which eventually led to their starting to ski again.  Finally, at age fifty, on a ski slope in Quebec, he met a blonde divorcee with two teenage children and decided that his life with Irma was over.

"I have no one," she informed me, fixing me with sad brown eyes, like a cow too long in the pasture. "My parents are gone. I was an only child and I never had children because of him. Now, all I have is my job which means nothing to me. He said he's got a new lease on life, a new woman and even two kids that he never had. I can't just walk away and let him get away with this."

I agreed with her. But there was no way that we could legally do it. They both had pensions worth approximately the same and they both made approximately the same income. It was a classic case of merely dividing all assets and each going their own way.  There was absolutely nothing in this marriage to entitle my client to an unequal division of assets. There was absolutely nothing to entitle her to support.

"I don't care, "she said defiantly. "I can't let him get away with this."

So, when the inevitable divorce petition was served asking merely for a sale of the home and an equal division of net family property, we answered and counter-petitioned, asking for a lump sum of one hundred thousand dollars.

Of course, it was legally unjustifiable and the inevitable phone call came.

"Are you out of your f-----g mind?" shrilled the female opposing counsel.  "How in the hell do you justify a claim like this, under these circumstances?  They didn't even have kids and she never missed a day of work."

That's just it, I thought to myself. She didn't have kids.

There was correspondence back and forth but no discovery. Opposing counsel refused to co-operate in discoveries on what she felt was a blatantly ridiculous claim.  Time and again she demanded an explanation. Woman to woman, I gave it to her.

"My client feels she has nothing," I explained. "She gave up everything: her social life, the family she wanted, absolutely everything, to nurse and cater to this jerk you represent, because of his Celiac Disease. And now, he has the gall to dump her for some divorcee with two kids and leave her with nothing."

"So, what else is new?" asked opposing counsel.

When you've been practicing long enough, you get tough and cynical. I was as tough and cynical as she was.

"I hear you," I replied. "But that's the way it is."

It settled. Not for anything like the sum requested, but my client accepted an extra ten thousand dollars. It was very poor compensation for a ruined life, but she said it gave her satisfaction.

"At least for once," she said, not without a little triumph in her voice, "I got the better of him. Just a little, but I did get the better of him. It doesn't make up for any of those years and the kids I should have had, but it's better than nothing."

As I often say, "Sometimes you gotta do what you gotta do".

**W**omen have a thing about premature ejaculators. It gives them a sense of unfairness and they ask themselves why they should go through the entire birth process without experiencing one tinge of sexual satisfaction from the whole process, from start to finish.

One woman complained to me that the only thing she had ever experienced that resembled a sexual orgasm was the delivery of the child. Thirty-five years of marriage, three grown, very successful children, thirty years of gardening, growing her own vegetables, making literally hundreds of jars of jam and pickles, which she both sold and kept for private use, working as a bookkeeper in the family business and running everything in the local church from Sunday night dinners to Saturday night bean suppers—and not a twinge of sexual pleasure!

"Before I die," she informed me, all five foot one inch of fighting woman with glittering eyes behind horn rimmed glasses and black hair streaked with grey in a bun on top of her small round head, "I want to have an orgasm...just one. But I want to have one."

She was one of the least sexy women I had ever met, but I found her determination enviable.

"No reason why you can't," I said encouragingly, wondering how she would meet a man up to the task, with all the hours spent organizing and preparing those church suppers and missionary meetings. And after all of that, he had the nerve to leave her for a younger woman — a much younger woman.

"She is obviously after his money," I stated. She agreed eagerly.

"What else could it be?" she questioned. "He never lasted more than ten seconds in his life. I couldn't believe I could have children. They must have been great swimmers, those sperm. I was so amazed every time I got pregnant. I couldn't believe it."

"I believe they have some sort of sexual counseling for that now," I interjected.

"Too late," she said flatly. And I silently agreed.

She must have inwardly vowed to make the case as difficult as possible — and it was. She broke into her own house sometime after the separation and may have assaulted him. He may have attempted to defend himself. In any event, he was charged with assault — a charge that was later withdrawn — but which left considerable bad feelings. He offered to buy out her interest in the home, but she fought it and obtained an order for sale. Eventually he did buy her out. She was angry and did not want him to continue to live in the home.

Then there was the business. She contested its worth and fought over all of the appraisals. Finally, her own appraiser came up with an assessment she believed to be satisfactory, but then she became incensed with her appraiser and her accountant. It was a nightmare from start to finish, and the legal fees escalated because of the tortured hours spent in attempting to obtain an agreement on figures.

I had liked and respected her at the beginning and I still do, but it was difficult at the end. It was a nightmare case which eventually settled after hours of negotiation, much to her dissatisfaction. It was a case that simply could not go to trial, because the issues had become so complex. No judge would have been able to follow them.

He did give in at the end, to an extent, although she always felt cheated. Her kids supported her. After all that wrangling about the money, it really wasn't about the money at all.

Incidentally, the girlfriend did not last. Money, after all, isn't everything!

# Chapter 7
## Nice Guys Who Didn't Finish Last

Mr. Rodrigues had the misfortune of marrying a woman who, every time he turned around, seemed to be engrossed in yet another affair. At first it had been a car repairman, and at one point, the man that came to fix the hydro. She then graduated to the children's music teacher, and finally, when they both took flying lessons to enhance togetherness, she had affairs with the pilots. The final straw came when he surprised her at her part-time employment, where she held a marketing position, and found her in an embrace with a co-worker. In truth, she never really had to work. He did remarkably well, acquiring various properties in both Canada and the United States.

He finally tired of it all. She had a good voice and spent thousands of dollars making records, which she then refused to market or promote. None of the children wished to follow him into his business, but they were all talented musicians.

A cross examination on the wife's filed court documents was conducted. She was a miserable witness, lying about everything, then forgetting what she had said and contradicting her own lies. Had her attorney been more astute, he would have attempted to settle, but the case went on and on much to my client's annoyance.

My client was extremely intelligent, and was well aware that after a long term marriage with four children, he would be responsible for ongoing spousal support, despite his wife's infidelities. However, she did not want ongoing support. She wanted a large lump sum payment instead.

Lump sums are often the choice of individuals immersed in an affair. These individuals want to cut the cord and not give the ex-spouse any excuse to later reduce monthly amounts should they remarry or co-habit.

Whatever the reason, the wife wanted a lump sum support payment, which would not have been awarded by any court, as there had been no defaults in support payments, nor any violence, which often define the criteria for a lump sum.

Monthly support payments, were, of course, to my client's advantage, as they were tax deductible and could be reduced in the event of a change of circumstances.[8]

Multiple offers were made by my client, all extremely reasonable. Professional appraisers evaluated all his properties and the wife was offered the entire matrimonial home: not a paltry inducement, as it was quite palatial. In addition, she was to get other transfers of property and generous ongoing monthly support. She refused all offers. And to my client's irritation, she also refused to make a counter offer.

"We have nothing to lose," I assured my client. "We are on the side of the angels. You have been totally reasonable and she is forcing us into an unnecessary trial."

In spite of this, he kept insisting on settling. I knew the market was appreciating rapidly, but this was basically irrelevant, as everything had been appraised as of the date of separation, which would apply to her assets, as well as his residential properties in the United States We finally settled on a figure, which I warned him appeared to be grossly unfair

---

[8] Monthly support payments are tax deductible by the payer and taxable to the payee in both Canada and the United States provided they are specifically made pursuant to a separation agreement or court order. Do not think that you can deduct your payments unless a separation or court order is in effect.

and over-generous. He merely shrugged and informed me that he wanted to settle the matter. This occurred six months before the serious slump in residential properties in the United States.[9]

At his wedding some six months later, I learned that he had sold one of his apartment buildings for what I considered to be an astronomical amount just before the recession. He was such a pleasant man, always so reasonable and balanced. It appears that he was also very knowledgeable about market conditions. In retrospect, the lump sum looked like a steal. He had tied things up nicely and had gotten on with his life. After meeting his new bride, who I presumed had been in the shadows for some time; I concluded that he had also traded up.

The lesson to be learned, of course, is that one does not always have to go totally by the book. Often, clients have said to me, "I want exactly what I'm entitled to, no more, no less." That, of course, is fair, and what I usually advise. There are times, however, when being a little more generous than one has to be, turns out well.

Charlie Massa was a local dentist who had yet to establish his practice. He had been unhappily married for some seven years and had two young daughters. He had, I suspected, met someone else, although he did not disclose it to me or to his wife, which showed considerable common sense. As I have already warned you, this type of disclosure opens the door to ongoing havoc and makes settlement much more difficult. In fact, it is one of the most viable reasons to lie your head off and keep that significant other under wraps for as long as possible, regardless of his or her complaints. Tell her you are

---

[9] In Canada and in some States your assets are evaluated as of the date of separation, although in some cases they are evaluated as of the date of trial. In an age of rapidly declining property values it is prudent to be able to evidence your date of separation and obtain appraisals as of that date. Ask your attorney about the rules for property division in your state.

worth waiting for, and if she doesn't accept that, then she's not the right one for you. Run from the woman who telephones your wife. It invariably turns out badly.

Dr. Massa was a smiling, pleasant client, with a dark moustache and a distinct space between his two front teeth — unusual for a dentist. He sat down with me while we went over his net family property. His dental practice had been evaluated and, due to the large debt accumulated for its establishment, had a negative net worth.

Incidentally, were you aware that you cannot have a negative net family property? The figure merely shows as a zero. This prevents a party from taking advantage of debts to the disadvantage of the other spouse. Some of my clients believe this to be unfair, but it's the law in Ontario. It may not be the law in your State.

In any event, after calculating the net family property, it was quite obvious that Mrs. Massa was owed very little, in fact, almost nothing at all. Not even her one half of the matrimonial home, which had a substantial mortgage.

"The home will have to be sold," I explained. You have to get your own place and both of you will have to scale down."

"No," Dr. Massa said definitely, "I want her to stay there with the kids. I want to see my girls as much as possible and I wouldn't want them to think that their Dad had pitched them out of their home."

I admit, I argued against it. His wife was a nurse and nurses were in high demand at the local hospital. She could easily have gone back to work and many children thrived in two bedroom apartments. And then there was the question about his debts. His share of the home would pay down the debt against his dental practice considerably. Once he had himself established, he could afford to be generous, but surely not now.

He had, however, thought it all out. Worse, he had assured his wife that she could stay in the home. I gave him the guideline amount for child support, which was modest enough considering his current income. These guidelines, incidentally, are quite rigidly adhered to in Canada and make life simpler for everyone, especially judges. No longer are amounts plucked out of the air, according to the whim of some judge, who may or may not be feeling generous on that particular day. They are, instead, taken from a guideline chart and child support is paid according to the payer's income. And now, in Ontario, we even have advisory guidelines for spousal support, which although only advisory, are also given great weight. Be sure to check with your attorney regarding child and spousal support guidelines in your specific state.

I note that in California judges follow guidelines for spousal interim support but for a determination of permanent support use their discretion. This could work in your favor if you have special circumstances that should cause you to receive more support than would be expected.

Dr. Massa, however, was having no part of it.

"It doesn't matter to me what you put in the agreement," he informed me. "I will be giving her extra for the kids. Perhaps, it would be even better if we just use the guidelines and then I can up the ante when she needs it. She says she wants support to help her with the mortgage until she gets settled into nursing again, and that should be about two years."

As an attorney, you take instructions from your client. My client knew the law. I had told him exactly what he was obligated to do, but he chose to do otherwise. His relationship with his kids and his wife, although he had apparently regretted marrying her after the first year, was more important to him than money.

"This may put pressure on any other relationship you may have," I warned. I suspected there was a current significant other, as such generosity indicated a fair amount of guilt. He only shrugged. He was not worried about it.

I saw Dr. Massa some two years later for a cracked cap. He was his usual smiling self, with his black moustache curled up at the ends and the space between his front teeth as prominent as ever. He showed me a picture of himself and his daughters. He had joint custody with generous access, although the girls resided with the wife on a day-to-day basis. He had gradually introduced his new fiancée, a dental hygienist, into the children's lives some six months earlier and he was planning to be married the following year. Things were going well financially and his wife had returned to nursing.

Lesson learned? Sometimes it's best, depending on the individual, to not always go by the book. It all depends, I suppose, on one's priorities. Dr. Massa did not wish to lose his warm relationship with his two young daughters. He wanted to have a friendly relationship with his estranged wife, who was very hurt by the separation he had initiated. He managed to sustain everything, although at a financial disadvantage to himself.

The future Mrs. Massa also deserved some credit. All too often, the new girlfriend or second wife is adamantly opposed to *her man* helping his former wife, even though she has been instrumental in the marriage break up. It takes a certain type of man to withstand a constant nagging barrage of complaints from a second wife, who all too often will fuel the flames of resentment that come from an antagonistic breakup.

The dental hygienist kept her mouth shut and stayed in the background. When she met the two daughters, she did not try to usurp the mother's position — a disconcerting practice used by second wives — but acted as a loving friend.

As such, the girls, and eventually the ex-wife, had a friendly relationship with her. There was none of the *you can call me Mommy* stuff, which sends the biological mommy into orbit. They called her "Alice" and they had fun together. There were no foolish attempts to discipline or become a second mommy. Smart guy — Dr. Massa. He really had his priorities in order. And to think at the time, I advised him against it!

# Chapter 8
## Children from the First Marriage

Kids from a first marriage can get you into all sorts of trouble, if you are the second wife or husband. I've had a multitude of male and female clients whose second marriages broke up directly as a result of their relationships with their spouse's kids.

For one thing, many children believe that their parents will eventually get back together and the new wife or husband is seen as an interloper who will prevent this hoped for eventuality. Therefore, second spouses have this hurdle to climb. In the case where the divorce occurred long in the past, was not caused by the second spouse, and mom and dad have gotten on with their lives, this impediment is removed, but, quite often, there are other problems.

"His room is a disaster. He plays rap music all night long and he's forever taking food out of the refrigerator."

My client was describing her husband's seventeen year old son who she blamed for breaking up her marriage. Her husband, she said, always defended him and had recently told her that things weren't working out and that he wished to separate.

Before the marriage, they had entered into a pre-nuptial agreement. My client was well established in a career and there were no financial issues. She was in her middle forties, however, and saw this collapse of a second marriage as a failure — and she was incredibly bitter. Her voice, when she spoke of this fairly typical seventeen-year-old, rang with dislike.

On her instructions, I wrote a letter suggesting counseling rather than formalizing a separation agreement. She explained to me tearfully that she still loved her husband and blamed the son for the entire breakup.

It was too late.

I had a similar case the year before. I represented a police sergeant who had been in the military prior to his police career. Both he and his wife had been previously married, but he had no children from his marriage. She, on the other hand, had two boys, aged fourteen and sixteen. Both were good students and involved in sports, but they were rowdy, careless about their clothing and prone to making the home a teenage hangout. In other words, they were teenagers — possibly better than most.

It all irritated him. He had taken on the role of being a surrogate dad, and as such was, as he put it, *straightening them out*. The straightening out finally resulted in his being charged with assault, a charge which was later withdrawn but which could have jeopardized his police career.

There were two tumultuous years of wrangling. The boys hated him, as eventually did his wife. The split up was extremely acrimonious and he ended up paying guideline support for the two boys, as he was considered by the court to be *in loco parentis*, which is a legal term for *in place of a parent*. Ironically, following the break up of the marriage, he became the father, at least financially, that he had attempted to be.

Both of these clients are examples of the disaster that can ensue when a new spouse moves in with the husband or wife's original family, and decides to play mommy or daddy, in the manner they believe a mommy or daddy should act. There is only one thing wrong with this. They are *not* their mommies or daddies.

You may get away with yelling at your own kids to pick up their clothes or *clean out your shit-house of a room*, because they are *your* kids. There is a bond between parent and child and your children realize you love them, in spite of their being slobs and gluttons. In your new *family*, however, they are not *your* kids. They will resent every move you make to dominate or discipline them. Eventually, if you go at them and play the heavy, your husband or wife will feel the same dislike for you that the kids do.

Your best bet? Go in there as a loving friend. Even if your new wife has made a mess of bringing up the kids, I'm sure they're not all bad. Be encouraging and lavish them with praise even if you secretly think the kids need a firm hand. Attend their hockey or ball games and give them a hand with their homework if you're up to it. With today's homework, many of us aren't. Let your wife/husband be the one to set the guidelines. If the kids are rude to you, don't over-react. They're finding it tough to adjust to having you around as well.

Try to capitalize on the few things you may have in common. This is not difficult if you are a new wife and the children are girls. Unless, of course, you have been instrumental in breaking up their father's marriage and they have heard gushes of animosity from their biological mother, who has called you the world's worst bitch or even more colorful names.

If they're living with you, it's a whole new ball game. You have to start from scratch to ingratiate yourself. Do it slowly. Take an interest in the purple they've streaked their hair with and the nails they've painted with black polish. Really make an effort not to be critical, even if you would just love to tell them that they look like the world's worst tramps and you're not so old that you don't know what the intent behind a tongue ring is.

In the case of body piercing and tattoos for both male and female children, I suggest that it doesn't hurt to say that they may regret this later on. You can also state that their removal, if possible, may be quite painful and that tattooing and piercing, if done under unhygienic circumstances, could result in contacting Hepatitis C or AIDS — both potentially lethal. Likewise, you should warn of the hazards of street drugs, alcohol and smoking.

Sometimes one has to voice an opinion to prevent present or future harm—softly and reasonably, if possible. But by and large, things like hygiene, or lack of it, for boys and monopolization of the bathroom by the girls, had best be ignored. Remember, when boys' hormones get going at about age sixteen, they become so immaculate that they sometimes compulsively shower three times a day. Age will take care of some of these problems.

The hatred I have seen some of my clients express toward these stepchildren is heart stopping. Was it, I sometimes wondered, a spillover of residual jealousy toward the first spouse? Or jealousy because the natural parent is much too doting—spoiling the children to death rather than spoiling my client to death, as he or she would much prefer.

If you're marrying someone who has custody of their kids, weigh in on your relationship with them prior to the marriage, if possible. Hopefully, you've taken your time to get to know them, not pushed intimacy at the first opportunity, and certainly not immediately after the father or mother broke up. Start off as a loving friend and remain one.

Do not join your spouse in bitter alienating tactics against the children's mother or father. In fact, you should be discouraging this type of behavior in any event.

If you're living with them, you may attempt to establish a routine, but keep it very flexible. Don't sweat the small stuff. Nobody ever died from a messy room or no milk left for your coffee in the morning.

If your spouse merely has weekend access, then don't try to monopolize him or her all the time. Give the kids a little time to spend with their mom or dad and don't always be present. In fact, sometimes it's not a bad idea to schedule something else on a Saturday afternoon so that they can be alone together.

Only enter into that second marriage or relationship if you can abide his children, or better still, genuinely like them. Things take time and relationships don't develop over night. Mussing your stepson's hair or playfully punching his arm is a good idea for a stepmother, provided he's under eighteen, but perhaps not to be advised for stepfathers.

Boys are sometimes much easier to handle than girls. Feeding them well and not being too critical over their baggy pants, which expose half of their buttocks, is a start.

Of course, if the ex-mommy or daddy were complete washouts as parents and had little interest in the kids in question, you're almost home free. If you're kind, loving and uncritical, they'll think you're wonderful. And so will your new spouse.

You'd be surprised how appreciative he or she will be if you can get along with his or her kids. I have known of cases where stepchildren have gone into business with their step-moms or dads and have attended weddings where the step-dad gave the bride away. There was no doubt about the way he and the daughter felt about each other.

Being a great step-mom or step-dad takes a certain kind of person. If you can't be that kind of person, then perhaps you shouldn't venture into the marriage or relationship in the first place. The dislike I have seen emanating from some of my clients toward their stepchildren is chilling.

If you're already in a marriage and feel an increasing irritability toward your husband or wife's teenage kids, perhaps you should head for some counseling or therapy. Remember, you'd probably be going through the same thing if they were your biological offspring. But you wouldn't get rid of them, would you?

Often, your new husband or less frequently, your new wife, may give in to your nagging and complaints about their kids and ship them back to the other parent. In the husband's case, he'll start paying child support according to the guidelines and start seeing them on a regular basis, without your being present.

If you cause this to happen, he won't forget it. In the long run, it will no doubt undermine your relationship and you may break up in any event.

Look upon this entire process as a challenge, one which you can meet and win, with substantial benefits from a positive outcome.

# Chapter 9
## The Financial Cheaters

She was a sixty-year-old Dutch woman with graying dark hair in a bun, fixed securely on the top of her head. She wore a tailored navy blue coat with laced black shoes and dark stockings. Her makeup-free face was flushed and periodically covered by hands that showed years of hard physical work.

Hennie Vandenberg was beside herself and for a good reason. Her husband, Joe, had sold the matrimonial home, without so much as consulting her, and now she was convinced he was going to pocket all the funds, just two days after informing her that the marriage was over.

He dropped this on her right after she had served him his second cup of evening tea and had informed her that she had best return to Holland.

She had been a schoolteacher in a small Dutch town near Amsterdam and at thirty-eight had reconciled herself to not having the husband and children she had always wanted. With her round pink face, steel rimmed glasses and severe hair style, she was not pretty, but heartbreakingly wholesome. I saw all this in the wedding picture she handed me, as if this were to be some essential part of her divorce.

One day, an ad appeared in the local paper from a Joseph Vandenberg, who was a native of the same small town, but who was now residing in Ontario, Canada. Vandenberg was advertising for a surrogate mother for five of the seven children he had produced with his first wife. He described himself as a hardworking and industrious farmer and set out that his five remaining children very much needed a mother.

She replied to the ad, setting out her credentials and stating that she loved children and was not afraid of work.

Within a month she arrived in Ontario, with Vandenberg as her sponsor. In less than a week, they were married. The children's ages went from seven to fourteen; three boys and two girls. She adored the children, but not Vandenberg. He had not stated in his ad seeking a mother for his children that what he really wanted was an unpaid housekeeper. Nor had he mentioned that besides being industrious and hardworking, he was also cheap and cruel.

His children were expected to work long, grueling hours on his twenty acre dairy and beef cattle farm. There was even an abattoir for the slaughter of the animals. She fed, cooked and cleaned for the children and, most importantly, protected them as well as she could from their father's assaults, especially when he drank. She washed out the blood stained clothing from the abattoir and often cooked for four extra farm workers during busy times. It was a hard and exhausting life and at times she yearned for Holland, but she could not leave the children — not to the tender mercies of Joe Vandenberg.

"But he can't sell the matrimonial home without your permission," I insisted. "You have to consent to any disposition of the home, even if it's a mortgage, let alone a sale."

Hennie shrugged helplessly. She would, she explained in her accented English, sign anything Joe asked her to. She had done that throughout the marriage, without having any idea of what she was signing. I later learned that the house was actually in both names due to the insistence of Joe's attorney, who was holding all money in trust. He had refused Vandenberg's demand for a check in both names, surmising he would no doubt place the funds in a joint account and then transfer them into an account in his name alone.

Joe Vandenberg was the owner of the farm where they had first lived upon Hennie's arrival from Holland. Five years later they had purchased another home where they began to live. The money from the sale of that home, which I finally retrieved for Hennie, was sufficient for her to purchase a new smaller home in Peel County, where she could continue her relationship with the children whom she considered to be her own; even playing grandma to their children.

She merely wanted enough money, she explained to me, not to have to borrow from anyone and to be able to afford to give gifts to the children.

At age sixty, she wished to pursue a modest social life, which had been denied her for some twenty-two years. In addition to selling the matrimonial home, Joe had, she confided to me in a heavily accented whisper, sold the farm for 2.8 million dollars. He had also sold all the cattle and farm equipment and concealed the money — only God knew where.

She told me, if she could have even a modest portion of the $2.8 million, she could live well, for she was quite certain that Joe Vandenberg would never ever pay her support.

During the twenty-two years of marriage, the farm had drastically appreciated in value. We were able to determine the original value of the property, because Joe had paid off his first wife and we had the documentation, which in a lucid moment, Hennie had hidden in a drawer. The first Mrs. Vandenberg had walked away with a relative pittance, after bearing seven children for Joe. I assured Hennie and myself that it would not happen to her.

The sale of the farm, unfortunately, fell through because Joe decided that he had been swindled by the real estate agents. With property values increasing, in a few years the money to be gained from his twenty acres would be greatly in excess of the $2.8 million. Besides, he did not wish to liquidate property and have "Hennie's whore attorney" grab it for Hennie and herself. In any event, he had no intention of giving Hennie any money whatsoever and considered her very lucky to have received one-half of the proceeds from the sale of their residence.

On her second visit, Hennie produced a letter written to Joe from Richard, the youngest son. It was an unforgettable letter, reminding his father of the cruelty the children had all endured as a result of his conduct, and finally asking him for once in his life to do a decent thing and give Hennie what she deserved. The letter was, in reality, an indictment against Vandenberg for his treatment of both the children and Hennie. It ended with the sentiment that the author neither wanted nor expected to receive any money from Joe, considering his character, but that he should at least treat Hennie with some decency, considering all she had done for them.

Any man, I thought, who would be the subject of such a letter must be evil incarnate. I was not far from wrong.

Joe Vandenberg's crusade against Hennie started from the moment she dared to ask for something extra besides her interest in the sale of the matrimonial home and only ended with his death some ten years later.

There were five attorneys involved, each one only lasting as long as Joe believed they were *on his side*. Essentially that meant agreeing to use any means possible to cheat Hennie out of any sums owed to her pursuant to the Family Law Act, which set out an individual's property rights in the Province of Ontario. When they urged rationality or suggested that he tender an offer, they were summarily fired.

The worst occurred when attorney number three, a soft spoken little Brit with an Oxford accent, badgered Hennie with questions during a cross examination that confused and upset her, and while relevant, were on a much too sophisticated level for a clear response. It was obvious that he had been instructed to attempt to intimidate and break Hennie down, and in spite of my objections and obtaining an adjournment at crucial times so that she could get herself together in a nearby washroom, the questioning took its toll.

The next day, Hennie had a stroke and was hospitalized for several weeks.

Offers were advanced on her instructions. Pathetic offers that were so modest that their acceptance would leave her with far less than the amount to which she was legally entitled. The stroke had done her in and she wanted to end it. Especially painful was the distance Joe was attempting to create between her and the children.

The Brit with the Oxford accent was soon fired. I knew he would be. His fees were notoriously high and although he had succeeded in giving Hennie a stroke which undoubtedly shortened her life, Joe Vandenberg was not a person to willingly pay legal fees. In addition, she received threats from the most painful source, the children.

She told me she was returning to Holland. Her blood pressure was high and she feared another stroke. She could stand the pressure no longer and could not go to trial. I was to settle as best I could, but she would not be here.

The fourth and fifth attorneys, no doubt inadequately paid, were as indifferent as our Oxford accented Brit was intrusive. Telephone calls were never returned and scheduled meetings ignored. Through it all, the property remained unsold and Joe's litigation with the purchasers continued. A renowned Family Court Judge held a conference in Toronto and recommended a settlement of five hundred thousand dollars. The fourth attorney said he would recommend it, but never did get back to me.

The threats continued, even in Holland, where Joe placarded Hennie's small home, humiliating her by telling her neighbors what a greedy, grasping bitch she was. Then letters were sent, with pictures of himself and an enamel-faced blonde of a certain age beaming away, informing Hennie that he had finally met *a real woman.*

I got a court date, but, as she had previously advised, she could not come. She had been moved into a home for the handicapped and could no longer get around. Over the phone, her voice lacked its vibrant accent and her will appeared to be shattered.

In the eighth year of litigation, Joe Vandenberg died, leaving the enameled-blonde a generous bequest and leaving his estate to one of his seven children — a daughter, who, he advised, could do what she wished with the money, insofar as her siblings were concerned.

It was a will calculated to cause dissension, upset, and hatred amongst the family. Joe Vandenberg would have been delighted. It succeeded in turning all of the children, except the youngest boy, against Hennie, who was then vilified for having a claim against the estate.

Suffice it to say, the land was sold for what I believed to be twenty million dollars. It was necessary to go to court against the one beneficiary of Vandenberg's will to arrange settlement. Even then, when a settlement had been agreed to, and a very modest one of less than a million dollars, the beneficiary telephoned Hennie in her nursing home and talked her out of it. I was subsequently asked by her to reduce the amount previously agreed upon. It was farcical, as she had intended to leave all her money to the children in any event. As it was, she told me feebly, it was much too late for her to enjoy the money. It would all go to benefit others.

When she died a few months later, I was informed of her passing by the youngest son, who also told me that his sister had reneged on her promise to divide the estate with his siblings. He had benefited through Hennie's will to an extent, but she had also left money to the others, including the main beneficiary of Joe's will, who was hardly in need of funds.

Poor Hennie, she once said to me in a rare attempt at humor, "They are, after all, all Vandenbergs."

And what, you may ask, could Hennie have done to avoid what appeared to be a legal travesty?

She should have remained in Ontario, in spite of her health and proximity to Joe Vandenberg. Hiding in Holland where she had only a handful of distant cousins, was not the answer. Despite her efforts to distance herself from him, he sought her out and harassed her. Had she remained in Ontario, the trial could have been expedited and most likely settled at the courtroom door, although with Vandenberg, one never knew.

In cases involving elderly people and illness, the courts are open to expedited trials. A speedy trial would have assured Hennie of at least one half of the amount of the litigated offer of $2.8 million, which would have been more than satisfactory.

Telling an attorney to settle no matter what, takes away bargaining power and without the impetus of an upcoming trial, the litigation drags on and on. Obviously, Joe Vandenberg believed that Hennie's illness would carry her off and in the end he would have millions to spend on his enameled blondes. But he died before she did, leaving calculated chaos behind him.

Joe would have met his comeuppance in court, but was able to avoid it, albeit in a drastic way.

**O**h these Dutchmen! But Margot Hornig was no Hennie Vandenberg, although at first I thought she might be. In her early fifties, Margot wore her dark blonde hair in fat braids, wrapped around her small round head. Her face, rosy and unlined for a woman of fifty-three, reminded me of a cherubic, menopausal milkmaid. She was devoid of makeup, jewelry or style and always kept her appointments dressed in a uniform of a grey cardigan and long pleated skirt, which served to emphasize her rather ample hips. Her English, except for a slight accent, was perfect and she brought me cookies at each appointment but the first. Having a client bring me homemade cookies, especially thin crunchy ones, warmed me. In addition, she confirmed my hourly rate in the written retainer when she entered the office and eagerly wrote out her check.

This was, assuredly, no Hennie Vandenberg.

Margot had married Hornig, who I shall refer to as Horny, twenty-five years earlier in Holland. They had two children, both attending university. He was a frugal and controlling man and *the children*, although one was in her late teens and the other in his early twenties, were afraid of him. He also, she confided, made her nervous and it was at his insistence that she had kept her long braids — *pigtails* as we called them years ago.

He had started a company that had proven to be very successful and which had dozens of employees.

She worked as the company's bookkeeper, and was awarded a modest salary for her efforts. Horny effectively considered this to be income splitting, because her salary was deposited to a joint account from which he paid household expenses. Their home, in the Greater Toronto Area, had appreciated in value and was in both names. The business, of which he was the sole shareholder, paid him dividends plus a monthly income. Of late, he had been making monthly trips to Holland and she had suspected that something more than business was going on there.

"Monkey business," she informed me with a smile.

It was not as if she intended to do anything. She was not a woman to inquire as to her husband's personal life. She continued keeping the house, doing her bookkeeping duties and attending church on Sundays and prayer meetings on Wednesday nights.

Then it was brought to her attention that Horny was selling the business for a considerable amount. He had told his employees that the new owner might want to bring in his own staff, but they could try to negotiate new employment contracts. There was no severance pay for those who wished to retire, nor had there been a pension plan. Justifiably disgruntled, some of these employees provided Margot, who was well liked, with the information that her husband had failed to relay — there was a girlfriend in Amsterdam, eagerly waiting for Horny to arrive with his pockets bulging from the corporate sale.

There was, she informed me breathlessly, no time to be lost. Apparently, Horny had no intention of giving her anything from the proceeds of the corporate sale and would, in addition, be expecting one-half of the proceeds from the sale of the quite valuable matrimonial home. Once the money was in Holland, where she suspected he had already stashed considerable funds, her chances of retrieving it would be difficult, if not impossible.

The sale was due to close within five days. A divorce petition was issued, seeking the usual relief, including spousal support and an equal division of net family property. To cover contingencies, exclusive possession of the matrimonial home was also claimed. As well, an order freezing all proceeds from the sale of the company was requested.

"He must not know zat vee are doing ziss," she exclaimed excitedly, her accent increasing with each sentence. "He iss great friends with his attorney, zey vill bring zee sale forward."

I did not see what Horny's hopefully friendly relationship with the attorney who did his corporate work had to do with sneaking money out of the country. I supposed it would help to ease the process. I proceeded to obtain an *ex parte* order freezing the money.

An *ex parte order* is an order obtained, signed by the judge, issued, entered and served as a binding order on the individual or his attorney without serving them with prior notice of your intention to seek it.

The judges, quite rightfully, dislike granting these orders. They are basically unfair since the opposition has had no opportunity to respond and they are based solely on affidavit evidence presented by the procurer of the order. In certain cases, however, when a child is about to be abducted or money is about to be taken out of the country, the order will be granted. This was one of those cases.

There were, of course, the usual irate phone calls asking me what in the hell I thought I was doing and threatening that if a sale were aborted, I would be personally sued. I could not understand why my freezing the proceeds from the sale would in any way prevent the sale from taking place and said so. There were also threats of sharp practice and reports to the Law Society, which sometimes occur when you attempt to do a decent job for your client. But the money remained secure, frozen in opposing counsel's bank account, although the location of the funds made Margot very nervous. She feared his attorney would somehow leak this money out to Horny so he could pursue his wicked ways in Holland.

One thing is abundantly clear. Attorneys do not release trust money or money relating to court orders unless they wish to take an early route to retirement. Opposing counsel was no fool, and friendship or no friendship, the funds were secured in spite of Margot's misgivings.

The attorney did, however, send a member of his firm who did matrimonial work, to ask the Court for the release of these funds, a sale of the matrimonial home and special costs because, he alleged, the *ex parte* order, had been based upon false affidavits and was unnecessary.

Strangely, *the pleadings*, which are what an affidavit and various materials used for a motion are called, also set out in detail a personal attack on Margot, claiming her to be a filthy housekeeper and lacking in personal hygiene.

These allegations were completely false. Margot smelled so strongly of soap that it wafted across the desk at me as I nibbled on her crisp, thin cookies during each appointment. She had shown me pictures of her shiny and well kept home. The attack was not only false, but also *irrelevant*. You will learn, if you are involved in litigation, that anything that does not directly or indirectly relate to financial matters is usually deemed to be *irrelevant*. An exception can be found in custody battles, where vile allegations abound and are sometimes considered *relevant*.

Finding these allegations personally offensive to my cookie supplier and totally irrelevant, I requested in our response to the motion that these offensive statements be *stricken*. Fortunately, the judge was also offended and proceeded to strike them, rightfully suggesting that it was somewhat late after twenty-five years to take such a position and in any event these personal attacks were quite clearly *irrelevant.*

Spousal and child support were ordered, even though, with his business gone and all of his funds frozen, it was argued that Horny had no funds. Child support was awarded, since both children were still attending university and under those circumstances, were considered to be dependent children pursuant to the Divorce Act.[10]

Most gratifying of all, exclusive possession of the jointly owned matrimonial home was also granted to Margot. One half of the proceeds of the sale of the company, however, were to be disbursed to Horny and the remaining one-half was to be paid into court pending a trial.

This incensed Horny, who had been muttering vicious threats against Margot and me as we walked down the courthouse hall. He fired his litigation attorney, contacted his friendly corporate attorney, retrieved his one-half of the proceeds of the company's sale and fled to Holland on the first available plane.

After that, it was downhill all the way for Horny. His new attorney, who Horny had retained hours before leaving for Holland, undertook discovery proceedings, which were an examination under oath of Margot and of all documents put forth in the pleadings. Horny's documentation, however, was not produced. Neither was spousal nor child support paid. As well, Horny's financial disclosure was defective, which, although not given the importance that it currently has, raised all sorts of gratifying suspicions in the mind of the future presiding judge.

Suffice it to say, two days before the motion to strike pleading was to be heard, Horny's second attorney went off

---

[10] In Ontario, Canada, child support can be paid up to the age of 23, provided the "child" is still pursuing an undergraduate degree on a full time basis. Many States cut off child support at age 18. Ask your attorney what your State's cut-off date is for child support.

the record, which left Horny on his own, unrepresented by counsel.

Incidentally, you may be wondering what it means to strike pleadings. This is a great device against individuals like Horny who ignore court orders. It literally means the same thing as it sounds. You eliminate the other side's affidavits and claims, which results in the Court granting all of the relief sought in your own petition, as if it had been unopposed.

It is quite a delightful position to be in for any litigant, especially when money is securely held by the Court and/or in a joint asset, like the funds from the sale of the matrimonial home would be, against which an order for exclusive possession has been obtained.

When Margot and I appeared in Motions Court that morning to strike Horny's pleadings, we were amazed to find that Horny had parachuted in from Holland and was now representing himself. He asked for an adjournment before a quite unsympathetic judge, who had read our claim but nothing from Horny, who had not filed any opposing material and who looked like the flight risk that he had already shown himself to be.

Having heard that Horny had not yet been examined, the judge directed that Horny was to present himself at a specific special examiner's office that afternoon so he could be examined in regard to his financial statement which he had attached to his counter-petition.

This was yet another delightful prospect. NEVER appear on your own against your spouse's attorney. You need your own attorney to object to certain questions and to protect you against the probing of opposing counsel. More seriously yet, without your attorney, you may even tell the truth, a prospect no litigant should relish. I am, of course, being cynical and sarcastic, but not about appearing for a cross examination without your attorney.

Horny, unnerved by the unsympathetic judge and me, as opposing counsel, who by now had developed a well-founded dislike for the man, blurted out the incriminating truth. There were assets in Holland, undisclosed on his financial statement. Although he was spending considerable amounts to live in Holland, at what could be seen as a luxurious level, he had not been able to afford to pay support to his wife and children. In any event, he did not feel that he had to abide by this court order as he felt his children disliked him and were siding with their mother.

There were all sorts of detrimental answers to questions, each one more damaging than the last. When I had finished examining Horny, I knew that the battle was over and that there would be no continuation of the war.

Margot, needless to say, ended up with the entire home, and the portion of the proceeds from the sale of the company that had been paid into court. She subsequently sold the home at the height of the real estate market and at last count was living quite comfortably from the income generated from the proceeds from the sale of the home and the corporation.

She visited me a few years later and was not recognizable, a fact that was commented on by my receptionist. In fact, the only thing that remained the same were the cookies. She had cut her hair, thick after all those years of braiding, and which now bounced off her shoulders. She even wore makeup and quite a smart pantsuit. She was dating a younger man who, she confided, she met at her prayer meeting on Wednesday night. There's nothing like a little extra coin to make one look smart and start off in a new direction. Horny apparently is still in Holland.

There are many lessons to be learned from the Hornig scenario. The first is, if you have a spouse who you believe is going to liquidate his assets and place the proceeds in unknown pockets of the world or even in unknown pockets of where you reside, you must absolutely and immediately obtain an attorney and deep freeze the proceeds of liquidation.

The judge may not like your doing this on an *ex parte* basis and it puts considerable pressure on your attorney, but an *ex parte* order is tailor made for this type of situation.

You must ask your attorney if he or she is too busy to move quickly and, if you are going to a larger firm, whether he or she intends to attend personally or have a junior carry this out. Juniors can sometimes be quite effective, but not as effective as the senior attorney you desire or are about to retain.

Get your money up front and write out a decent retainer to this attorney. You may have to borrow the money but it's money well spent. Well-retained attorneys move much more quickly than those who receive a small retainer and are promised money from certain proceeds.

Impress upon your attorney the urgency of the situation and the dire results if something is not done forthwith. Be assured, everybody will be very angry, and if there has been physical abuse in the past, then this may be the time to get a restraining order so that your furious spouse cannot come near you.

Legislation in the United States and Canada makes the breach of a restraining order a criminal offense. This means that you can call the police if your spouse is so incensed by your freezing his assets that he decides to deep freeze you. I know it's no laughing matter and there has been the occasional homicide, but most of these bullies show amazing decorum once you have started legal action and call them to account. I have seen some of these characters as mild as milk when it comes to an actual court appearance. Of course, they are not all that way so prudence is the order of the day.

Secondly, if you are on the other side, and your spouse happens to get a plethora of orders against you, all of which I know you feel are repugnant and unfair, please comply with them regardless. Non-compliance with court orders sends a red flag to any judge that you have no respect for the legal system and this usually makes them most annoyed and even punitive. It is then that charging orders are made against assets and lump sums are awarded for payment of future spousal and child support.

The one-half of the matrimonial home which was in

Horny's name was charged with all arrears of support and future support. It all ended up in Margot's hands and was not an inconsiderable amount. And don't forget the costs. If you show bad faith and thumb your nose at court orders, then most likely your spouse will get costs against you which can be charged against any asset available.

In the Hornig case, Horny's attempts to flee the country with his assets, combined with failure to disclose his finances for a considerable time, meant an award of costs, which paid some, if not all, of Margot's legal fees.

The third thing to remember is that appearing on your own behalf is legal suicide. Even if you feel your attorney is the worst financial rapist ever born and that he has inadequately represented you throughout, he's better than representing yourself. Sometimes, if your spouse is unrepresented, you may take a shot at representing yourself, but it would still give you a leg up to have an attorney.

Although judges will do their best to represent the unrepresented and make efforts to be fair, they find them a great annoyance as they waste the time of the court on unimportant issues — issues which do not concern money and are, as we have discussed, *irrelevant.*

The fourth thing to remember is: Don't leave the country. If you have a girlfriend or boyfriend living abroad, then by all means visit them — briefly. Better still, sponsor them to come to your place of residence, but don't just take off for prolonged periods if you are in the midst of litigation.

Your wife or husband's attorney has the right to examine you, unpleasant as it may be. Your attorney should see you the day before the examination and prepare you for the type of questions you will be asked. Known as *woodshedding*, this is not looked on favorably, especially in criminal court. I personally call it common sense. You should not be forced to submit yourself to a cross-examination or discovery, and certainly not to a trial appearance, without having some idea of what you will be asked, given the opportunity to get all information together and to prepare yourself.

As a bookkeeper, Margot Hornig was meticulously prepared. She even had a binder with special tabs to indicate various financial matters. She put my legal clerk and me to shame. There is nothing worse than arriving at a discovery without having the requested documentation. For example, your last three years of income tax returns. You certainly will have to produce them and explain certain write offs if you have your own business. Be prepared to justify your write offs. Sometimes it is prudent, even if expensive, to have your accountant with you, if you have your own business. After all, you've been paying him for years and the least he can do is substantiate the figures detailed in various financial statements. If he refuses to help, then perhaps it's time to get a new accountant.

The fifth point to remember is that nasty, aggressive spouses require aggressive opposing counsel. The nicest guy in town, who you met at a wedding, may not be the one you need for litigation. Get someone who is experienced in the area and who has done a great job in a similar instances for your friends. Be sure it is a similar action and not a case where a husband or a wife, either guilt ridden or anxious to get out of the marriage, co-operated fully in negotiating a separation agreement. There is nothing wrong with having a satisfactory separation agreement — in fact, it is the only way to fly in most cases — but the attorney who negotiates a good separation agreement, may not be the attorney you wish to represent you against a devious, asset hiding, threatening spouse.

I permitted one of my clients to attend a mediation. She wanted to settle as cheaply and as quickly as possible and as such wanted to attend a local mediator without counsel being present. The husband, a controlling bully who she suspected was hiding considerable assets, did not change his character in front of the mediator. In fact, he used his superior financial position and aggression against her nervous, nonconfrontational personality. Not surprisingly, nothing was resolved and the mediator had the decency to withdraw stating that the husband was using the entire mediation process, not only to bully the wife, but the mediator herself, into some result favorable to him.

Remember this, you can only use the many forms of alternate dispute resolution if both parties have made full financial disclosure and are not using the alternate process as a way to circumvent the demands of legal process. If the parties are acting in *good faith,* by which I mean full disclosure of their assets with supporting evidence of their income, and demonstrate that they are not using the alternate forum as a way to befuddle and pressure the other spouse into a lopsided settlement, then any of the alternates to litigation — mediation or collaborative law — can be very worthwhile.

Most upsetting is the spouse who has had little to do with his children, but upon separation decides he is a born-again father. He demands custody, and the children, suddenly inundated with expensive gifts and given all sorts of attention by a daddy who had previously ignored them or when he did pay attention, was critical and irritable, naturally respond.

The wife, panic-stricken that she will lose *her* children, is willing to acquiesce to anything, provided that they remain with her. This is short sighted and unwise.

Forfeiture of the entitlement to your legal share of Community Property could place you in a position where you must seek immediate employment which, even with spousal support, might provide insufficient income. This may restrict your ability to create a home environment conducive to your kids' happiness.

Unfortunately, teenagers are a greedy little group and can be bought off with designer jeans, motorbikes, a sports car or anything else with wheels. After a while, some of them realize, after choosing to go with the more affluent partner, that Daddy hasn't really changed — he's just more generous and — they miss their mother. So you have the circus of teenagers bouncing back and forth between parents. In the meantime, their grades suffer, while their social lives do not.

Do you really want to use your kids in this fashion and see that son or daughter, who was absolutely bound for college, settle for far less? Of course, if they're with you, you won't have to pay child support and this could even influence in some respects, spousal support. However, unless you genuinely feel you can provide your kids with a more structured and wholesome environment and are determined not to undermine the relationship with the other parent, I urge you to think long and hard before making this custody move.

It's happening all the time. It's used as a form of intimidation and very often the kids, because they're not all dumb, end up where they were in the first place, with that parent who has been the main caregiver throughout the marriage.

When negotiating, be guided by such mainstays as child support guidelines and the advisory guidelines for spousal support. Be guided by the fact that an equal division of property will be ordered by the court in any event and attempt to do what's fair.

If you know your partner had a certain amount of money when you were married, which he or she cannot now prove, giving credit for it goes a long way toward showing your good faith. You don't have to. The law says such deductions have to be proven. You can deny that there was any money there altogether. It will color whatever else transpires, so don't be surprised if your spouse also can't remember little gifts he's given away just prior to separation.

You can each *out-sneak* the other to your heart's content, but who really wins if you end up in a five-day trial? You can spend your kids' college money and pay for your attorney's new deck on his expensive new home.

## DON'T DO IT THAT WAY!

✦ ✦ ✦ ✦ ✦ ✦ ✦

There are those of you who absolutely will not accept the

inevitable: that your spouse simply does not love you anymore or, even worse can't stand the sight of you. This is very hard for you to understand, although you do admit that at times you have been a mean, bad tempered prick or a strident, conniving bitch.

But think of the good times, you say. Think of all those things I've done for him or her. It doesn't matter. They want out, and nothing you can say or do will make a difference. If there's a significant other lurking in the shadows — hopefully well obscured — if your spouse has taken the advice given in this book, then your chance of reconciliation ranges from zero to no chance at all.

You can, if you wish, always make life as unbearable as possible for your spouse, believing that in some weird way this will force him or her back into your arms.

Mrs. Bennett, her soft accent tinged by the north of England and her black hair and eyes revealing her Maltese descent, married her husband when she was pregnant at age seventeen. He was a short, controlling, East End Londoner. After they had immigrated, he became extremely successful manufacturing machine parts for the transportation industry. They had a great lifestyle, expensive home and cars, and enjoyed many trips, all of which were written off as they occurred simultaneously with business conventions.

Success, however, did not sit well with Mr. Bennett and he progressively became a household bully — sneering and belittling his wife, who had not finished high school because of her dyslexia and pregnancy, and picking on his teenage son, who suffered from the same learning disability. Neither was he kindly disposed toward his teenage daughter, but doted on the unexpected and unplanned three-year-old son who arrived seventeen years after they were married.

The marriage ostensibly ended when Mrs. Bennett accosted Mr. Bennett, who was leaving a motel with a stripper with whom he had spent the afternoon. The stripper peddled her wares through "The Bada Bing," a strip club located close to Mr. Bennett's office. The marriage ended as most marriages do, long before that, although that afternoon became the significant date of separation or *triggering event*.

Mr. Bennett wanted his wife back and convinced himself that if he made life miserable enough for her, she would see the error of her ways and return to the fold, duly chastened. He refused to pay support until ordered by the court. He insisted on access to the three year old which was unduly disruptive but to which Mrs. Bennett acquiesced. He played up to the teenagers, giving them expensive gifts under the table and even employing both at his company for the summer so that they would be beholding to him. I am, incidentally, not against one employing one's children but, as stated, Mr. Bennett's intentions were suspect.

He intentionally twisted his financial disclosure, suggesting that his highly successful business was, in fact, barely making it. It would have been impossible for this couple to have maintained their past lifestyle, had the business been as impoverished as alleged by Mr. Bennett.

To prove her case, it was necessary for Mrs. Bennett to retain financial experts, namely a business appraiser and an income evaluator to prove that most of Mr. Bennett's allegations regarding his business and assets were total lies.

In the meantime, she went back to school and completed her final grade of high school, leading the class. This was not made easy, as Mr. Bennett stole her car on the first day of school — there were two keys to the SUV.

While carrying out his horrid little scenario, Mr. Bennett went through five attorneys. Many attorneys will do anything for money, but there is a limit. Even some of Mr. Bennett's more aggressive attorneys became jaded by his lack of financial disclosure, which necessitated constant returns to court. Things were finally settled with the fifth attorney, by means of Minutes of Settlement, which took three days in a court corridor to negotiate.

Not surprisingly, Mr. Bennett refused to conform to any of the Minutes. It became necessary to obtain enforcement orders and register them against various properties so that his signature to transfers could be dispensed with.

Mrs. Bennett ended up with the home, several properties up north, and all of the children. Even jobs and motor vehicles cannot make up for living with a puffed up, cantankerous, vicious parent.

Mrs. Bennett acquired the designation of Certified Professional Accountant and works as a bookkeeper, receiving a modest salary. She prefers this, however, to the affluent, but humiliating life with Mr. Bennett. Mr. Bennett has had a stable of strippers and the like since the breakup, but unfortunately still wants Mrs. Bennett back. I really believe he loved her, but had the damndest way of showing it!

His conduct following the break up had the unfortunate result of making a bad situation even worse. Counseling was attempted through another attorney noted for success in this field. She informed me that Mr. Bennett's attitude precluded any movement toward reconciliation.

This whole rotten case stretched out for over five years. To Mrs. Bennett's credit, she refused to use the youngest child against him and produced him obediently, even though at times, it was decidedly against the child's interest. She has her pride and Mr. Bennett has his money. He does not, however, have Mrs. Bennett — all that money and all that angst!

## DON`T DO IT THAT WAY!

Is there a lesson to be learned from Mr. Bennett? There are several. Although it appears obvious, one lesson would be that being a total prick, and doing everything possible to torture your wife in the misguided belief it would influence her to return is lunacy that bears no chance of success. In this day and age, it is dubious whether one afternoon spent in a local motel with Autumn Haze or Steamy Rain will really cause any straight thinking woman to terminate a twenty-year marriage.

However, the concern of a sexually transmitted disease, coupled with Mr. Bennett's behavior in the home where he constantly criticized, belittled and acted condescendingly toward his wife and the older children, made the ground ripe for separation.

Besides this, Mrs. Bennett knew all about the business. She knew about the phony write-offs and the fact that most of the renovations and furniture in the matrimonial home, which she would eventually end up with, were not bona-fide corporate write-offs, as claimed on Mr. Bennett's income tax returns.

And, of course, she knew that the pricey trips and fine dining, also written off as corporate expenses, were in fact expenses incurred in promoting the Bennett's comfortable lifestyle. She knew the company did well, as Mr. Bennett regaled her on a nightly basis with tales of his success. As such, it was ridiculous in the extreme to have Mr. Bennett's six hundred dollar-per-hour attorneys blatantly set out his poverty in page after page of his pleadings. It was an insult to Mrs. Bennett, who may have been dyslexic, but was certainly not mathematically retarded.

Mr. Bennett spent well in excess of two hundred thousand dollars on his various attorneys. They were not incompetent attorneys; they had just been deceived by Mr. Bennett's misrepresentations concerning his finances. He paid them to be gullible and when he stopped paying, they sent him on his way to another attorney. Mr. Bennett was not a good witness when questioned about his business. He sat with a picture of his youngest child in front of him, oozing self-pity and lies. He was a piece of work.

Advice to male clients who have their own company: the courts are not stupid and neither are accountants. Constantly lying about your assets and corporate profits, which you have to disclose to the IRS and which must be given to your wife's attorney is a futile exercise. Your wife is going to get her share of the division of Community Property or an Equitable Distribution depending on your resident State.

It may or may not come from your one-half share of the matrimonial home, other properties, bank accounts or IRAs.

It should be some comfort to you that the courts will consider the fact that your wife has a very expensive home together with other properties which she may be able to liquidate so that she can be assured of an income. This may influence support under the Spousal Advisory Guidelines.

In the past, an ongoing support order could, and sometimes did, go on forever, incensing my male clients. Sometimes support could be varied or at least be revisited within perhaps a five-year period should *material changes* ensue. However, there was no inducement for a woman to become independent, knowing that if she did, her generous support would become much less generous or even eliminated.

Recently, the courts appear to be more stringent in demanding that a wife attempt to re-establish herself. Under these circumstances, it is very wise to fund your wife while she obtains a R.N., C.A., or a B.A. plus a teaching certificate or anything that will result in her obtaining future financial independence.

If your wife is over fifty-five and has spent her entire life parenting your children and never did finish high school, then you are out of luck. It looks like a lifetime proposition in all probability, unless there is the *material change of circumstances,* such as her winning the lottery or marrying Donald Trump.

So determined are some men not to benefit their wives in any way, they actually destroy their businesses deliberately. The husband of one of my clients systematically liquidated everything in his business and ran up debts to the extent that he forced himself into bankruptcy. It was a ridiculous situation and one in which it was difficult to have my client attempt to put a stop to the husband's financial insanity. She dragged the matter on, refusing to move for months, until his company was in shambles.

I last heard that he was in arrears of child support and she was forced to sell the home. She had been awarded generous child and spousal support by a sympathetic judge, which was followed by the husband's filing bankruptcy and becoming unemployed.

Bankruptcy does not let you off the hook for spousal or child support, although you can avoid an equalization payment. Moreover, now courts have a habit of imputing income to formerly successful CEO's who suddenly find they cannot make a living. I reminded my client of all of this, but she simply wanted no part of it.

When I last heard, she was doing extremely well as a real estate agent and was receiving some child support from the husband on a reduced basis. She was a talented woman who had an impressive corporate job before her marriage and she was able to re-establish herself. The husband's actions, however, greatly impeded his corporate future.

Sometimes help comes to people in the strangest ways. Lou Thompson was, what is known in his British birthplace as "a bounder and a cad". He married Florence, a large, good-natured, bottle blonde. Within five years of their marriage they had four children. After this, Florence saw very little of Lou and certainly even less of his money.

He worked for the government and made a respectable salary, with regular increases throughout the years. But his money went to his two main loves, horses and gambling. The horses were housed on a ten-acre piece of land Lou had purchased, together with a home, for a modest amount during the early years of their marriage. Periodically, he would encumber the home to buy yet another horse, but he usually paid the mortgage. In reality, this was almost his sole contribution toward the family.

Florence worked as a waitress at a nearby restaurant and babysat the children of local families. Somewhere along the way, Lou also sponsored his widowed mother into the country. She lived in a small flat nearby and babysat the children when Florence was at work.

For many women, this would have been enough. But Florence hung in, believing that Lou would eventually straighten up, reminding herself that, after all, he was the father of her kids.

The final blow came when it turned out that Lou, during one of his visits back to Blackpool, met an old schoolmate, impregnated her and promised to sponsor her into Canada. It was the cruelest cut of all, especially when Lou expected Florence to take care of his five horses, mucking up the barn and supervising them while he was gone.

Even then, things could have been settled, but Lou refused to co-operate. His pension was none of Florence's business, he told her. She hadn't earned it. Nor did he believe he should pay for the kids. After all, they were lazy and wouldn't co-operate in helping him take care of the horses. And although he made three times Florence's income, including her tips as a waitress, he refused to pay spousal support. In fact, later on he demanded the house be sold, even with four teenagers living at home and five horses still out grazing.

It was one of those situations where a court case was inevitable, although Florence could ill afford legal fees. After firing his first two attorneys, who I suspected tried to instill some sanity into Lou's perception of family law, we ended up before the presiding judge, a former criminal attorney, in the small town where the home and ten acres were located. The judge knew little about family law, but a great deal about *bounders and cads.* And he knew one when he saw one.

The Star Witness, however, was neither Florence nor Lou, but rather Mrs. Thompson Sr., Lou's mother and the grandmother of the four grandchildren she had babysat for over ten years. A tiny woman, with fierce black eyes and grey and white hair bobbed to her ears, she gave His Honor the straight goods.

"Don't listen to a word he says," she cautioned the judge, in an accent that resembled Lou's, but was much stronger. "He's nothing but a *bluffah.* You never could believe a word he says and now he's gotten worse."

When she left the witness box, all ninety-five pounds of her, glaring at her son as she walked by, there was no doubt who was telling the truth in this matter and who His Honor should rule in favor of.

Help comes from the strangest sources. Mrs. Thompson thought, of course, about the grandchildren she had been babysitting and to whom she was extremely attached. She could not sit still and watch her son, regardless of his sponsorship, turf his family out of their home and continue to pursue what she characterized to the judge as *his evil ways*

Florence got the house and Lou moved the horses else-where. It was in the days before the Family Responsibility Office attempted to collect child support, so Lou became a deadbeat dad, ignoring his support orders. His mother certainly had his number.

I thought I was through with Lou Thompson, but within a few years another blonde, somewhat prettier, appeared as the second Mrs. Thompson. She had shared his enthusiasm for horses and indeed had invested some of her money in a horse farm. Lou, however, had turned nasty and she separated and wished to force a sale. Lou blamed her menopause, which he insisted had ruined an otherwise happy marriage. This time there was no mother and Lou pushed his new wife into signing an agreement, which was later set aside. The matter ended up settled, with no one very happy.

Lou continues with his horses and I am told a third helpmate. Sometimes you can't keep a good man down!

What's the lesson? Sometimes, if someone is impossible and can be proven to be so, you have to go to court even if you can't afford it. In addition, it's prudent to keep the same attorney. Lou's third attorney knew nothing of the case, had been hired at the last minute and had not even read the discovery transcripts. I know, because he asked me if I had a transcript.

Ignoring court orders, letting his wife struggle financially while he played the horses, and taking care of his own five fillies in good style at the expense of his family, was not impressive — even to a judge whose background was restricted to criminal law.

If you have a good witness, like Lou's mother, by all means use her. Usually, it's the kiss of death to use your opposing spouse's relatives to give evidence against him or her. Blood is thick when it comes to the crunch and family members are known for supporting their own — regardless.

I let one client persuade me to call her husband's sister who, she assured me, would support her claim. Of course, she didn't. I had to have her declared an adverse witness so that I could cross-examine her. It was more than embarrassing and it taught me a lesson. Never subpoena anyone unless they are absolutely willing to help and they do not have to be persuaded to testify.

There is an old adage among attorneys: you never ask a question of a witness unless you already know the answer. A poor witness is much worse than no witness at all. Judges know that family members are notoriously reluctant to give evidence against their own. This is why Mrs. Thompson Sr.'s evidence rang so true and was so believable.

Of course, you can't underestimate a grandmother's affection for her grandchildren. As a cynic might say, they have yet to disappoint.

# Chapter 10
## The Emotional Abusers and Trial Hazards

Dino Rossi stated, "My wife is the meanest bitch alive, but she's very intelligent."

Thinking, in some weird way, that it was essential to obtaining a divorce, he produced a wedding picture. From what I could tell from the picture she had also had been very pretty twenty years earlier.

Sleek and slick in his dark suit, polished shoes and hair shining with Brylcreem, Dino looked very much the same. Priscilla, on the other hand, had been driven to food, which, although preferable to drink, had other insidious side effects.

Dino had been a chaser for years, and was good looking enough to have the much younger and much slimmer objects of his desire reciprocate. The latest affair, which was still ongoing, had Priscilla Rossi ballooning up to two hundred and fifty pounds. When I saw her at court for the first time, she was bursting out of her print dress and fat spilled over from her swollen ankles onto her scuffed low-heeled pumps. It was obvious that Priscilla needed get rid of Dino, if only for her health.

They had both been driving instructors, and both had terminated their employment to ensure that neither would have to pay the other support. As a result, neither had money and both subsisted on unemployment insurance, which was about to terminate. There were no assets, except the matrimonial home with its small mortgage.

Their only son left home the previous year, rather than put up with his parents' ongoing animosity, which was worsening by the day. Priscilla wanted to continue to live in the small bungalow with her son at home and Dino out.

She assured me, when examined, that Dino was working construction on the side and she wished him to pay the current expenses and the mortgage. It was, she stated, "the least he could do."

Every morning, complained Dino, she'd wake him up at five a.m.

This, I thought, with some sympathy, would be extremely hard on Dino, who no doubt had spent the night before drinking wine and making love until the early hours with his young girlfriend. The girlfriend would not permit him to move into her apartment, which she shared with her sister.

Not only did Priscilla vacuum for two solid hours from five o'clock to seven o'clock, she threw out all the food which he had purchased from the local deli.

"It's a waste," howled Dino. "I wouldn't mind so much if she would eat it. But she throws it in the garbage, where I can see it, and covers it with coffee grinds and sometimes toilet paper."

"Used toilet paper?" I inquired.

Dino nodded his head. His clothes would be next, he feared. Because of this, he folded his two good suits and one sports jacket and placed them under his bed, transporting them to the trunk of his car when he left the house.

As well, she had taped his syrupy conversations with his latest girlfriend and played them on full volume whenever he was home, causing him considerable annoyance. This was before cell phone use became widespread. "There is no doubt," I told him, "that the house must be sold. In fact, any judge would order it, especially under the circumstances."

He could not, I cautioned him, retaliate in any physical way. If he did, he could be removed from the home and then she would have exactly what she wanted — exclusive possession of the home, rather than a sale. I advised him to walk out when anger got the best of him.

A court motion was made and Priscilla represented herself. She informed the presiding judge that she could not afford an attorney. The house was ordered sold.

There was, in reality, no reason not to award a sale. Both parties were unemployed and there were no small children at home. There had been no violence, except on the part of Priscilla, who was waging a psychological battle second only to the Russians during the Cold War.

The Court Order made no difference to Priscilla. True, she signed a listing with a local agent, but she managed to be unavailable whenever he produced a prospective purchaser. The family pet, a Rottweiler, who had hitherto been Dino's friend, had suddenly turned nasty and threatened all who entered, including Dino. Dino suspected a combination of dog biscuits and coercion.

"There's no stopping her," he complained.

A motion for contempt against Priscilla was brought, but adjourned by a judge on the condition that the parties cooperate in the sale of the home and "civility be the order of the day."

*Civility?* I thought. This couple does not know the meaning of the word. And, just when I thought nothing else could happen, something did. Dino was charged with dangerous driving: a charge which was brought by the police after Priscilla insisted he had tried to kill her with his car while she was driving on Highway 401.

"It was," he assured me, "all lies."

It was Priscilla who had tried to kill *him,* and it was only by using his driving skills, which no doubt he learned in order to qualify as a driving instructor, had he been able to avoid death.

Priscilla was an excellent witness. Swollen cheeks and neck quivering with indignation, her plump hands chopping at the stale courtroom air, she described a horrific scenario worthy of a James Bond chase scene. It was not Dino Rossi's fault that she had not been killed. His attack on her, cutting her off and attempting to drive her into the guardrail, was relentless and unyielding. It was only by God's intervention, she insisted, raising her small dark eyes in their pillows of fat upward, and fingering the crucifix which Dino had given her in happier days, that she was still alive.

Dino's evidence paled by comparison.

Her Honor, however, dismissed the charge, not without commenting that she believed Mrs. Rossi, but some doubt lingered, especially as the couple was in the midst of "acrimonious divorce proceedings."

Priscilla, no doubt, saw this as a moral victory and waddled from the courtroom with a slight smile.

Dino felt that the judge had no business at all finding him not guilty, and then stating that she believed his wife. I agreed with him.

"But she had a doubt, Dino," I said.

The house was finally sold. Unfortunately, for a price somewhat less than the first purchaser had been willing to pay. It had gone stale on the market and had become the house where the Rottweiler lived.

"There were two Rottweilers," grumbled Dino, "Priscilla and Bruno."

Five days before the closing, Priscilla suddenly surfaced with an attorney, moving to freeze all money, despite the fact that neither of them had alternate accommodation and both were in desperate need of funds.

Dino wished to counter, asking for some compensation as a result of the hindered sale and delay. I did not do it. It was simply not worth it and too hard to prove. Besides, there had to be some end to the litigation. A consent judgment was finally entered into giving Priscilla an extra five thousand dollars, which Dino stormed was completely unfair. Of course it was. But things have to stop somewhere.

In retrospect, one can only ask what would have been a better course. Five o'clock vacuuming and food theft are dangerous pursuits. But Priscilla knew her man. A philanderer he was, but a physical abuser he wasn't — except perhaps a psychological one.

Had Priscilla attempted to make a deal and tried to persuade Dino to give her a disproportionate amount of the house proceeds earlier on, she may have done better. In that case, she probably would have fully co-operated in the sale of the home and would have had more money to start over, if indeed that was ever possible.

Of course, no judge would order this, as both were unemployed and Priscilla's allegations that Dino was working under the table in construction could not be proven, even though I suspected she might be correct. One does not court a young woman, pay an attorney and have a wardrobe like Dino's, without receiving something more than unemployment benefits.

Charging one's spouse with dangerous driving, a serious criminal offence, is a dangerous ploy when fabricated. I always believed that Priscilla initiated the hazardous pursuit on Highway 401, which could have resulted in a fatality, not to mention leaving Dino with a criminal record had he survived. Had they not been driving instructors and extremely skilled, the question of divorce might have become moot.

The lesson: If something is inevitable — like the sale of the home in this particular case — try to make some lemonade out of the lemons. Attempt to get more money from your share of the home or if the person is employed, or will be employed in the near future, attempt to obtain some support if you are less qualified than your spouse.

If you are both under the same roof, there is nothing to be gained by methodical torture. Stay out of each other's way. If things become dangerous, leave. A report to the police of an incident in which you do not lay charges, but detail what has gone on in your home, is a good idea and will soften things, should they be called in the future. Neither Priscilla nor Dino called the police during the 401 driving battle, leaving no evidence as to its reality.

After all the fuss, stress and legal fees, the parties were left with exactly what the court would have ordered — an equal division of the home proceeds, less some of the joint debts incurred prior to the separation which were due and owing at the time of sale. As an inducement to settle, Priscilla did get the extra five thousand dollars, but I suspect a considerable amount of this went to her attorney in any event.

It was similar to many other court battles, the results of which are easily foreseeable.

An expensive waste of time!

Carmela Grotteria came to Canada as an eighteen-year-old immigrant bride. Twenty years later, her English was still hesitant and deeply accented, a fact her husband Giuseppe — whose accent was not much better— constantly brought to her attention.

It was, he would rave, yet another example of her stupidity. He had assaulted her on their wedding night, some twenty-two years earlier, for being too nice at the wedding reception to relatives that he despised. He proceeded to batter her on a regular basis from that day forward.

The battering was for a variety of reasons: her housekeeping, the pasta that was not cooked al dente and which he subsequently threw against the wall, and for being one of a number of employees laid-off from a factory assembly line — there was always something.

Her daughter, Liliana, who accompanied her and translated, and her son, who simply did not want to be involved, had witnessed most of the abuse. Liliana detested her father, who had thrown her beloved white cat into an incinerator and who called her a whore because she wore eyeliner and lipstick. The son, on the other hand, emulated the father. Although he had never assaulted his mother, he treated her with the same disrespect that his father appeared to believe she deserved.

It was, I expressed, a horrible situation. I wondered out loud why she had not at least seen an attorney earlier or called the police.

Carmela, who came from a small village in Calabria, gave me a look of surprise and concern.

"This was," Liliana explained, "not something mama would do."

Police were apparently only called in cases of murder—and sometimes, not even then.

Liliana went on to explain that the reason her mother had sought me out was not for a divorce on the grounds of cruelty. Her father had acquired a Canadian girlfriend — a divorcee, with three small children — who her father believed to be superior to her mother because of her ability to speak English.

Strange how it happens, I thought. A woman endures abuse that would drive a saint to homicide and does nothing about it, but when the abuser acquires a girlfriend, is suddenly driven into action. Carmela finally wanted out.

The Grotterias had one substantial asset and that was a mortgage-free bungalow located in Etobicoke, a western suburb of Toronto. Giuseppe also had a fixed benefit pension of some twenty-two thousand dollars with a company he had worked for since his immigration and where he earned a respectable income as a skilled craftsman.

Carmela had not even considered receiving any money from Giuseppe for herself or the children. Although he had paid off the mortgage and paid the expenses of the home, including utilities and taxes, Giuseppe had never given Carmela any money. He did give his son an allowance, but not Liliana, who he believed would spend it only on makeup and the type of clothing that her *whore friends* would buy.

From a series of jobs, which had included commercial cleaning, factory work and occasional stints at kitchen work in various restaurants, Carmella supplied all of the food for the family, and clothing and money for Liliana.

All she wanted, she informed me, not wishing to wait for Liliana's translation, was the house. If she had the house, she could manage without the help of Giuseppe, which would not, she was certain, be forthcoming in any event.

"Of course he'll have to pay you," I said naively. "Liliana and your son are still in high school. He'll have to pay child support and spousal support. It's been a long-term marriage and from what you tell me, he makes three times as much as you'll ever make. And while you may not get the entire house, you'll certainly get one-half of it. Considering all the circumstances, including the violence, I might even get you exclusive possession. That means that you could live there for perhaps three years before its sale and get off to a good start."

Wrapped in dark clothing, with her grey streaked hair coiled at the nape of her neck, she sat there looking at me with large brown eyes. She looked a good ten years older than her forty years. She spoke rapidly to Liliana in Italian and Liliana translated.

"Mama says, he will fight you all the way." And she was right.

Giuseppe's attorney, an inexperienced, and, dare I say, incompetent fellow, seemed to be receiving bizarre instructions from a source that I later determined to be Giuseppe's girlfriend. The welfare mother of three in some strange fashion fancied herself an authority on family law.

Upon the court case commencing, Giuseppe moved in with the girlfriend and then took the position that he need not pay any support whatsoever for his wife and children as he was no longer living in the home. It took a court motion and a judge's order to attempt to convince him otherwise. Even then, the support was not forthcoming.

The judge had ordered Giuseppe to produce three years of income tax returns and recent pay stubs. Giuseppe did not comply. An order was obtained directing his employer to produce proof of income for a three-year period and documentation relating to the worth of his pension. The employer listened to Giuseppe's instructions and refused to comply.

This case occurred before the time of the Family Responsibility Plan, which was enforced by a government enforcement agency that collected child and spousal support and support arrears. But even then, a party to an action was under an obligation to disclose his income. Of course, in today's courts, lack of financial disclosure is viewed with such seriousness that some judges would not hesitate to strike pleadings as a result of non-compliance.

An application was made to do exactly that, but instead, a trial was ordered, expedited, and the matter immediately added to the Court docket for the next court sessions.

His Honor, it seems, was hesitant to wipe out Mr. Grotteria's pleadings, contemptuous of the law as he appeared to be. The judge, however, gave Carmela exclusive possession of the home, which had effectively been given in any event, and ordered Grotteria's employers to give financial disclosure.

They ignored the court order.

Incredibly, Carmela, by dint of holding down two jobs, together with help from Liliana, who was failing her high school year while doing dishes at night, kept things going. The son, who suddenly realized that his father may just not be the man he thought he was, acquired an after school job. Giuseppe was providing for his new love and her three children, even though I discovered at court that she was still receiving welfare benefits.

Sometimes, things really go right at a trial and you know it immediately. The judge was a relatively young, attractive, and bright woman, who had just gone through a well-gossiped about divorce herself. She was patient and sympathetic with Carmela and her halting English. A translator had been ordered but Carmela attempted to answer many of the questions in English herself, which gave her additional credibility.

The employer had been subpoenaed and sent the company accountant as his representative, with full proof of Giuseppe's income, which was quite impressive. Certainly, there appeared to be no reason why he had not complied with court orders. The reason given by the accountant for non-compliance with earlier court orders was that they had been urged by Mr. Grotteria not to get involved. This excuse appeared not to go down well with Her Honor, who informed the accountant the company was on very dangerous ground.

Liliana appeared, nose ring and multiple earrings intact. She was, however, a sincere and supportive witness who eyed her father with narrowed eyes, complete with the eyeliner he detested. At the end of our evidence, there was little doubt that things were definitely leaning to the side of the angels.

Giuseppe's attorney, obviously failing in what may have been his first trial, asked irrelevant questions, which I later found had been supplied by Giuseppe's girlfriend. Needless to say, this made matters worse for Giuseppe and with each answer, better for Carmela.

Giuseppe's first witness was his girlfriend. This was shocking in the extreme, as she had never met Carmela, and any information obtained was based on hearsay from her live-in-lover, Giuseppe. Undaunted and happily ignorant, she launched into a diatribe of criticism concerning Carmela's poor housekeeping and lack of personal hygiene. All of this was delivered in a sneering and barely controlled voice.

It was grossly inappropriate, offensive, irrelevant, and highly inflammatory. The girlfriend was only some three minutes into her diatribe when the judge abruptly asked for an adjournment and ordered both myself and Giuseppe's attorney into a mid-trial conference before an experienced judge. He knew a thing or two about non-compliance of court orders and girlfriends who give offensive evidence against wives of twenty-two years.

He asked me what my client wanted. Smelling burnt flesh and flushed with oncoming victory, I naturally launched into a long list of requested relief which included everything but Giuseppe's left toe.

"I know you've got them on the run," said His Honor, "but I want to speak to your client, in your presence, of course. I want to know what *she* really wants."

All she really wanted, of course, was the house.

He then spoke to Giuseppe and his attorney alone in chambers. I don't know what was said, but I do know that the attorney appeared flushed and upset and Giuseppe white-faced, with fists clenched in fury.

Needless to say a deed was prepared over the lunch hour by an accommodating law firm near the courthouse and the house was signed over to Carmela. Child support was ordered commensurate with Giuseppe's newly-disclosed income. There was no spousal support, as Giuseppe's one-half share of the home was to be considered as a lump sum payment; a remedy sometimes relied on for those parties who have a history of non-payment of support and violence. Mr. Grotteria was permitted to keep his fixed benefit pension of approximately twenty-two thousand dollars, which could, reminded his Honor, be attached for arrears, if necessary.

All of this was agreed to in Minutes of Settlement drafted by his Honor and executed by the parties. It was a way to avoid an appeal, explained his Honor, and, he told Giuseppe, a way to avoid costs, which under the circumstances could be considerable.

Incidentally, costs have become much more considerable in recent years. Several years back, the courts were reluctant to award costs in matrimonial matters, especially in custody matters. Much of this has changed. Now, substantial costs are ordered against parties who lose on most of the issues at a trial, or who do not make reasonable offers or accept them, especially if they are similar to the judgment received.

This is something to be very concerned about as in one recent case I noticed that the costs were much higher than the equalization payment which, of course, means that a great deal of work was done to benefit the attorney representing the payee. This means that the party had a moral victory but not a practical one.

Carmela was delighted. This was what she wanted all along and this was what she received. To the best of my knowledge, she still resides in that same bungalow in Etobicoke, West Toronto.

Giuseppe's mistakes were classic and destined him for legal oblivion. His choice of solicitor was an error. He had, I learned, chosen his young attorney because he had closed a real estate deal for a friend and had incorporated a company for another. Giuseppe failed to ask him how many trials he had participated in as lead counsel or about his level of experience in the area of matrimonial law.

Besides, Giuseppe's girlfriend had liked him because he had listened to her and obeyed her instructions. This was a gross error on the part of counsel. To parade in an arrogant, loud spoken, much younger girlfriend and to have her vilify an abused wife for the most irrelevant of reasons was unheard of strategy. To have a girlfriend make up the questions for cross-examination and then let her take the stand and spew forth a vulgar and offensive diatribe against a wife whose husband she had somehow enamored was stupid beyond belief.

Of course, Giuseppe did everything wrong. He ignored court orders, probably with his girlfriend's encouragement. He did not pay a cent to Carmela or the children. He then instructed his company's administrative offices not to comply with court orders to disclose his earnings. Strangely, they agreed. I could never understand why they would not have checked with their corporate attorney, who would certainly have advised them that compliance was necessary.

If there is an eleventh legal commandment, it should be do not produce a girlfriend or boyfriend at trial, unless it is a custody case and that individual is there to put forward her closeness to the child in question and her willingness to assume parental duties. There is something about producing a girlfriend or boyfriend that in some way is especially off-putting.

I learned my lesson when I permitted a gorgeous second wife to attend a trial and take notes. It went over badly with the judge. I have even had my clients persuade their siblings or business associates to sit at the back of the courtroom, so that they would not be perceived by the judge to be a significant other.

Elderly parents, of course, are a different thing. It is touching to see an elderly solicitous father sitting with his young daughter who is on the verge of divorce. Sometimes even a concerned mother may help in a son's case, provided she does not fix him with the words, "he's only a *bluffah*," as did Mrs Thompson Sr. in our former case.

Had Giuseppe left his girlfriend at home and complied with court orders, I hazard a guess that he would have at least ended up with one half of the home. Carmela may, however, have been permitted to stay there a few years for re-establishment reasons as a result of the history of abuse.

The abuse should have been documented. Even if she were averse to calling the police, which she assuredly was, pictures should have been taken of various bruises and medical reports of emergency trips to a doctor. All of this had occurred, but she had confided in no one and had lied about her injuries to her fellow employees out of embarrassment. It was Giuseppe's word against hers. I am emphasizing the abuse, as it is one of the reasons that a party may be given exclusive possession of the matrimonial home, or even a lump sum to avoid further contact.

It did end well for Carmela. A few years later, however, Liliana appeared in my office with a swelling the size of a purple and maroon mouse under her eye. She had acquired a lover from the Middle East, who had set her and her mother up in a successful franchise selling fast Italian food. She had a child by the man, who was quite obviously an abuser — a worse one than her father. She wanted to know her rights concerning the franchise. Unlike her mother, Liliana had reported the abuse to the police and her common-law husband had been charged. Like her mother, however, she had gotten together with the abuser again. She never returned to my office after that visit.

These things have a way of becoming circuitous and unfortunately children appear to emulate the parents' conduct and continue their mistakes — another reason for leaving after that first slap and never going back.

The world has changed and there is much more awareness of domestic abuse. There are many places where you can go, including local shelters, if you find yourself in an abusive situation.

Do not stick around if you fear for your life. Unfortunately, sometimes abuse appears to be cultural and the women remain silent for religious or familial reasons. Often there are language difficulties and inability to obtain employment so there is complete financial dependency on the abuser, who takes advantage of this.

The longer the abuse continues, the lower the self-esteem and the harder it is to escape from it. Eventually, women appear to believe that they deserve this type of treatment and they acquiesce. Sometimes, some of the sons adapt the same methods as their fathers, so that the wives are abused on all fronts.

At times, throughout my practice, I have cautioned women in this regard, told them of their rights and urged them to take a stand against these perpetrators of abuse. I have recommended counselors and assertiveness training and begged them to notify the police. All too often, my advice has been ignored and they simply disappear. Too often, they only want me to write a letter to their husbands advising them that if their conduct continues, more stringent measures will be taken.

This, of course, is not the answer. It may shock the perpetrator into good conduct for a month or so, but in time he will revert back to his old ways and the abuse will recommence, in many cases on a much worse scale.

Occasionally, the avowed separation will trigger an even worse episode of abuse and, on occasion, murder, as in the previously mentioned Woodbridge case where the wife returned to the home to pick up clothing, only to be murdered by her husband. This, I stress, is rare and quite often abusers are merely bullies who retract into their shell and stop their abuse once they are called on it.

As for you guys who've been guilty of pushing your wives around and bullying your children, your abuse will define you in court and will certainly bias a judge against you. If, after the commencement of an action, you feel inclined in any way to resort to violence, leave the home.

If your wife is the perpetrator, don't even try to restrain her if she attacks you. Go to the police, have them document her conduct as an incident, and stay away if you can, returning only to reside in a room with a locked door.

My client's wife told him she had every intention of performing a castration while he slept. Why she thought he would not wake up during the operation is beyond me. Needless to say, it made him a nervous wreck, especially as I had urged him to stay in the matrimonial home because I believed it would further the settlement of our case.

And gentlemen, leave the girlfriend out of it. She shouldn't even exist for some time, even when you have access to the kids and perhaps more especially then. Don't parade her like a new trophy at court or elsewhere.

On a personal note, there is nothing worse than to have a client come in with his girlfriend at every appointment. Girlfriends, unfortunately, work themselves up to having a real antipathy against the first wife. I had one very successful government official come in to see me with his second wife, so I could explain to her why he had to pay child and spousal support. It seems that she was haranguing him day and night about giving any money to "that bitch and those damn kids."

He was visibly relieved when I informed the second wife that it was his responsibility to follow a court order and even if she believed money he was paying was not being used for the kids' benefit, they would not succeed in a motion to vary support based on this assumption — in addition, the amount he was paying was not unfair.

I am always amazed at second wives who break up a marriage and then do everything possible to undermine the financial position of the first wife and kids. It makes for considerable trouble and stress for the husband, who is torn between his legal obligations and the haranguing of a second wife.

Keep your mouth shut honey, you got him didn't you?

Now back off.

# Chapter 11
## Alienation
## The Most Dangerous Game

In 1985, Dr. Richard Gardner defined the *Parental Alienation Syndrome.* He classified the behavior of a spouse, who would deliberately alienate the children from the other spouse because of resentment and hate following a marriage breakup, as a disease. The disease had various characteristics and one of the ultimate cures for it was the deprogramming of the children.

At that time Dr. Gardner was looked upon as somewhat radical, especially for his suggested treatment of the alienating parent, which involved incarceration as a last resort. Several psychiatrists attempted to disassociate themselves from him, claiming that alienation per se was not a disease. They did, however, believe in alienation as an existing force and although they could not define it with clarity, as did Dr. Gardner, they knew it when they saw it.

Fortunately, many more judges are now seeing it, defining it and confronting it. This is excellent. Unfortunately on occasion, they see it when it isn't there and Daddy is, in reality, an abusive stinker who the kids have decided they don't wish to see. Maybe this should not be classified as alienation, but merely a form of selectivity. However, human judicial error aside, alienation is one of the most savage ways known to man to destroy a child. Stopping it by any means possible is laudable.

Ricky Barnes was a smooth as custard and as sleek as a riverboat gambler. When he entered my office, looking like Burt Reynolds before his face-lift, with his full head of dark hair, sharp dark eyes and well-trimmed moustache, he caused a minor commotion in the reception area.

"There is a real hottie coming up to see you," panted my receptionist.

As if to further explain, she referred to Ricky Barnes as a *hunka burning love.* While I certainly did not judge my clients as a result of the expletives of hormonally-charged receptionists, Ricky Barnes was a very attractive man and at this point in time, a very self assured one. I mention this specifically because when the pressures of his life weighed ever more heavily upon him, both his self assurance and attractiveness faded. Litigation will do that to you.

He informed me that he had met his wife, Tempest — not her real name, but an appropriate one, in medical school. He was instantly attracted to her, because, he informed me, she was brilliant, sexy, and fun to be with. She was the daughter of East European immigrants who had sacrificed to send her through university and then medical school.

He was the son of a fourth generation, very successful businessman and one of five children, all of whom, at times, were recipients of their father's largesse. That generosity, of course, varied with his approval or disapproval. In any event, his father had considerable investments in a small European Principality and it was his wish that Dr. Barnes go there, not only to practice medicine, but to keep an eye on and perhaps even expand these investments.

Tempest had not wished to go. She wanted to become licensed and to practice in one of Canada's largest cities or perhaps even go to the United States. He persuaded her otherwise, so instead of doing an internship as planned, she went with him to the Principality and settled in.

It did not take him long, however, to expand the list of original adjectives that he applied to Tempest with words such as *high maintenance, temperamental and hysterical*. She considered the children, of which there were three in quite rapid succession, as unduly trying, although there were a multitude of nannies available and she went through literally dozens of them. She screamed when the children would not eat, demanded instant obedience and complained incessantly about trivial misbehavior. The kids, he felt, were afraid of her and for good reason. Their only son, especially, was upset by her temperamental outbursts.

At parties she drank too much, flirted too much, and embarked on what he suspected, and in time felt sure, were a series of affairs with persons whom he considered *low-lifes* — craftsmen and an individual who had been hired to renovate the matrimonial home.

He had come home late one night and found her naked in the pool with the husband of a close girlfriend. She pretended it was innocent, but he knew it was not. He made the decision then, he informed me, to get rid of her. But most importantly, he did not wish to rid himself of his three children. They were a handsome trio, two girls and a boy, and he showed me a recent picture. Three great looking kids: two who bore a close resemblance to him and the youngest, he stated, the image of Tempest.

He intended to be fair, he assured me. She would get one-half of the value of his considerable properties and he would buy out her interest in the matrimonial home. She would return to Toronto, as she had become an embarrassment in the Principality, and, in any event, the children, especially the oldest, were nearing a time when local schools would no longer be appropriate. The wealthier expatriots all sent their children to the United States and some as far as Canada for private schooling.

Despite the fact that he wanted the children one-half of the time so that he could maintain his close and loving relationship with them, he was prepared to pay very generous child support. The sum mentioned caused me to raise my eyebrows. This was before guideline support for children came into effect and the sum mentioned was far greater. It would support Tempest in a style superior to that of eighty percent of the population in Canada or the United States.

The girls, he informed me, especially the youngest, were *Daddy's Girls*. The son looked up to him and adored him. There was no way he intended to have this relationship disturbed, especially not by a screaming, hysterical banshee who couldn't keep her legs closed and had soiled their reputation. He would acquire an apartment in Toronto, or purchase a condominium, where the children would visit with him one-half of the time. It was the only way he could hope to keep up his relationship with them. And, of course, he would have the children on expensive holidays and for at least one-half of the summer, alternate Christmases and during the Easter break.

"But your practice," I reminded him. "How can you carry on your practice?"

"It'll be quite all right," he assured me. "My patients would never go elsewhere and besides, I have a junior working with me." Then, he added thoughtfully, "I would think Tempest would wish to resume her medical studies and update her credentials. She was much better than I was in medical school, you know."

An agreement was signed in the Principality, a mistake to start with. If one is proceeding under Canadian or American State law and the children and wife are to be residing in Canada or in a particular State in the future, surely an agreement executed in that particular Province or State and reflecting their specific family laws would have been preferable.

Instead of this, Ricky Barnes had insisted on having an agreement drawn up in the Principality, which did not reflect the law where Tempest and the children would be residing, and which also set out the exorbitant amount of child support, which he had been willing to pay.

Even more serious, there was no variation clause, so that presumably the amount would remain steadfast in spite of changes in circumstances which were not predictable.

Ricky used all the money he had to buy Tempest out of the matrimonial home and half the value of his practice and business interests. Any other properties were to be divided upon sale. It was a generous agreement. In fact, some aspects of it, mainly the child support, were much too generous. When reminded of this, he replied with a shrug. It was not his wish to deprive his children of anything.

Tempest arrived back in Toronto, bristling with hostility. She had decided she had not wanted to leave her friends, especially her masculine ones, and accused Barnes of bamboozling her into leaving. She had, he informed me, become physical the night of her departure. He hoped her anger would subside upon her returning to Toronto. After all, her parents were there.

Then, as an afterthought, he casually mentioned that he had a friend who was close to his children, who had taught them music and had been their favorite babysitter. She would, he was certain, help pave the way for the children's adjustment and could conceivably be a reason why the children might eventually wish to stay with him.

Ricky Barnes had definitely underestimated Tempest's rage and animosity. The children were, as I recall at the time, eight, ten, and twelve. Naturally, they had felt some hesitation at leaving their school and friends. This was further fueled by Tempest, who assured them that their father had thrown them out of the Principality and wanted to get rid of them. This was, of course, untrue.

True, my client had wanted to get rid of Tempest, but certainly not the children. In fact, he had been unstinting in his efforts to keep up his relationship with his children and I suspect that was one of the reasons why he selected their little Scottish music teacher to be a fill-in mommy for Tempest.

Tempest blew hard and relentless. For a girl to have known her way around Europe and to have, according to my client, a number of married lovers, she was livid at what she perceived as being dumped for a *little nothing.* She worked on the children, so that when my client, who had flown hundreds of miles, came to pick them up for a long weekend, they informed him they did not wish to see him.

He was physically attacked by this tribe of shrieking Lilliputians, who, to his horror, spat, kicked, and even jumped on the hood of his shiny, leased, black Cadillac. Tempest stood in the doorway of her new luxurious home, obviously enjoying the spectacle which she had helped create. It was not until he had headed for a mall and lavished the children with gifts, despite their bad behavior, that things simmered down and they became themselves.

The weekend after the initial opening scene was a pleasant one and the children behaved, except when "Mommy Dearest" phoned. The call upset the kids, especially when Mommy informed them how lonely she was without them.

Unfortunately, this was only the beginning. After that, the scenes became worse and my client threatened police action, although there was no court order directly involving the police. Then, the oldest child, who we can refer to as *Tempest light,* refused to go with Daddy at all. She was, she informed my client, staying with Mommy. She hated him and did not wish to see him. Then the youngest child, who he had stayed with in the hospital when she had her tonsils removed, who sat on his lap nightly and who he often referred to as *Daddy's Little Girl*, also decided that she had to stay with *Tempest Light* and Mommy.

This left the boy, who adored his father, but quite obviously felt guilty about deserting the pack. It was all too troubling and my client wanted them to be seen by a psychiatrist.

One of the most eminent in the city was chosen. To bring all this about, there were constant applications to court. It was endless. The parties needed their own private attorneys.

The psychiatrist interviewed the children. He determined that the hostility toward their father appeared to be unfounded and attributed *alienation* as the cause in a subsequent report. On the next visit, the children were even more obnoxious and uncontrolled, speaking disparagingly of the psychiatrist's dirty, dull office and of his appearance.

Things worsened — and he was habitually denied visitation. At one point they visited the Principality. The children's much-loved Scottish music teacher was present. She was ugly, *like a witch,* the girls told her. Besides that, she was sleeping in Mommy's bed and using Mommy's bath. In fact, she was trying to take Mommy's place. My client adamantly denied all these allegations, which no doubt emanated from Tempest.

Fun in the family pool degenerated quickly after a phone call from Mommy, who had insisted that the children be allowed to contact her and vice versa. My client taped the call. There was no doubt that Tempest was blatantly coercing the children into outbursts of hostility against both my client and the music teacher.

There were a multitude of motions to various judges. One particularly astute female judge threatened Tempest with contempt, should she continue her obstructive conduct and brainwashing of the children. Yet another assessor was appointed: a soft-spoken woman, who could calm the devil himself — or should I say, herself.

The warm beginning between the new assessor and Tempest was very short lived. Within a few months, the assessor became the enemy and the relationship terminated when Tempest became hysterical and threatening in her office.

To do a complete report, the assessor traveled to the Principality and watched the two youngest children relate with their father. The oldest child, Tempest Light, appeared to be irrevocably alienated and adamantly refused to go.

Unfortunately, she had considerable influence over the other two. In any event, she was a big, well developed, twelve-year-old and I could not see having her board a plane against her will.

The assessor wrote a thirty-page report. She concluded that the mother had attempted to alienate all the children from their father and had succeeded with the oldest, to the child's detriment. She had partially succeeded with the middle child, who still expressed affection for her father, although she wished to live with Mommy, regardless.

The boy, however, in an unguarded moment said, "I really wouldn't mind living with dad."

There was a lengthy pre-trial in front of the most effective pre-trial judge in Canada or, I suspect, in the United States of America. She was a woman who could settle anything and who would stay until midnight to bring about an effective agreement — a woman who had saved the litigants in various court actions thousands of dollars in legal fees.

Her recommendation: The mother keeps the two girls and the father keeps the boy. At last, on the date of the trial, this was agreed to. But, it wasn't the end. These things never end. All of the above took years. The husband had neglected his practice to such an extent that it collapsed. As well, he was neglectful in supervising his father's business interests.

It became a financial calamity.

He could no longer pay the exorbitant child support agreed to in the other jurisdiction. She fought him for it and succeeded in keeping the sum the same, even though she only had two children now and he had one. It made no sense to me, as surely there was a change of circumstances which should have varied the support although such had never been referred to in the primary agreement.

He again applied to reduce the large amount of child support, which had, in fact, supported the entire family, including Tempest. The amount was as much as many senior civil servants make in their final years on the job. He was refused. The agreement, on which the support was based, had been negotiated and drafted elsewhere and as such, the safeguards which would have been placed in it, had it been drafted in Ontario, were missing.

It perplexed me why he should be paying the same for two children as he had been paying for three. As well, why should he be treated with such severity when there had been such a drastic change in circumstances financially?

Tempest, a qualified medical doctor, had chosen not to attempt to re-qualify, but decided she preferred to become a law clerk. It was all unbelievable, and when last heard from, Dr. Barnes was living in a small hamlet in Scotland where he was trying to re-qualify as a doctor. Tempest was receiving none of her huge child support payments, which were accumulating arrears, and was attending a community college for accreditation as a law clerk.

The results of all of this on the children's psyches could not be anything but detrimental. How could even the most well-balanced child survive hours of consistent brainwashing by a hysterical mother and then bursts of extreme generosity by a father who simply could not do anything else to contravene his former wife's brainwashing?

Breaking up a family so that one parent can enjoy the custody of one of his children — the one who was not as thoroughly brainwashed as the others, is a sickening scenario.

Aside from the children, let's be crass and look at the practical aspects of this case. Dr. Barnes ruined himself financially in his determination to pursue a relationship with his children, in spite of the unmitigated efforts of his wife Tempest to prevent it. The bills for the psychiatrist and assessor were no less than eighty to one hundred thousand dollars. There must have been at least ten court applications, with endless affidavits. An individual cannot pursue this type of litigation and do much else.

Dr. Barnes' absence was construed as neglect by his business partners and his patients. He effectively went down in flames and left the Principality with a pittance of the money he had formerly enjoyed. Besides, he had become a nervous wreck. He was hospitalized for bleeding ulcers, brought on by stress. His new relationship suffered.

Of course, the greatest victims in this type of wretched scenario are the children. Confused and unsure of themselves, they constantly feel disloyal if they side with one parent over the other. However, should they not, they are subject to the wicked probing of the alienator, who spends hours attacking the other parent in every way known to man.

Dr. Gardner believed the methods used are strangely consistent in all cases. The other parent, the object of alienation, becomes increasingly diminished in the eyes of the children and eventually he or she is detested. The circumstances surrounding the separation of the parties are distorted and the children are traditionally told that their father or mother has deserted them and has no use for them. This perceived rejection has the effect of not only diminishing the children's self esteem, but places them in a position where they fear that the alienator will also reject them if they do not follow her lead in despising the other parent

**J**erry Crawford was only five foot five but he packed a lot of muscle. During the day he escorted prisoners from the court to the detention centre and back, and in his spare time he coached a variety of kids' hockey and baseball teams. He had a ready, wide smile and a blonde brush cut. He was apple pie wholesome and invariably pleasant. Everyone liked him, including all the staff at the Head Office of the Court.

"You have to help Jerry," they chorused every time I entered to file a document. "You're the only one to help Jerry. It isn't right what's happening to Jerry."

Of course it had to be pro bono. Twenty-five thousand dollars a year with a holdback for pension didn't leave anything over. But sometimes you do what you have to do and hope that you can settle it really fast.

She was a slim girl with shoulder length blonde hair with bangs that half obscured her eyes. She wore very red lipstick, which matched her long red fingernails. And she suffered from cystic fibrosis. That was one of the reasons he married her, he told me. He wanted to take care of her. To always be there for her. But it didn't work out like that.

She had been spoiled. Perhaps that was natural as she was an only child with an incurable disease that required constant monitoring and hospital visits. A cold could require a hospital visit and her parents were protective. They always thought she would continue to live with them and were shocked when told by their daughter and Jerry that they wanted to marry. The mother was especially hostile and he knew she did not like him or believe he was good enough for her daughter. Besides, she was frail, he was told, much too frail to withstand the rigors of a marriage.

Jerry's in-laws insisted that he and his bride move into their home and live with them. Jerry was uncomfortable living with his in-laws and wanted to move into a place that would really be their own, but when his wife mentioned that, her parents became so upset the subject was dropped. However, their dislike for him increased.

Then his wife became pregnant and her parents were as distressed as he was ecstatic. He had always wanted a boy with whom he could enjoy sports and it was a healthy boy, with good lungs, who was quite easily extracted from the wife's frail ninety-eight pound body.

Although the parents had not wished the birth to occur and had indeed mentioned an abortion in the earlier months, they now doted on the baby. Jerry tried to hold him, walk him, give him his bottle, but his mother-in-law objected. She would interfere with everything. She objected to his teaching his son to ride a three-wheeler and then a two-wheeler with training wheels. She did not want him to teach his son to swim. At the end, she objected when he took the child to the park or to McDonald's.

The child was three when the wife told him to leave. He

had been uncomfortable and even his placid nature was ruffled by his mother-in-law's constant interference, but he would never have left. Not leave his son and his wife.

He could not afford to fight her, but said that he must see his son at least every second weekend, with a couple of visits in the evenings after work. He did not want his son to forget him. He showed me a picture. Same brush cut, same broad smile, only the shoulders were unlike his dad's. Of course, he had yet to work out.

It was on the second weekend, when he had gone to pick up his son, that he knew something was wrong. The mother-in-law answered the door and used the words, *filthy degenerate.* He knew what filthy meant, but not degenerate, so he looked it up. He did not understand.

The first weekend had gone well. He and his son had gone to the park and played ball. He had taken him to his parents' home for dinner. He had purchased a small bed for him and placed it in the same room as his in the one-bedroom apartment he was renting. They had Egg McMuffins for breakfast. The boy was happy and clung to him when he was delivered home.

They had, he informed me, accused him of sexually molesting his son. They said that the boy had informed his grandmother of this. She had taken the boy to a social worker with an M.A. in psychology, who specialized in assessments. The boy had repeated the same words to her. Daddy, it seemed had pulled his *dickie bird* and his own *dickie bird* and what had come out was bright green.

It was, he told me in a choked voice, his head lowered, *really unbelievable.*

"Why would I do that to my son?" he asked.

"Relax," I told him, "you didn't."

It was a four-day trial. The key witness for the wife, her mother, the child's grandmother, did not appear. The grandfather appeared, but stated he knew nothing of the allegations of sexual abuse. The wife gave evidence that she had questioned the boy after hearing the information from her mother and had heard the same story. The social worker with the M.A. gave evidence that the child had repeated this story to her and, of course, she believed the three year old.

"Children seldom lie about sexual abuse," she stated with conviction.

A second expert, a psychiatrist who had been paid the total value of Jerry Crawford's IRA, informed the court that he believed the child had been brainwashed and that the case was indicative of alienation.

No one in the wife's case could stand up under cross-examination. It was all so patently false.

"How could you do this?" I asked opposing counsel. He was a friend of mine, and I liked him. Perhaps his business was down and her parents paid his legal fees.

He shrugged and said, "Well, I've got to go ahead now." It was obvious he didn't believe his client or clients.

The presiding judge, smart, practical and a mother herself, didn't believe them either. She didn't give us costs, however. She felt that this might only worsen a tense situation. I believe she should have. They already hated my client enough to falsely accuse him of child molestation, so how could a few thousand dollars make things any worse.

Jerry was given generous access to his son and there was no reluctance on the part of the wife to let the child go. She had a new boyfriend and it was obvious that she hadn't believed the story.

As far as I know, Jerry still sees his son, is close to him, and is training him to be a major league hockey player. I got a lot of respect from security staff for that one, and I still feel close to Jerry. I'll never forget watching him day by day as all this evidence piled up, watching his face get whiter and whiter and thinner and thinner.

I'm really glad it ended the way it did. It was a case that had to be won in any event. Whoever heard of bright green sperm?

**T**ommy Fraser was an ace salesman. Balding, round bellied and constantly smiling, he was what some of my female clients begrudgingly acknowledge after expressing a litany of sins, *a good provider.* He was also a good dad. Although, maybe not great in the sports department for his youngest, an energetic little kid who looked like a miniature shrunken Tommy with hair, who was known as "Little Tommy," but he made up for it in other ways.

They *hung out,* he told me. They were great spectators. Little Tommy accompanied his dad to dozens of games, hockey, baseball and basketball, for which Big Tommy's grateful customers had provided tickets. When it came to his girls, they cuddled at night and he read to them, dramatizing their stories as only a good salesman could. They always wanted him and not their mother. He told me they were healthy kids, except for the oldest girl, who had a serious problem with constipation, attributed to much too rigid toilet training too early by *my crazy wife.*

Of course, men always believe their wives are crazy and I normally only half listen. When I hear the words, *high maintenance, screaming banshee, a really rotten mother, and like sleeping with frozen gristle,* I mentally turn off. Except for the last category, I found all the other categorizations of this particular mother accurate and I could have added a few more, like *vicious, manipulative,* and opposed to having her children share any relationship whatsoever with their father.

When I saw her in court, all five foot ten of her — a gum-chewing skeleton with narrow, hostile eyes, I knew there would be nothing but trouble ahead. I classified her in my cerebral directory as a hysteric with a borderline personality disorder.

"She yelled day and night," he complained, "and the kids are afraid of her. In fact, I should be tryin' to get em' but I gotta work and they're not gonna to take em' away from a stay-at-home mom. And she'll never get a job. Within a week she's fightin' with everyone in the office and comes home tellin' me they're all pickin' on her."

I mentally added *paranoid* to my cerebral classification and dug my heels in for the long haul.

And a long haul it was.

On the first access visit, she said that the kids were all sick and couldn't see him. And no, he couldn't see the kids or even talk to them. They were too ill. Besides, Amanda, the oldest, hadn't gone to the bathroom for three days. How was he going to cope with that?

On the second visit, it continued. It had been snowing and she didn't trust the weather or his driving. It didn't matter that he'd driven one hour to get them, he could just drive back. They didn't want to see him anyway: They hated him for leaving them. What was she supposed to do, push them out the door?

The third visit followed a court order. The kids were screaming and crying, saying that they didn't want to go with Daddy. Mommy, they were told, would be all alone.

Once the car pulled from the driveway, all was pleasant and the oldest child whispered, "Sorry Daddy," about two miles down the road. They ate at the Swiss Chalet, Amanda actually went to the bathroom, and everything seemed great. But three telephone calls the next day from *Crazy Mommy* temporarily upset the kids.

On the fourth visit, she said she did not care what the court ordered. She knew her kids better than any court. They had been having nightmares ever since the last visit and there was no way she was going to subject her kids to that.

Both the young ones had colds and Amanda had her usual bathroom problem.

"No, you're not getting the kids, and you can call the police if you like and drag them out of the house screaming. Is that what you want for your kids?"

On visit number five, "Your attorney is a gum sucking bitch," she screeches. "How could you serve an order giving the cops the right to take the kids from the matrimonial home and escort them to the car! How sick can you be? Really sick, that's how sick. Are you recording me? That's about as low as it gets. Officer, is he allowed to record me?"

The two girls were somewhat intimidated by the police presence, but little Tommy thought it was "neat." After all, how often do you get a police escort to your dad's car, especially when you really want to go there?

I could go on and on, but I will spare you more details. Suffice it to say, my client was systematically blocked on every turn, so that seeing his kids became a Saturday ordeal and I knew I could predict a phone call or two.

In addition, the wife dragged the kids to a counselor, an unqualified fellow, who had apparently never heard of alienation and who wrote a letter attesting to the fact that the children did not wish to see their father. My client knew it was all untrue. After all, the kids whispered their apologies to him and expressed their love as soon as he herded them into his small rented home some twenty-five miles away.

One judge, a former female crown attorney or prosecutor, gave the wife, who was present in court, a stiff lecture on permitting the kids to have two parents, threatening her with sanctions if she did not abide by the court order.

It was water off the banshee's back. By the time she was through, the kids were the emotional wrecks that she had falsely stated them to be at the beginning of access to their dad.

When I last heard, the mother had prevailed upon the police to charge Tommy Fraser's son by his first marriage with sexual assault of the children. It was, of course, all totally fabricated, but my client sounded as if he were at the end of the road. He was certainly at the end of his legal fees. Naturally, Mrs. Fraser complained that as a result of "protecting her children," all her money was gone as well.

There is some good news. One of Toronto's most tenacious attorneys recently obtained a cost award of two hundred and fifty thousand dollars against a mother who regularly and without cause prevented her physician husband from having access to the children. In addition, the kids were sent for *de-programming* to a center in the United States that specializes in giving psychiatric treatment to children who have been exposed to a parent's alienation tactics. They were all brought to court on that day and physically handed over to the father.

I am proud of my colleague and hope that this sets a precedent against these alienators, who make it their life's work to sever the ties between their spouses and the children of the marriage.

However, let's think about it. The husband's costs in the aforementioned case, as set out and delivered to the presiding judge, were some five hundred thousand dollars. They were reduced by fifty percent, leaving what I suggest is still a hefty tab. How many parents in this world can afford this kind of expenditure in order to undo the lethal effects of alienation and resume a relationship with their kids which has been savaged by a vindictive spouse? Not very many, I suggest.

Had my colleague's client not been a successful professional, he would have been irreparably cut off from his children. His wife could have continued to go along on her mendacious path, doing everything she could to punish the spouse for what she, no doubt, considered justified personal animosity between them.

Hopefully, this recent case will set a precedent and members of the judiciary will follow the lead of this quite valiant judge.

I would actually suggest jail time, or at least an overnight visit to impress on Mommy or Daddy the danger of the path they are pursuing. Of course, there may be a backlash. The innocent victim of the alienation will likely be told by his children, "You put mommy in jail."

In the old days, I would be told time and again by the judiciary, "We agree that Mrs. Vicious' conduct is really unfortunate, but the children are attached to her and we would not wish to disrupt them at this time, regardless of the unfairness to your client."

A caring mother or father does not deliberately alienate the children from the other parent. The effect of using alienation tactics on children is so detrimental that there have been documented cases of suicide by tortured and confused children as a result.

There has long been a legal holding imposed by both statute and case law which sets out that the parent who has custody should be the parent who is most ready to facilitate access. For years, this sensible legal provision has been all too readily ignored and parents who thwart access on a regular basis until nothing really remains of the original relationship the children had enjoyed with the other parent, have gotten away with their behavior.

"He's a born-again father," sniffs the wife. "He never wanted to do any of this stuff when we were together."

Well, so what? Thank God he is *born again*. Why not let the kids get the benefit of it. It is a well known fact that the other parent, whether responsible for the breakup of the marriage or not, often becomes a much better parent upon the separation. The children should get the benefit of this, rather than have the man vilified for not being up to snuff before the marriage break up. Parties to an unhappy relationship are often poor parents and the kids are all too often the recipients of spilled over bitterness.

I can think of a long line of horrible examples of alienating tactics I have witnessed during my practice. A Ukrainian client of mine, a scholarly and introspective accountant, was beaten up by *mommy's new boyfriend* every weekend he approached the home for access. In spite of my protests, he refused to fight and gave up.

**B**rian Ghastly, which is not his name, but an appropriate one, who unfortunately was my client for a brief period, deliberately alienated his son and thwarted access between the boy and his mother, who was dying of cancer. I could finally stomach Mr. Ghastly no more, but when I last heard, the boy had been placed in a foster home. I can only imagine his state of mind after his mother's death.

In another case, where the mother had succeeded in severing the father's formerly close relationship with his two sons, the boys had dropped out of sports, their school marks plummeted and one became seriously involved with drugs within one year. She, blamed the father for walking out on them, and denied that her own vicious meddling in preventing access contributed to the problem.

Now that judges have become somewhat enlightened as to the causes and effects of alienation, they are, as judges are prone to do, seeing it in every case. One of my former clients telephoned me recently, crying that her twelve year old had been threatening suicide if she had to continue seeing her father. He had attempted to choke her the weekend before. This had been relayed to a counselor at school, who had reported it. The Children's Aid Society became involved and questioned the child in the presence of the father. Of course, she lied and said it never happened.

My client feared going back to court, as she had already been penalized by one of our more erratic judges, to the tune of eleven thousand dollars in costs, because she and her new husband wished to move to a less expensive area, in order to live more cheaply. The ex-husband was paying less than two hundred dollars per month in support of the children, although he had a new home, new car, and took the children on exotic vacations.

My client went bankrupt after the trial, because the female trial judge, a former Crown prosecutor, soundly trounced her after listening sympathetically to the elders of her church, no doubt to prove her great tolerance for all sects and to support them in their shunning of adulterous wives.

The Office of the Official Guardian, which is now known as The Office of the Children's Lawyer, refused to produce their social worker, who had done a balanced and fair report on both the children and the spurned husband. It's this kind of trial, packed with irritations, that makes you question the system.

Occasionally, judges and some psychiatrists hang onto a concept like alienation much like a dog with a bone, and see it when it's not there. Others, for years, did not see it at all, but now fortunately the majority has taken over.

Alienation is in.

In the last custody trial I endured, the cards were well stacked against my client who had already spent some hundred thousand dollars in legal fees on her former attorney. It was the judge's first trial. He had been a Crown prosecutor and knew nothing about custody or family law. He was the last person on earth who should have been appointed to hear this particular case, which had gone on for four years and had even reached the Court of Appeal at times.

Opposing counsel had become so personally involved that all rational thoughts had long fled. The psychiatrist, hooked on alienation, detected it in every nook and cranny of the issues, and even announced, "I like bad boys," when being presented with a list of the husband's quite serious lapses of character.

The husband had stolen my client's credit cards, running up charges to entertain his girlfriends. He had consorted with a known criminal element. He had been fired from his bank job for fraud. Most seriously, he had been physically abusive to the child, who had been unceremoniously dumped between the warring couple, week on, week off, for a two year period.

The child's lack of stability had prevented any school progress, and indeed, he was thought to be developmentally handicapped. To cap off the entire situation, my client informed me that at one point, the husband had told her that he didn't really want custody of the child at all. His mother had insisted upon it and she was footing the legal fees.

Eventually, it all worked out, even though the Judge's endorsement showed he simply didn't get it. Luckily, at that time, the Court of Appeal had expressed in other cases the belief that it may not be good for some very young children to be juggled around like hockey pucks on a week on, week off, basis.

The husband had owed my client a considerable amount of money but she never collected it. The only way the trial could ever be heard was if the issues were restricted solely to custody. That may have been just as well, as His Honor, swimming his way through the rocky waves of his first divorce trial, found that sufficiently challenging.

Although she was quite willing to have the father see the son on a regular basis according to the judgment, he simply did not bother after the trial. He paid no child support and the client, who was sick of judges, attorneys and legal fees, did not believe it was worthwhile to pursue it. It was one of those nightmares that make matrimonial work so daunting and make it all so *not* worthwhile.

Additionally, within the next two years, my client's father, a shockingly stressed witness, suffered a stroke and the psychiatrist, who was cross-examined for days, much to his chagrin, had a fatal heart attack. Then, I got sick.

The child, incidentally, is fine.

# Chapter 12
## Harmful Parents

Sometimes a parent will actually turn on a child when dumped by his or her spouse. Fortunately, it has happened only a few times in my practice. It is a phenomenon which is, thank God, quite rare — but not rare enough!

The first time it happened was with an introverted individual of about thirty who had been dumped by his wife for a better, probably more outgoing, prospect. He just wanted to get everything over with, which wasn't difficult, as the wife was sufficiently guilty and the assets sufficiently sparse.

He was quite willing to pay child support, but did not ever wish to see his six-year-old son again.

I couldn't believe it. Somehow, in his convoluted mind, he associated the child with his unfaithful wife and wished to completely sever ties with both.

Apparently, contact was too painful.

"You can't do this," I told him. "Your son will believe you've rejected him and he'll feel guilty. He'll think it's something that he's done instead of something his mommy has done. This is a vicious thing for you to do."

My words were wasted. He was adamant and unfortunately stuck with his position. Some ten years later, he came in to see me with his second wife, who was having problems with her first husband. I inquired as to the son and their relationship. I was horrified to hear that he had no contact with the boy, despite the fact that as a teenager, the son had reached out and attempted to contact him. His second wife was decent enough to agree with me when I voiced my disgust.

A judge at a recent seminar told a story of what had happened in court the previous week. A father had refused to see his ten-year-old son, who was so devastated, that he carved his father's initials in his arm with a knife.

What sick, twisted individuals these fathers must be — placing their wounded feelings and vulnerabilities ahead of the mental health of their kids. Shame on them!

And what can you do about it? I guess you can't compel anyone to be a decent human being. Sick, sick, daddies.

If you feel that your marital breakup has made you so vulnerable that you can't even continue to have a relationship with your kids please seek therapy. The damage that you're doing to your rejected kids is boundless.

Then, of course, there are those *parcels of insensitivity* that never pick up the kids when they say they will. When they do, they refuse to take them to their hockey or baseball practice; although that's the only way they can make the team, *because it cuts into their time.*

Or those real sweethearts who shower their new addition with all sorts of love and goodies, making the child of the former ruined union feel like chopped liver. And, there's always the occasional daddy who has the kid for the weekend and goes off on Saturday night with his new doll, leaving the kid alone to watch TV.

Ironically, these characters are often the ones who really fight for access and then, like a dog chasing a car, don't know what to do with it when they get it.

Give your kid some love and attention, idiot. Make him feel he's important and that you didn't leave him, just his old lady. And don't fill him with stories about what a miserable, old bag she is. She's his mother and you're his father, and unless he thinks well of both of you, he's going to have problems. It makes him feel badly when you run his mother down, no matter how justified in your mind. If she's the bitch you want him to think she is, unfortunately he'll find out soon enough. You don't have to enlighten him.

This also applies, of course, to those mommies who spend hours regaling their kids about their daddy's shortcomings. It's all part of alienation and will inject rot into any relationship.

Just remember this, *Mommy Dearest*, your son believes he's a part of that no good bastard you had the misfortune to marry. If he's rotten, your kid may also believe that he may be rotten too. He couldn't have always been the worst piece of garbage on earth. You married him, didn't you?

I once had a client whose husband stripped their son down completely and left him naked in front of the apartment door after every visit. His beef was that his wife did not keep *his* clothes pristine between visits, and in any event, he feared they would not be returned.

I wonder what goes through the head of a naked little boy standing in front of an apartment door, in view of all the neighbors, waiting for the door to open, while daddy walks up the corridor with his clothes and any toy he might have given him during the visit in his arms.

I know what goes through my mind. Not fit to be a dad — that's what.

Some dads want to pack every bit of living possible into that two day weekend they spend with their kids twice a month — to hell with homework and tooth brushing. Open the door to fries and two-scoop cones. Forget veggies and fruit. Drop in at McDonald's or Mr. Sub. Piano lessons and sports practices dig into *your time* and you don't want to have to spend an hour and a half hanging around when your kid sits on the bench anyway. And who wants to get up at six in the morning on your day off just so your kid can make hockey practice?

You should Mister, that's who!

Some dads think that they've done a real state of the art job when they bring their exhausted kids home, usually late on a Sunday night, crammed with crap food, totally exhausted and with unlooked at homework. Do you really think that you're showing your great love for these kids of yours if you expose them to a fast food circus every weekend? By all means do some things with them and bond as much as you can, but attempt to give them the occasional home cooked meal and buy some fruit and veggies for snacks.

Take them to their scheduled activities, even if you believe that their mother has deliberately over booked them to exhaust you or to cut into your time. If this is the case you do have a right to object. Ask yourself, is this for my ego or to torment the hell out of their mother, who will be asking them as soon as they get back how they spent their weekend?

Or am I really trying to work in my kids' best interests? You must ask yourself these questions. That's what being a dad or mom is, isn't it?

There's one thing to remember about custody. I learned it many years ago, long before the reliance on experts. It was one simple fact. The parent who gets the children immediately after the break up is the parent who continues to keep them. In other words, *thems that have keeps.* This has a bad ring; you'd almost think that the child wasn't real at all — just a chattel and possession.

Fortunately, most parents don't think that way, although you get the odd one that does. Most parents know that their kids are bundles of rights and obligations. They want them to grow up as decent, law abiding, drug free, hopefully employable, and well educated, even if the parent never finished grade school.

It's all right to feel like that though, even if it is perhaps sometimes a little unrealistic. Every now and then, we have Presidents and Premiers who come from very humble beginnings and make their way by means of scholarships and parental encouragement. How many of the superstars in football and baseball leagues do you hear say, "I owe it all to my mother?" Unfortunately, they seldom mention the father — except perhaps for Tiger Woods!

Anyway, let's take it for granted that you want to be a really good parent and that you feel that it's in your kid's best interest to remain with you. You are willing to let your spouse see your child on a regular basis, provided he or she's not a drunk, drug addict or pedophile, regardless of your differences. How do you bring this hoped for custody about?

If your child is with you at the time of separation and remains with you except for generous periods of access which you give to your spouse, then in all probability, you will be the custodial parent of that child until he leaves home to attend college, pursue employment, or even to get married.

The courts will not interfere with a good thing. It's called *maintaining the status quo*. If your child is well adjusted, doing well at school and you are attentive and caring, a court will not disturb the relationship.

Courts have a strong repugnance to disturbing happy, well-adjusted children, who are doing well in school and have not become little arsonists or small animal killers.

It is for this reason that it is important for a parent not to leave the children with the other parent should there be a marital breakup. This act of "abandonment," although I don't like using that word, says to the objective observer, *you can't really be a bad parent because I left the kids with you.*

There are a million reasons why you *had to* do it. You had no other place to take them. You didn't want to disrupt them from their school. There were kids in the neighborhood that they saw on a daily basis, and besides, you had to obtain employment as he warned you that he would never support you.

There are dozens of reasons why you must leave the children in the matrimonial home. I understand and accept them. However, don't believe for one minute that this won't undermine any future hope you have for custody.

Daddy or Mommy, whoever is left with the kids, most definitely has a leg up. If they go to court on an emergency basis, dispensing with any pre-trial conference, to ask for interim custody, he or she usually gets it.

Now, this doesn't mean that you can't agree to joint custody later on. Joint custody is extremely important to fathers as they tell all their friends at work that they have joint custody of their kids. And even if the situation is exactly the same as just being an access parent, that is, having custody on every second weekend with weekly visits on the other weeks, it makes a great difference to the parent having that particular label.

It is for that reason that I could never understand the great kafuffle parents make about agreeing to joint custody.

# Chapter 13
## Joint Custody

As a joint custodial parent, it's good for a Dad to see teachers and doctors. It's also good when they coach hockey and speak to the parents at the rink. It makes them feel important and involved with their child. Isn't that a good thing?

You may argue, "I can let him do all those things without giving him the label. If he has the label, he'll try to push me around and run things like the controlling bastard he's always been."

Probably so, or maybe not. You can always specifically place in any agreement a proviso that you are to have actual care and control and that you will be primary decision maker in scholastic, medical and sport matters. It's a pretty heavy responsibility, isn't it? But you could have all this and still give him that joint custody label. I have known couples to go to court and spend hundreds of thousands of dollars because they fought over joint custody.

I think they're crazy.

Unfortunately, there's the occasional nut that gives joint custody a bad name. Willy Newton was given joint custody by a judge after a three-week trial in which the parties argued over absolutely every bit of minutiae possible, including prior to marriage deductions, bank accounts, stolen BBQ's, stock portfolios, that increased after separation, and mutual spousal abuse. The wife was even accused of child abuse, although The Children's Aid Society, who had been involved, did not accept the husband's allegations. It was a bitter, endless circus and the much too long suffering judge, who I suspect wished to avoid an appeal, rendered a one hundred page judgment.

The children had remained in the home and the parents had visited them on a one-week on, one-week off basis. On hearing interim motions, sometimes Judges do this in an effort to be fair to both parties, as they are well aware of the first premise of custody being determined by the individual who has the children in the first instance and continues to have them.

As I have told you, the courts will not remove a happy, well adjusted child from the custodial parent. Stability is a cardinal rule for judges, and who can really question this? Perhaps it is unfortunate that so much weight is given to the fact that the parent seeking custody has had actual possession of the kids since the breakup. What if the parent who has not had actual physical care and control can expose the children to a vastly more enlightening lifestyle and a more tolerant world view, in addition to providing them with the amenities of life? But that's the way it is, so suck it up. It means all sorts of manipulation and trickery to make sure that you are the one with the kids and it also means that if there is a serious claim for custody on behalf of one of the separating parents, then that parent should not leave the matrimonial home.

There are other reasons for not leaving the matrimonial home: one of the most important being financial. But we are discussing custody, and the problem is that while living together with great animosity under the same roof, parents sometimes carry on an ongoing battle in front of the children. Still, as attorneys, we always tell them to stay and it sometimes leads to the most horrendous situations. On the other hand, the one week-on, one-week off situation, at times turns the children into disrupted little hellions. If, however, you can really pull this off, without having the kids upset, all the better.

It has to be conducive to your employment, and hopefully you can afford accommodation in the same neighborhood. There should be minimum disruption to the kids—schools, friends, and activities. And you must be able to work together, in the kids best interests. The kids will take their cues from you both.

If this equal sharing drives one of you crazy, the kids will pick up on it. To make this successful, you have to be special kind of people. Ask yourself, do you and your ex fit into that *special* category? Also, you must ask yourself, does one of you have a specific agenda? Reducing child support or using that extra time to brainwash the child to stay with you full time are ugly possibilities I don't even want to think about— but you must!

Sometimes, pending trial, it is reduced to which parent can spoil the kids more, Mommy or Daddy. That's when the assessor's report, which carries great weight, when it is considered, hopefully won't repeat one kid's words who said, "I really want to live with my daddy because he doesn't make me brush my teeth and he gives me candy all the time."

Lovely — one up for Mommy in that report.

Anyway, watch those experts. You don't want to use an assessor if the other attorney is really pushing for him and if you find that his firm constantly uses the same expert. It should come as no surprise that this expert will be leaning very hard toward opposing counsel's client, even if he or she is the worst parent in the world.

I would hate you to think that these laudatory experts could be bought, but it's certainly a great coincidence that they tend to be much warmer to the solicitor who constantly uses their services and this warmth runs off on the client who is asking for custody.

Unprofessional and unfair? Absolutely. Even judges are beginning to discern this and there is a much less tendency now for judges to rubber stamp these reports instead of seeing them as yet another piece of evidence to consider when awarding custody.

# Chapter 14
## Joint Custody Problems and Access Errors

Let us get back to our preliminary couple who fought like cats and dogs for nineteen days and were then awarded joint custody, with his Honor taking the sunny view that he felt in spite of all their differences, this couple loved their children and could function as a unit in deciding their best interests. Fortunately, my client, an extremely intelligent and reasonable individual, somehow managed, despite being told after every visit by the children how wonderful Daddy was and how terrible it was that he was forced to pay child support.

Poor Daddy, with his $200,000 a year plus income, being drained to the max by having to pay support for his three kids. And the kids were made well aware of this, telling Mommy that she should be buying them new skates, new clothes and everything else because of *all that money Daddy gives you for us.*

Of course, there were fights about everything — ongoing fights. This couple could not even be in the same skating rink. It was finally agreed that only one parent could accompany a child at a time. There were even battles about who was to change the skates in the change room. Parents at the rink took sides and, after listening to Daddy's propaganda, decided Mommy really had no business there at all, and as a group refused to speak to her.

Everything brought about a run-in, including the wife's wish to have the children at her parents' cottage for one month in the summer and the husband's wish to break up this well-established tradition, although he would not be personally present to parent the kids during *his* summer custody.

An ongoing travesty, with endless trips to court and both individuals representing themselves, with their exhausted attorneys long gone, together with thousands of dollars in legal fees.

Both these parents, by the way, were supposedly intelligent, highly-paid professionals. I am convinced both loved their children. It's just that if one party is constantly quibbling and showing irrational behavior, then the entire concept of joint custody is disrupted.

In this particular case, the husband had to be restrained from visiting the school where the wife taught. He actually visited the pediatrician who had been the children's doctor for years and was so annoyed with her after she testified to the wife's good parenting, that he reported her to the medical association. This type of behavior bodes badly and I marvel at the judge's optimism when he gave out the label of joint custody, which represents cooperation and sharing in the fullest sense of the word and not a stick with which to punish the other parent at every opportunity.

Surprisingly enough, the children are fine. The mother, intelligent and insightful woman that she is, has actually permitted the children to have a relationship with their father in spite of the fact that he has done everything to undermine her and has caused hours of stress by the litany of litigation which he has pursued for years. Under the circumstances, it is remarkable that these children are as balanced and as high achievers as they are.

At one point the boy did express nervousness and showed signs of the father's brainwashing, but survived it and is doing well. It was, assuredly, not a case for a joint custody judgment. Even the psychiatrist, who wrote a long report and appeared as a witness at trial, did not recommend it. I do give credit to the wife in this case for surviving and for helping the children to survive.

I suggest that there are some practical criteria to consider if you and your spouse wish to contravene the financial and emotional stress of a contested custody trial. Custody trials are the last really dirty aspect of matrimonial law. In the old days, grounds for divorce were often based on the intolerable behavior of the other partner. These set out, in graphic detail, all sorts of abuse and cruelty which sent the victimized partner barreling into the psychiatrist's office for prescriptions of tranquilizers and a supporting letter for the judge. The presiding judge could take all of this into account in granting a divorce based on *cruelty of such a kind as to render future cohabitation intolerable*.

This and adultery, in which the same correspondent was often pictured flying from the bed when photographers burst into the room, were the main grounds, as no one wished to wait a three-year period for a divorce. Now, however, there is literally no fault divorce and you can get a divorce after a separation of twelve months in Canada, or even less time in many States. You can still get together during this period to attempt reconciliation and there is no waiting period at all in some States provided the parties agree that there are irreconcilable differences.

Of course, you can still get a divorce on the grounds of cruelty or adultery and a few other choice grounds, but hardly anyone ever does. It's actually considered rather bad form and not appreciated by most members of the judiciary.

Custody is quite another matter, however. One party characterizes the opposing parent as drunken, drug addicted, vulgar, abusive, neglectful, cruel, totally unfit and unable to meet that special criteria of custody, *the child's best interests*. Things that are said about the other parent in these custody actions are seldom forgiven. Long gone are the hopes that the parties could ever attend their children's weddings or, for that matter, their grandchildren's birthdays together. It rankles and stays with them forever, but, in spite of this, the wars continue.

In cases such as extreme alienation, there is no other choice. If a parent wishes to have any relationship whatsoever with his or her children, it is necessary to get him or her away from *the alienator*. *The alienator* will not permit a relationship with the other parent.

The criteria that I am now putting forward are for most of you who sensibly see the importance of children having two parents and who aren't willing to spend all the kids' future education costs on a battle in which there is no winner.

The following are custodial considerations which should be taken into account upon separation.

From a practical point of view, ask yourself which of you has been the most proactive parent with respect to meeting the kids' day-to-day needs — meals, homework and activities. If you are that parent, then it may be most logical that the children spend their day-to-day custody with you.

Forget fussing over that joint custody label. Unless your partner is some sort of nut who wishes to use this label to take over and embarrass you and the children, then by all means have joint custody. It's the specifics under the label that really matter. It's who has day-to-day care and control and makes medical, sports and academic decisions. Who is going to take the kids to their sport activities or other activities? How much time will be allocated so that the children will not lose contact with the parent who is not physically present, but wishes to remain a part of their lives?

Don't underestimate the daddy factor. It is absolutely essential that the children continue to have a relationship with their father, even if the mother is the main custodial parent. Boys suffer psychologically if they do not retain a close relationship with their fathers and mothers have got to realize this.

Check out the achieving women, many of whom have reached CEO status in various public companies. A large majority of these women had fathers who did not place them in the *little princess* category, but who urged them to compete with their male counterparts on, dare I say, an *equal basis*.

Recent psychological tests have come to the interesting conclusion that girls, believe it or not, have their father's brain, while boys have their mother's. As a result, captains of industry who wish their sons to follow in their footsteps were urged to marry intelligent, achieving women. I thought about this premise after I read it and found it amazing how many daughters, rather than sons, have taken over their father's companies.

In dividing up the time to be spent by both of you as parents, please give some consideration as to how your children, as they approach their teens, may feel about having their time cut up so that they have to spend time with their non-custodial parent—or for that part their custodial parent!

Parents sometimes don't realize that after the age of thirteen or fourteen, friends are much more important than parents. This should not be an occasion for hurt feelings or belief that the other parent is in some way attempting to obstruct access. This is just the way things are.

If you want to compromise the situation, then resign yourself to the fact that you may have to take your son or daughter's best friend with them when you have access and you may end up taking a tribe to the movies or McDonald's as well as your son or daughter. It may mean less of the bonding that you wish to establish, but at least you'll have happier kids who won't resent your usurping time they wish to spend with their friends.

And yes, you do have to take your kids to early morning hockey practice and to afternoon ballet class on Saturdays. Access is, after all, for children. If you and your spouse were still together, they'd be attending these functions wouldn't they?

I know of one mother, rotten creature that she was, who deliberately scheduled different activities for the daughter and son, at the same time during the father's access period. It meant, of course, that my client was placed in a position where he had to bring the son to hockey practice and the daughter to piano lessons at the same time, each at the opposite side of town. His only solution was to have his girlfriend take the daughter to piano lessons, which brought about an even angrier response from the frustrating wife.

Sometimes you just can't win.

If you want to maintain a civil relationship with your ex, please make an effort to be pleasant when he or she arrives to take the children on their allocated weekends. Don't hang on the children's neck and tell them that Mommy will be so sad and will miss them so much so that they leave with little clouds of guilt hanging over their heads.

Don't inundate Daddy, and I'm not going to say Mommy because it's usually the mother who is guilty of this, with a list of instructions as to how you believe they should spend the weekend. By all means, give details of activities that the children are scheduled to attend with times and addresses, but don't be so intrusive that you are dictating every aspect of your children's time spent with your spouse.

Do caution the father if one of the children appears to be getting a cold or is just coming off a bout of the flu. Many mothers see this as a reason for canceling access. Certainly, if a child is seriously ill, moving them from their usual place of residence would not be wise, but if the child only has a slight cold or is recovering from one, surely their father can monitor this as well as the mother.

I have actually known cases where the children are on medication and the mother has not delivered the medication to the father in some deliberate attempt to thwart his nurturing an ill child. This has never made any sense to me. In fact, the child for whom the medication has been prescribed is being punished for some parental animosity. The father ends up taking the child to a walk-in clinic and getting a brand new prescription which may, in some way, counteract the medicine the child has been taking.

I have also known fathers who have refused to give a child medicine on the pretext that the mother may be over medicating the child. Any of these actions are inexcusable, dumb, and dangerous to the child's health. I did not even wish to mention them, but unfortunately these tactics are resorted to by immature and vindictive parents, who, in reality, should not be parents at all.

Do not — I repeat — do not, sweat the small stuff. Again, it is the mothers who are the worst offenders if they are the actual custodial parent, although the label may be joint custody as recommended. Ask yourself, is the apocalypse really going to occur if the father gets stuck in traffic and is ten minutes late in picking up the kids? Hopefully, he'll be considerate enough to call you on his cell phone and inform you of his predicament. If he doesn't, there's still no reason to slam the door in his face, take the children elsewhere, tell the children that Daddy doesn't think enough of them to pick them up on time, or tell him he's missed his chance at custody for the weekend.

Your real bitch should be if he doesn't appear at all and has two kids looking out the window for hours waiting for someone who doesn't come. I knew of a father who, I suspect, consistently did this, because in some sick way he wanted the reaction of his children to help establish how much they wished to have access with him — a particularly ugly way of assessing his children's affection. Of course, what eventually happened was that the children, to insulate themselves from hurt, decided it was best not to go on access weekends when the father finally did show up — and it served him right! But not right for the kids, who should be at least able to trust their parents.

If dad brings the kids back five or ten minutes late, ask yourself is this really serious? Is this ten minutes really going to prevent them from functioning the next day and irrevocably put off their bed times and render them exhausted the next morning? Of course, if this is a consistent pattern and the children are invariably brought home up to an hour or more late, then surely you are justified in saying, "Hey, make an effort to try to bring these kids home on time."

Say this in an even tone. Do not scream or yell in front of the kids.

You must encourage the children to say a fond goodbye to the access parent. One of my fathers informed me that his daughter and son insisted that they hug and kiss him three blocks away from the home so that their mother would not witness this display of affection. This is similar to the case where the children were supposed to show great reluctance at seeing their father by clinging to their mother. As soon as the car rounded the corner, they would settle in and tell their dad how glad they were to see him, apologizing for their preliminary reluctance, which had been deliberately initiated by the mother.

This is sick stuff, mommies, and you are hurting your children. Stop doing it. They will remember it when they are older and think poorly of you.

And daddies, why not put a dollop of shampoo in a tub and let the little darlings submerge themselves an hour before returning them home. You can't imagine the complaints I've had about daddies — and yes it's usually daddies — returning the kids *filthy*.

I refused to write to the other attorney complaining of this. It was too petty and silly. But if you know your wife to be petty and silly and this is one of the reasons why you broke up in the first place, then don't do things that make her even pettier and sillier than she ever was.

*PLEASE*, don't cut the kids' hair without telling their mother. I have had more hysterical telephone calls on Sunday nights than I care to remember, from mothers whose spouses have *sheared* their kid's hair over the weekend without their permission. It's a violation, like severing their right leg or left arm.

It sometimes happens when Mommy has her son with shoulder length locks and Daddy believes she's giving him a passport to become a clothes designer and model, which conflicts with his baseball player image.

Not satisfied with a brush cut, some of these dads relegate their kids to skinhead status. Why should there be a problem in saying to their mother, "Any objections if I get a bit of this hair cut off?" And as for cutting off curls, please don't do it.

"But it's hot when I take her to the park," complained one exasperated dad, who had tired of his daughter's complaints about the way he attempted a ponytail. He took her to one of the city's finest salons and had a professional haircut done. From the reaction of his wife, I would have thought he had dropped her in hot oil.

Of course, the child then became upset as her mother told her she wasn't pretty anymore and her dreams of becoming another Britney Spears were forever blighted.

Silly? Extremely. Avoidable? I believe so. Remember, in that agreement you signed agreeing to joint custody? There were certain areas of responsibility which fell into the authority of one or the other of you. You didn't include haircuts. Include them.

My fathers sometimes complained that their wives delivered the children *in rags*. This was an indication, they always told me, that the mother was spending all those tax free dollars given for child support on herself rather than the kids. Time and again I have had fathers say to me, "She doesn't spend any of that money on the kids. What can I do to see that she does?"

Not a damn thing, Daddy.

Most of you are paying for the kids according to Child Support Guidelines, which vary as to State, are reasonable, and, some men feel, over generous. Then there are extraordinary expenses, which include special costs for sports, education, camp and other activities. These are usually paid in proportion to your income, so if you make a hundred thousand dollars a year, father, and you make fifty thousand dollars a year, mother, then dad will be paying two-thirds and mom one-third of these extra costs.

As these costs are traditionally not paid through the Family Responsibility Office or any government collection agency in your State there is much too often constant controversy as to how they should be paid and, indeed, whether they should be paid at all. Sometimes the payor believes his regular support cheque should cover ALL the child's expenses which is hardly fair. Ideally, the parties should get together in a civilized way and proof of costs should be produced and joint checks sent to the appropriate place.

Strangely, this seems quite insurmountable for many parents and the father ends up paying all the costs of hockey, because he wants his son to play hockey. But that appears to be the only extraordinary expense he's willing to shoulder. On the other hand, he does not want to pay the costs of a tutor for the boy's failing math marks. "She should be helping him with his homework," he states, not taking into consideration that today's math would challenge a Ph.D.

Again, I would ask both parties to show some maturity and fairness here. If the individual actually having physical custody has to pay all of the activity costs, she will resent it and it will come out in other ways. On the other hand, the father believes that all too often, the mother is living off his child support. Accordingly, he is not disposed to paying any extra costs.

"Let the bitch pay," is his mantra, although most have the decency not to say it, even to their attorney.

One way to get out of this is to quantify what you believe will be the husband's share of extraordinary expenses and have him give you a check for this amount. Some mothers, in an effort to be *fair*, are satisfied to pay one-half of these expenses. I am not sure this is fair at all if the father is making two or three times more than the mother. However, it can prevent constant dissension and friction, which the children witness and are disturbed by.

About that old chestnut of a complaint, *she's not spending all the money on the kids,* there's not one thing you can legally do about it. The judges are hardly going to have third parties go in and monitor the mother's expenses. Remember, she does have to pay rent or mortgage and utilities to provide accommodation and she does have to feed your kids.

And even if you feel that your kids are wearing rags, which many of my fathers have complained of, some mothers, I suspect, deliver their children in their worst clothes so that their fathers, ashamed of their appearance, will buy them new ones. Some of my fathers keep an entire wardrobe in their home for that purpose and have the children change as soon as they come for their access visit. This gives some sort of message to the kids that I don't even want to think about. At least, I suppose, they don't strip them at the door as in that other case. They are, however, returned in the *rags* they arrived in.

There are, unfortunately, actual cases where despite encouragement by the custodial spouse, the children are very reluctant to go on their access visits. The reasons are numerous. It may well be that they have picked up on the fact that you are reluctant to see them leave and insecure over their enjoying their time with a former spouse with whom you have had an unhappy relationship and a painful breakup.

If you think this may be the case, and that in spite of the fact that this was not something you contrived or plotted, they don't want to leave, march them to the door the day of the visit, give them a good hug and kiss, tell them to have fun and assure them you have made plans for the weekend. Do not keep phoning to see if they are still alive. They have your home phone number and if they want to, they can phone you. If they don't, take it as a good omen and know that they are getting alone fine.

When they arrive back, ten minutes late, in their *rags*, *filthy and exhausted*, as these children were so often described to me by my clients, give them a positive hello, ask them if they had fun and do not cross-examine them. If you have a close relationship, which you probably do, they will volunteer some details of their weekend. Enough, hopefully, so you do not believe they spent all of it watching horror shows and playing violent video games.

# Chapter 15
## The New Significant Other

There are very few kids — really very few — unless Daddy was an abusive drunk and the parents spent hours in screaming matches and fisticuffs, who do not secretly harbor a hope for their parents' reconciliation. If the parents are reasonable and loving, and luckily many of them are, kids hate break ups. They want their parents together, and anything that intrudes on this wish is viewed with suspicion and at times hostility. As a result, you often see a fair amount of dislike shown towards the new girlfriend or boyfriend.

They are impediments to Mommy and Daddy getting together again, particularly if Bob or Barbara, or Alice or Alex, was in the picture and caused the breakup in the first place. After all, as Mommy said time and again, "If it weren't for that woman, Daddy would still be with us" and Daddy has said, after an evening beer, "Uncle Alex took your mother away."

How do you expect the kids to feel about this third party who prevents reconciliation and who broke up his or her parent's marriage in the first place? Not very much, I suggest. In fact, I have already spoken of the reality of having the children break up the second marriage.

In the case of access, what role should your significant other play? At the beginning, I suggest, a very limited one. So limited, that the best you can do is to accidentally run into him or her at a designated place and have the kids meet the interloper on a casual and limited basis.

Of course, your kids aren't stupid and eventually they'll figure out that this was all a set up. However, it works quite nicely for younger kids and it prevents your significant other from being catapulted into a situation where the children will see her as an interloper. If you're living together, this little ploy won't work, but I do suggest that you have a period of at least three or four hours alone with your child.

For example, you pick your kids up on Friday night and take them back to your new home. Hopefully you have a room set up for their visitation so that they will not be sleeping with you, or even worse, you and your new love. I have had clients who informed me that the children have slept in bed with *him and his whore, buck naked.* This is not a good idea; in fact, it's a very bad one.

I'm not advising you to kick out your live-in for the weekend, but during the time the kids are there, please wear your pajamas — or something, and restrain your lovemaking for a time when the children are not visiting. The next day, by all means, have breakfast together, either at the pancake house up the street or prepare breakfast at home. Either hang out or drive the kids to any activities agreed upon. I then suggest that you and your child go on your own, to Wonderland, a park, downtown, or any place the child shows enthusiasm for. I suggest you have some bonding time with your children — alone. If your significant other feels shunned, so be it. If he or she is so insecure that you can't spend time with your kids, then perhaps it's time to reconsider that relationship — perhaps it's a forewarning of things to come.

Relationships develop. They shouldn't be forced. Let the new person in your life find out what your son or daughter really enjoys and share it with them. If you do it right and your new squeeze is a warm and loving individual — I'm sure you would not choose otherwise — then he or she will gradually develop a relationship with your kids.

Your former wife or husband may feel threatened by this. One of my clients said to me, "I've lost him and now I'm losing my kids to her."

I know it's a lot to ask, but try not to feel threatened if your husband's significant other gets along with the kids. After all, the more loving, accepting individuals your kids have in their lives, the better. If you badger the kids about their access time, pressure them to relate every detail to you and cross-examine them after every visit so you can criticize the quality of time spent with your ex, you will add unnecessary tension and stress to their lives. They may eventually decide that they do not wish to share their experiences with you at all.

On a cautionary note, there are some significant others, mainly women, but on occasion men, who decide that they will become the children's new mommy or daddy and immediately attempt a parental role and, if you believe it, attempt in every way to disparage the biological mother or father to the children.

These individuals often have borderline personality disorders and are happiest when focusing hatred on a third party. The object of this hatred does not remain constant, but drifts from person to person. I could usually spot them within five minutes when they accompanied my client to the office.

You really should get rid of this type of significant other before your relationship becomes too entrenched, regardless of how wonderful you are together sexually. They are nothing but trouble and eventually will decide that they hate one of your children, or in the end, you. Your life with them will lurch from crisis to crisis, for they are happiest when creating chaos. Believe me, getting rid of them is much harder than meeting them in the first place. Telephone calls will be made to your former wife and even your employer. Some will even call the police and attempt to lay charges. Just remember, if you become involved with one of these disturbed individuals, you have only yourself to blame if you continue with the relationship.

At first you will make excuses. You'll say she or he is insecure, had a bad childhood, and will change after you get married. People don't change, dummy. A borderline personality disorder is not curable. Therapy may mitigate their conduct and teach them some coping skills, but beneath it all is a seething, restless, even dangerous individual who is only happy when creating chaos.

One of my clients, a professional man, finally concluded his separation and divorce from wife number one. Although they never did wind up in court, the negotiations were endless and he was left fragmented and annoyed by the fact that he had been forced to forfeit the matrimonial home in exchange for his professional practice and large IRA.

He brought future wife number two to the office. She was a British blonde, very attractive, with a London accent and a ready, but nervous laugh. They were getting a prenup, he advised me, as they both had assets to secure and had agreed that neither wished to make demands on the other should the marriage not be successful.

During the fifteen minutes spent in my office I noted that she spoke disparagingly of one of his children, comparing one unfavorably with the other and comparing them both unfavorably with her three. She spoke resentfully of the fact that my client might wish to benefit his own children financially, rather than her children, even though his involvement with both her and her children had been relatively brief; and she was quite harsh in her assessments of others. She was obviously madly in love with my client, in an almost school girlish way, although she was over forty.

I had great misgivings and I privately told him so. I was not invited to the wedding, where she wore her new seventy-thousand-dollar engagement ring, which she had insisted upon.

Needless to say, it was a nightmare from beginning to end. The beloved object soon became a figure of abuse. He could not, and did not live up to her expectations. He did not wish to make love in the mornings, which ruined her day. If he read a book at night, he was ignoring her and depriving her of sex. She yelled at her own kids, which made him uncomfortable. After a few drinks, she also yelled at him. He left some eighteen times and even sought counseling with her as a couple. The counselor warned him that there would be continuing problems. The breakup dragged on and became increasingly bitter. Strangely, she was quite fair financially, I presumed because she earned more than he did. Ironically, her kids really liked him and commiserated with him for having had the misfortune of having married their mother.

Luckily, they had a prenup, which they abided by. She purchased his interest in the matrimonial home in downtown Toronto. He reclaimed his interest in his own children, which was seriously under attack during his time with her. Her children keep in touch and have no resentment over the breakup. In fact, they understand. Unlike my client, they knew their mother.

The answer to this type of union is, of course, not to marry him or her in the first place. There are certain badges you can rely on that signify whether there is something serious going on that will disrupt your future. Irrational dislikes, especially of your children and your former spouse, of her own parents, unless there is truly a good reason for it, her sisters and brothers and former close friends and relationships consume a great deal of her time. Temper tantrums and scenes, often in front of groups or other individuals abound. You do forgive him or her time and again— but it becomes harder.

With a male, disorders are usually reflected by irrational jealousy, accusations, and a refusal to accept your parents or family. While these individuals can be quite endearing for brief periods when you are alone, and especially prior to marriage, these other aspects of their behavior should be a real warning sign. These are the types who will attempt to cut you off from your family and friends, resenting any close ties you may have with anyone but themselves and who will target family members and even your children with irrational animosity.

If, in spite of this, you decide to marry one of these individuals, then I implore you to obtain a prenup which is rock solid. She or he must see his or her own attorney and you must be sure to make full financial disclosure, hiding nothing and doing nothing that could invalidate your agreement in the future. Your marriage, of course, will not last but at least you can protect yourself financially.

My client is just recovering his sanity, some three years after the breakup. He's over fifty and the tumult of living with Ms. London aged him twenty years. Thank God for the prenup. Of course, she didn't really want one, but for once he did the right thing. Be sure you do, too.

Your proposed spouse — hopefully not your present one — rather than having a hysterical personality disorder may have a narcissistic one. This can be diagnosed by a battery of psychological tests, but there are certain badges even a layman can discern. As the name signifies, there is an intense preoccupation with self, which is, occasionally extended to the individual's children, who become a projection of self. These individuals almost always find it difficult, if not impossible, to feel empathy for others. If you have a headache, his or hers is worse than, but not as bad as, the back ache that he or she has experienced for years. There is invariably one-upmanship and if the conversation turns to anything but her, watch her eyes glaze over.

These individuals stay in terrific shape and live forever, as they are quite often totally preoccupied with gym workouts, special diets and various forms of cosmetic surgery. They are the center of their universe and you are out there somewhere on the fringe, only important to the extent that you can buttress and aid in the well-being of their much adored self. Anything that could usurp or distract from the attention they believe they should receive may be treated with hostility— or at least boredom.

At times, his or her children are expected, and even compelled, to fulfill any of your spouse's unfulfilled fantasies of being a famous actor, television personality, or even a literary nonsuch, goals which could have been realized but for your coming into his or her life and drowning away all this promise in a sea of domesticity.

I suggest running as hard and as far as you can, but if you won't do that and you're willing to overlook some of these personality traits, which become even more pronounced and irritating with time, then at least get that iron clad prenup.

Remember, he or she must have his or her own attorney. It's pointless for you both to see one attorney, as the prenup can be set aside on these grounds — although either of you would still have a right to sue for negligence.

Men — don't present that prenup within a few weeks, or worse, within a few days before a wedding. It'll be set aside as invalid. Insist on the signing of the prenup at least two months before this fatal marriage. To justify it, inform her that your company's officials insist on it or even that your parents insist on it as a condition of your inheritance. Don't worry about how he or she feels about them. He or she will hate them regardless, on one pretext or another, following the marriage. Get it signed, witnessed and tuck it securely away in your safety deposit box.

In all probability, she'll fight you tooth and nail on certain clauses and inform you that you obviously don't love her or you wouldn't be insisting on such a stringent contract. Ignore this. But don't make the contract so stringent that it could be set aside by a sympathetic judge who could classify it as unconscionable — or grossly unfair.

Let's face it guys, if you're married long enough, you're going to have to pay support — and it will be according to your ability to pay and her need. If she's giving up her employment just to concentrate on the home, you, and a future family, then your support will be compensatory in nature.

You'd be surprised how many women give up their dreams of being a brain surgeon just for that home in the suburbs and the two children that follow. Never mind that she couldn't pass grade nine math. She could have been "somebody" had she not married you and cast away all those dreams. And you will have to pay for that.

Even if she hasn't given up that illustrious illusionary career, it'll be a great economic disadvantage for her to dissolve the marriage in any event. After all, she's only an executive secretary making fifty thousand dollars per year and you're making three hundred thousand dollars as a marketing whiz. There would be a tremendous downward spiral in lifestyle: no more trips to Hawaii or dining at those high end restaurants with a bottle of Dom Perignon. You may have to pay for the difference — for quite a while.

A lot depends, of course, on how long the marriage lasts. If you come to your senses within a year or so, the economic results will not be nearly as dire. Without wishing to seem crass, I would advise my male readers to encourage their wives in their careers and not to stop everything dead upon having children.

While a mother can be expected to spend some time after the birth with the child, to have a temporary hiatus lengthened into a lifetime of work abstinence is not a wise financial choice, unless you're totally convinced that this is a lifetime commitment. In any event, it's a tad too draconian to cut off future support in your prenup. I usually left that clause out and, of course, child support is a must according to the guidelines, in any event. What you want to do is to protect your assets, especially corporate assets, not only at the time of the marriage but for any future growth.

# Chapter 16
## Going to Court

### **Pre-Trial Considerations**

Y ou have had at least four meetings with your spouse and opposing counsel, followed by a full day of mediation. Evaluations have been completed concerning both spouses' pensions and business interests. Your attorney has given you some idea as to the expense of a trial, including his daily fee. If this is a custody matter, the psychological or psychiatric expert will have completed his report and made recommendations and, as such, will make himself available at trial for examination by both parties.

Your attorney has informed you of, or you have gone on line to obtain, information about the amount of support you may expect or be obligated to pay according to the Child Support Guidelines of your particular State or Province. You and your spouse, through your attorneys, have discussed the extraordinary expenses which we have spoken of including special tutorial help, artistic and sports activities, summer camp and any other special expenses which do not come within the ordinary range of child support.

Your attorney has told you what you may be obligated to pay according to the spousal support advisory guidelines, or if female what you may be expected to receive. Your attorney has also told you that the amount shown in your income tax as taxable income may not be the amount attributed to you by a judge, who may impute income to you if you have been too aggressive in your write offs.

Remember, allowable write offs in your income tax, such as depreciation of various assets etc., may not be allowable when considering your income for spousal or child support. In fact, if you have been very aggressive in deductions from your income, be prepared to have some of them factored back. This may have already been done when your spouse went to court on an interim motion for spousal and child support. If this is the case, unless you have had a drastic change in circumstances, be prepared for an almost similar amount to be awarded by the trial judge.

You must seriously consider costs. Some clients quite quaintly believe court costs to be the costs one pays to the court, like the price of admission at the movie theatre. Court costs are based upon legal fees, either those of your counsel or opposing counsel.

If you or your spouse have been consistently unreasonable and unwilling to pay within the range of what is set out in various state codes or statutes, have refused to agree on paying an equalizing payment according to your and your spouse's Community Property, or have been devious and dishonest in disclosing your financial position, then one side may well be awarded costs.

These costs can be atrocious and at times, depending on the fees which are based on the experience and expertise of opposing counsel, may even be worth more than the contested amount. In view of this, it is absolutely necessary that you make a sensible and reasonable offer to settle based on the current law of the State or Province in which you reside.

These offers should be exchanged at least seven days before commencement of trial and I would suggest even earlier. If your offer is more reasonable and better than the judgment given at trial, you should receive your costs. Of course, costs are within the discretion of the trial judge, but even a judge's discretion is limited by various rules.

For example, if you have hidden your assets by misrepresenting your net worth and opposing counsel has had to dig deeply, even hiring an investigator to ferret out your actual worth, you may expect to be penalized for the costs. A finding of fraud, misrepresentation and deceit on the part of a party is invariably followed by an assessment of costs — or certainly should be.

Again, forcing your spouse to constantly go to court so that he can enjoy access to his kids according to a court order, which you have disallowed on a continuous basis on some pretext or another, may also warrant costs. Be careful. Get that offer to settle out and sign it. Get it out in time. I have been constantly amazed at attorneys who do not send out these offers. It is foolhardy and reckless and I can only believe that they have clients who are so unreasonable that they do not wish to put any compromise in writing. That wouldn't be you, would it?

Remember, once that offer is accepted by your spouse, without any changes, you have a binding agreement and your counsel can apply to the court for judgment.

"Why should I do that?" you complain. "After she has forced me to run up all these legal fees and now, just before trial, all of a sudden she wants to be Mrs. Reasonable?"

You should do it, darling. If you don't, your costs can even be more astronomical, as they may well include your spouse's legal fees, if she has been smart enough to make a reasonable offer. They will also include your counsel's costs for the oncoming trial, which may be at least five thousand dollars a day. Think about it.

## **Dressed to Kill**

Some of my clients would ask me what they should wear to court as though they were attending a costume ball. I told my female clients to dress as though they were attending the funeral of a close friend. In other words, a dark suit, a white blouse, non flashy jewelry and sensible shoes, as you may be standing for a while in the witness box — although usually a chair is provided after a few minutes and you are given a drink of water.

When I said suit, I meant not only a skirt and jacket, but, of course, a pant suit. If you wear a skirt, it should reach your knees and you must wear pantyhose. You are not Sharon Stone, for God's sake! You want to impress the judge with your sensible and modest appearance, which reflects your sensible and modest claims.

One of my litigants, who was as promiscuous as all get out, appeared in court looking like the most wholesome cupcake on the planet. In fact, I hardly knew her when she met me outside the courtroom door. The judge just loved her and beamed his approval.

If this is a custody case, you should be attempting to look like Mother of the Year and not Miss America or Canada's top model. I can't believe I'm writing this, but I have to. Every time I didn't warn my client about dressing properly, believing they had a molecule of common sense, they appeared in some outrageous outfit, totally undermining the image I was attempting to convey. At one point it got so bad, I kept an extra black jacket in my closet to cover a multitude of fashion sins. The jacket, more often than not, did not fit well and because of the stress of trial or absence of deodorant was never the same again.

I have always believed that a male witness should wear a suit and tie. I believe it impresses a judge and shows respect for the court. Some of my friends disagree and believe that if your witness is a working man, he should come to court reflecting his status, which would be a constant reminder to the presiding judge that he is just a simple hardworking guy who should not be pummeled financially. Those who work for UPS, for example, should come to court in their UPS uniform. Besides, it is argued, this is the day of relaxed dressing and even high-end restaurants that required a tie to enter many years ago, have dropped the requirement.

"I don't even have a tie," my clients would argue, "and I don't have a dress suit."

"Well, someday you'll need one," I would reply. "Somebody will die or you may be best man at a wedding. You should have a dark suit."

I stick to my guns on this one and I still believe you should be dressed in a decent suit with a tie or a sports jacket with a tie. If you want to soften the image, then wear a v-neck sweater over your shirt and tie. But there must be a jacket over that. Then, unfortunately, you'll have all these layers and you're going to sweat when you're going to give evidence. In fact, you'll sweat even more when your wife is giving evidence. Use a strong deodorant.

A warning to both sexes: **NO TATTOOS SHOWING**. Cover them up. I know that tattoos are to a degree the order of the day and Hollywood types have their bodies packed with them, but you are not a rock star. Tattoos, body piercing or nose rings give a sniff of something not quite kosher and may not be appreciated, especially by older judges. The worst sight in a courtroom is a male litigant with a heavily tattooed chest, his shirt half open to the waist and enough gold chains to drown him if he leapt into a swimming pool — which is probably what he'll feel like doing after the judge renders his judgment!

If you are the female party, do not show any cleavage. We congratulate you on that full bosom, natural or synthetic, but the courtroom is not the place to give the girls an outing! Female judges, especially, may not appreciate it. As far as makeup is concerned, extremes are to be avoided. Jet black or platinum blonde hair should be toned down and makeup should not be an inch thick nor should eyeliner make you look like a vampire.

And guys, if your hair is long, either secure it back in a bun or better yet, cut it off. Flowing locks have all sorts of connotations, none of them good. Where are you going anyway? To American Idol, or to court to show what a serious and responsible fellow you are? And take off that earring. The judge won't like it and again, it gives all sorts of negative connotations.

Do I want you to look like a nerd? Yes! Yes I do! And don't wear dark glasses, regardless of gender. The judge will think, quite unfairly, that you've something to hide. Besides you have to look him or her squarely in the eye as you testify.

Don't look at your attorney. It looks as if she is coaching you — which has hopefully been done before the courtroom hearing!

And don't, and this deserves a paragraph of its own, chew gum. I know you're nervous and your halitosis is equal only to a bulldog in heat, but don't under any circumstances chew gum. I have known clients who have actually cracked gum while in the witness box. Chewing gum vigorously makes a statement as to your respect for the process and your chintzy background. While at this stage you probably have no respect for the process whatsoever, and your last few years have been spent working as a bouncer in some of the worst watering holes in town, it's not necessary to expose this part of yourself to the presiding judge.

In one of my most successful custody trials, I represented an individual who ran the Hot and Heavy Massage Parlor. He handled himself well and gave no indication that he was not the manager of the local bank. In fact, his profession was much more lucrative than that of any banker. But that is another story.

## Behaving Yourself

Hopefully, you will have spent several hours before your trial going over your evidence with your attorney. This is not to say that your attorney will feed you answers to questions asked. This is not considered ethical and I, on occasion, have heard it said, "Mrs. Hillier's witness' evidence is good, perhaps too good," — at which time I have defended myself indignantly.

What was implied, was that I had *woodshedded* my

Suzanne L. Hillier

witness by going over the answers so that they fall into the correct slot of the information that is being put forward. What an unkind presumption!

In preparing you, your attorney should put to you the questions you will be asked and listen to your responses. There is no reason why you cannot answer any questions in a clear, concise and candid fashion. But you must be prepared for these questions and the resulting cross examination. In reality, what it means is that you present information you have accumulated in such a way that it is conveyed properly to the presiding judge.

If this is a custody case and you are asked why you are attempting to obtain custody, you can honestly say, "I believe I should be the preferred parent because I am willing to put in much more time and effort than my spouse."

If your child has any sort of disability, dyslexia or otherwise, you should emphasize what special efforts you have made, or will make, to help him meet this challenge. You should be able to provide details, without hesitation, as to your efforts on this child's behalf. Positive evidence is often better than negative, but if there is negative evidence, and there often assuredly is, then this must be expressed in a clear and moderate way, without tainting your evidence with an accusatory or hysterical ring.

I personally dislike having a client burst into tears while on the witness stand. At that point, it is usual that a judge adjourns the matter for ten minutes so that the witness can regain composure. If you are sincere, and hopefully you are, your voice should show this. Do not let animosity and hatred show through on your evidence. A restrained rendering of an emotional incident is much more impressive than an over-dramatic one. I have had clients who have attempted to give an Academy Award performance and it embarrassed the whole court, including myself.

Speak up, be natural, and look the judge in the eye. The judge will make findings as to your credibility. Is he able to believe what you say? This is important if the other party is

204

refuting your facts.

A good attorney will never ask a question to which he does not know the answer. Likewise, do not make outrageous statements, which you may be called to task on by opposing counsel. A temperate, reasonable delivery will by far take precedence over a strained, hysterical one. And do speak up. There is nothing worse than having to be asked to repeat yourself because you are mumbling into your blouse or shirt instead of looking at the judge and voicing your evidence clearly.

Do not drink the night before and do not dose up on sleeping pills or take tranquilizers on the day of trial. I once had a witness who was so drugged up during her trial that her evidence took ten times longer than it should have and the thread of everything she was attempting to say was lost. She infuriated the judge and annoyed counsel, including myself. I tried to wake her up during the court recess, which usually occurs around eleven thirty and then again at lunch by force feeding her coffee, but it had little effect. The results were not as I had anticipated or hoped. She had effectively sabotaged her own trial.

My client, Doris the Drinker, simply could not be relied upon to go to trial. She had an excellent case and should have received millions from her highly-successful husband, who she had diligently helped for years in his business enterprises. Her alcoholism, however, was so pronounced that she could not be depended upon to keep an appointment at the office, let alone arrive at trial in a sober state. Moreover, she became exceptionally hostile when drinking and I could not risk her erupting into a tirade at the presiding judge.

It was a distressing situation, which did not rectify itself after I forcibly persuaded her to enter a treatment center. She would not acknowledge her alcoholism to her treatment group and acted as if she were a visiting Queen, looking down with kindly interest at all these poor, addicted, drug-addled and recovering alcoholics. It was all quite farcical, as was the settlement, but I really had little alternative.

If you have alcohol and drug problems and you are facing a trial, I would prevail upon you to attempt to get yourself under control before the trial date. There is nothing wrong with attending a treatment center and then continuing to attend A.A. on a regular basis or going on Methadone to curb a drug addiction. If you have impaired driving convictions and have been dismissed from employment for being drunk or using drugs on the job, the judge may certainly suspect you have a problem.

As such, the best you can make of this is to show at least you are obtaining treatment and attempting to conquer it. If your problem is alcoholism, then it is most impressive if you had entered the treatment center several months earlier, have been attending regular A.A. meetings, and have not had a drink since. Similarly, your drug use should be treated as something you have acknowledged, and for which you have obtained treatment.

I found, toward the end of my courtroom career, a relaxation of the condemnation of marijuana use; in fact, it seemed to be almost acceptable as a recreational pastime. At this point in time, the use of pot is still illegal in both the United States and Canada except for medicinal purposes. As such, I was somewhat surprised to see a lackadaisical attitude by a presiding judge when a wife referred to a husband as a *pothead*.

Remember, however, doing drugs with your child is a distinct no-no and should never occur. You are his or her parent, not friend. Some feel that pot use sometimes leads to bigger and better addictions and a parent's acceptance of this, or any encouragement whatsoever, would certainly cast a shadow over any custody claim.

Do be candid and straightforward with your attorney. I was one-half through a trial on behalf of one client and things were proceeding very well. She had experienced a long-term relationship with a successful attorney and there was no reason why she would not receive monthly support on a reasonable basis.

Right in the middle of the trial, however, opposing counsel disclosed the fact that she had received a relatively substantial inheritance some weeks before that had not been disclosed on her financial statement. She had told me nothing of this, which made me irate and embarrassed. Worse, she had undermined her own credibility by not declaring it, so that the judge mentally dismissed all her other evidence which was, I am convinced, substantially true.

The case ended horribly, and the judge informed me in chambers, in front of opposing counsel, that he would have given my client substantial, ongoing support if she had not been proven to be a liar — very disheartening and upsetting to my client and to myself.

The spouse had alcohol problems and my client had left her employment several years before. She had devoted herself to taking care of him and his hobby farm. There was definitely a claim for compensatory support for her efforts and she doubtless suffered an economic disadvantage from the break up. I still think the judge was somewhat harsh, but that's what happens when you are caught in a lie. It permeates all of your evidence, which is then discounted — even if you are telling the truth!

During the trial, do not roll your eyes, comment loudly under your breath, or make faces as if you are entertaining a two year old. As you listen to all those lies pour from your spouse, just keep your head lowered and if you feel you must, very gently shake your head to show your negative opinion of this verbal onslaught. Better still— don't make any gestures at all! It irritates the judge to have you grimacing and distracting your attorney the whole time your opposition is giving evidence.

I usually gave my clients a pad of paper and pen and told them to make notes of what they heard and what they disagreed with, so it would enhance my cross-examination.

I know I do not need to tell you to turn off your cell phone. That is the ultimate insult and will annoy the judge to distraction when he hears it. Remember, he believes that you should have already settled this matter and that he should have been out on the golf course hours ago. He is compelled to listen to all this, however, and as such wants you to make it as easy as possible for him.

With that in mind, sit quietly in your seat. If you have anything to say to your counsel, write it down. Stand up and bow respectfully when the judge enters, always refer to him or her as "your honor" or "sir" and under pain of death, never refuse to answer a question he asks. Indeed, answer it meticulously and respectfully, even if you believe some of his questions indicate that he has not been listening to all of the evidence.

Don't be rude. I know you wouldn't be rude to the judge — that would be a fatal mistake, but I suggest you not be rude to opposing counsel either. Regardless of how you detest this man or woman who you believe has acted miserably throughout, misrepresenting evidence and playing every dirty trick in the book to undermine your case, when he or she questions you, answer with great respect and call him Sir, Mister, Ms. or Mrs., whatever the case may be. If he or she is sneering or is sarcastic, do not let it upset you, even though it assuredly will, and answer in a restrained and even voice.

This may be difficult after all those months of abusive letters and those days of cross-examinations in which you were sneered at and ridiculed. You agree exactly with your attorney's assessment of him or her, as a *real scumbag*, but don't for a minute show it. If he is hectoring and abusive, his honor may tell him to restrain himself, inform him that you have already answered that question, and on occasion may give you sympathy as a result.

If he is really heckling you to death, your own attorney should stand up and complain that you are being harassed. All this is very effective, provided you are not the one to turn to the judge and ask, "Do I have to answer that, your honor?" I had a client who kept doing that and it bothered me as much as the trial judge.

Of course you have to answer, dummy, provided that the question is not irrelevant. If the question is irrelevant, your own counsel should get up and object to the line of questioning. When he does this, hopefully the judge will stop opposing counsel.

In this day and age, with so much emphasis on mediation and pre-trial conferences at every step of the way, few cases should be going to trial. If, however, your case is one where one of you is being manifestly unreasonable, there may be no alternative. If so, make the best of it. You have nothing to lose but your money — or perhaps your children, which is much more serious.

# Chapter 17
## Your Attorney: Sleazebag or Redeemer?

Y ou chose your attorney because your neighbor, Peggy
Harris, used him and obtained, she assured you, "an
amazing result." On this recommendation, you retained
this awesome fellow. You found him to be impossible to talk
to, ineffective in court, and overcharging you for what you
considered to be his paltry efforts.

What went wrong?

There is nothing wrong with taking a recommendation
from a neighbor or friend, when seeking an attorney. In fact, it
sure beats the yellow pages, which I adamantly warn you
against. In fact, attorneys who take out huge ads in the yellow
pages are usually seeking clients. Good attorneys are
invariably busy: sometimes so busy that you may have to wait
a few weeks to get in to see him or her.

In a panic, because your spouse has either left or
expressed a wish that he or she is in the process of leaving,
you seek the first available attorney. Big mistake. It is better
for you to wait for the busy one.

If you receive a letter from your spouse's attorney,
then telephone his office and advise him that you are in the
process of seeking legal counsel and to have the courtesy to

wait for a reply. If, on the contrary, you are served with a Divorce Petition, plus a case conference date or emergency motion, then better than obtaining the first available attorney, appear on your own and request a brief adjournment so that legal counsel can be acquired. It would be very unusual for this request not to be granted.

If you are served on relatively short notice with divorce papers, without even the courtesy of a preliminary letter, then you may be forewarned that your spouse has acquired a very aggressive attorney and you should act accordingly.

Now, let's get back to Peggy Harris and her awesome attorney. Don't just take this commercial and run with it. Ask Peggy just what this attorney did for her. It could very well be that her husband, Joe Harris, started a water cooler affair with one of his co-workers. As a result, he was full of guilt and urgency and instructed his attorney to give in to most of Peggy's demands, provided he had enough to survive. Exchanging financial information and drawing up a separation agreement under these circumstances is hardly a daunting task.

If this is your situation, and you and your spouse have already discussed settlement, and for reasons that you may not be quite aware of, but which your spouse undoubtedly is, he appears to be ready to be quite reasonable; then Peggy Harris' choice of attorney may very well be your man.

On the other hand, if your spouse appears to be anything but reasonable and has announced more than once that by the time he or she is finished, you are going to be "destroyed," then you may very well need a more aggressive attorney who is able to withstand the aggressive tactics of the attorney your spouse has retained.

It will not help your case to have an easy, laid-back attorney, whose main interest is in doing real estate — but who does do separation agreements on the side — to represent you in court against some Rambo, whose unrestrained, aggressive and zealous delivery reduces him to mush.

Choosing the right attorney for your case is of great importance. If you believe you are headed for a prolonged courtroom battle, then make inquiries of any of your friends who have been in a similar situation and find out who represented them and how satisfied they were with his or her services. You may also inquire as to how their spouse's attorney conducted him or herself in the courtroom.

If you have the time, sit in at motions court, or even a trial in progress, to watch any attorney you are considering in action. Are you impressed with his confidence and expertise when representing his client? Does the judge show him respect and appear to listen to his representations? Check the court's online services and see if any reported decisions or assessments have been documented.

Do not telephone the legal monitoring body in your state and ask them to recommend an attorney. I was the second attorney in one case where my client, who had a long-term marriage and extremely good prospects, was referred by the Law Society to a criminal attorney who botched the first motion to such an extent that the rest of her case was irreparably damaged.

The Law Society has a list of available attorneys. Many busy, competent, sought after attorneys may not be on this list.

Incidentally, there is nothing wrong with seeing two or even three attorneys before deciding on the attorney you wish to represent you. You should have an attorney who you feel relaxed enough to talk to. I always had my clients refer to me by my first name, but that may not be the style of the attorney you see. We all have different styles. Some attorneys charge their hourly rate for your first visit and perhaps more, if he or she is your second attorney and they have had to review a lengthy file.

If this is your first attorney, then expect to pay his hourly rate for an hour of his or her time. Before or at that first meeting, you may be asked to fill out an information sheet which the attorney will most likely clip to the inside of his file.

This sheet will ask for your address, telephone number, email, and you and your spouse's profession, income, number of children and children's names and birth dates and level of education. It should also clearly set out for you the nature of your attorney's retainer, that is, his hourly rate, his fee for an attendance at a pre-trial conference and motions court, and the daily rate he charges at trial. You may then be asked to sign this retainer form, attesting that you understand the nature of your attorney's fees and are willing to pay them.

It is against the Rules of Professional Conduct for any attorney to represent both sides of a case. Do not go to the real estate attorney, who represented you and your husband on the purchase of your home, and who did your wills. He cannot, or certainly should not, represent both of you and actually shouldn't represent either of you in drawing up a separation agreement, even if you have agreed on everything.

I know that if you and your spouse have agreed on everything and want to reduce this to paper and, more importantly, do not want to spend money on legal fees, this proposition is tempting. It is especially tempting if you have had a pleasant relationship with this individual and you both feel comfortable with him or her.

There are many reasons why this should not be done. One reason is you need a specialist in matrimonial law to represent you. If you have a heart problem, you go to a cardiologist, not a dermatologist specializing in acne. This is an age of specialization and knowing the law in a certain area and keeping up with the constant changes is quite enough for one individual.

I recall some attorneys, during a real estate collapse, taking up matrimonial work as they thought it would be "easy." One of these friends telephoned me on a constant basis asking what to do in certain cases. He had absolutely no idea. One woman came to me with an agreement she had executed upon the advice of my friend. It was a disgrace. She was cheated out of a large part of her equalization payment because this individual simply did not know how to do a statement of Community Property and had prevailed upon her to settle because it *seemed fair*.

Of course, it wasn't fair, and her recourse was to sue to put the agreement aside and to add this real estate attorney as a party. I don't enjoy suing friends, so I did send her to another attorney, who started an action against my friend for negligence.

Remember, all attorneys are insured against negligence claims and some have a five thousand dollar deductible. If an attorney has been the object of several lawsuits, his deductible may be up to ten thousand dollars or more. In any event, the Law Society or the governing body for attorneys in your State through their legal insurers obtains an attorney for the allegedly negligent one and it is up to the parties to prove whether negligence has existed and damages incurred.

So, I strongly suggest that you retain an attorney whose practice focuses upon divorce work, to represent you in your marital problems. I have a friend, who assures me that he does both criminal and matrimonial work, because if he didn't, he'd go crazy. I strongly suspect he is not totally competent in either field. I quite understand his comment that restricting one's practice to divorce work may indeed lead to madness, but at least you become a mad expert in what you do.

The mindset of a criminal attorney and of a civil litigator is very different. You have every right, when considering retaining your attorney, to ask if his or her practice is restricted solely to matrimonial work.

I have already told you that you and your spouse cannot have the same attorney. Indeed, either of you can have an agreement put aside if this occurs. In fact, if your attorney has interviewed your spouse or talked to him or her in regard to the case, he or she cannot represent you.

For example, if you live in a very small town and there is one renowned attorney who specializes in matrimonial work, you cannot retain him if he has already seen your spouse. What usually happens is that there is an unseemly race for one or the other to acquire the services of this attorney. If you have heard that this attorney is very aggressive and client focused, you may wish to retain him for yourself or you certainly wish to prevent your husband or wife from retaining him or her. The way to do this is to at least set up an appointment and see him or her for advice. Once he or she has seen you, then that is the end for your spouse.

This can be carried to extremes and can be quite annoying. I had one woman who telephoned my office, spoke to my receptionist and was told that her husband had already retained me. She actually went to court to prevent me from representing him, as she said she had contacted my office. I was able to continue to represent my client, but was very disconcerted by the fact that the judge made very thorough inquiries as to whether my receptionist had given her any legal advice. This particular receptionist had trouble even answering the phone, let alone give legal advice.

An even more irritating occurrence happened when a family member begged me to speak to a close, personal friend who she told me very much needed some comfort in regard to his marital breakup, although he was in the process of retaining another attorney. I foolishly spoke to him for about forty-five minutes on the phone, strictly on a pro bono basis. In other words, I gave free advice. Sure enough, the next day, the wife telephoned to retain me. Naturally, I couldn't take her as I had already spoken to the husband. It was a very good case and considerable funds were involved. I was annoyed.

The Rules of Professional Conduct state that an attorney must be honest and candid when advising clients. You have a right to know exactly what you are entitled to and what your obligations are. It is very unfair to you to have an attorney who builds up unrealistic expectations and runs up a fat fee, on the premise that he can in some way prevent your wife from obtaining an equalization payment, or save you from paying spousal and child support.

The law is a creature of statute and the *Divorce Acts* and the *Family Law Acts,* in addition to other statutes and codes, very clearly set out what the parties' obligations and rights are in your particular State. These rights and obligations are further extended by a body of case law, which is forever changing and reinterpreting these statutes. You have a right to be angry if, after court applications, pre-trial conferences, prolonged cross-examinations and discovery, the end result is that you settle at the courtroom door at approximately what was offered by you the week after separation— after incurring all those legal fees!

I knew an attorney for whom I had a great deal of respect. He was extremely bright and had detailed knowledge of divorce work, which he had specialized in for dozens of years. His clients were usually quite wealthy. This is fortunate, as this particular attorney would never settle a case, not with me in any event, unless he had run up approximately one hundred thousand dollars in legal fees.

As his hourly rate was much higher than mine, it meant that I would be running up somewhere between thirty and forty thousand dollars. When I saw him on the other side, I would caution my client that she had to be prepared to pay between thirty and forty thousand dollars in legal fees as the matter would go on for at least a year, but that at the end we would absolutely settle and she would get a quite fair result.

This attorney never went to court — with me in any event. He was usually in the Court of Appeal or pursuing, I am sure, much more important matters. After a while, I became used to his way of operating and went along with it, knowing that at the end my client would get a very fair deal and would walk away satisfied. He did not, ever, take custody cases. A rather sensible choice, as there is nothing more upsetting and frustrating than custody cases. He loved the intricacies of the law and was very good at them. Knowing the law, he knew a good offer when he saw one and knew what was fair.

"But isn't it ridiculous?" you ask. "Running up costs like that when you could settle so much sooner?"

Probably, but in fairness, he did know the law, was quite ingenious in transferring funds to avoid income tax to both parties and was straightforward and candid. I could not see his aiding and abetting a lack of financial disclosure and I had no doubt that any advice he gave to his client would be based on the law and would be reasonable. He did not grandstand and went about his work focused and efficient. Of course, as he invariably represented wealthy men, he drove my female clients mad with impatience. I always felt, however, that his good qualities far outweighed the running up of legal fees.

His conduct could be contrasted with another attorney, who I will refer to as *Slick Willy,* a blustering egotist. Willy's knowledge of the law was questionable, although he was a *specialist* and had practiced for some thirty years. I represented the husband and he represented the wife, who luckily had family money, as again costs were run up in an absurd fashion. There were endless motions and cross-examinations. The motions would, however, always be settled at the courtroom door. He never had his client present and I strongly suspect that he told her that the Minutes of Settlement we entered into, and which he agreed to on her behalf, were really orders of the court. In fact, I overheard him speaking to her on the phone and telling her exactly that, after we had signed yet more Minutes of Settlement. Two offers of settlement, both infinitely reasonable and better for his client than the final agreement, were ignored and I suspect not shown to his client. This went on and on and doubtless culminated in a huge legal fee.

The matter was abruptly settled when there was a meeting with accountants, appraisers, and opposing counsel. Endless posturing and tirades finally enlightened his not unintelligent client as to what was in reality transpiring. My client got to his feet, and simply and plainly expressed to his wife that he was not interested in her inherited money, never had been and even if it had increased from the date of marriage, he was willing to waive this increase and to settle without it. Of course, he had always been willing to do this, but obviously it was never conveyed to her by her attorney.

Much, I am sure, to *Slick Willy's* disappointment, the matter was settled with all due haste. He should not have been disappointed. He had, after all, squeezed the lemon dry.

Remember, your attorney is compelled to show you every offer of settlement that comes from the other side. If he does not do this, but wishes to promote litigation and keep the meter going, you can sue him. My client and I compiled what we believed to be a reasonable offer of settlement within a few months of commencing a divorce, and after all of the necessary appraisals of business and pension had been completed. Our offer was ignored. Some ten months later, prior to the commencement of trial, yet another offer was made, this one much more generous to my client. It was accepted.

After the settlement my client and her husband started speaking again and my client asked with curiosity why the preliminary offer had not been considered, as the final offer agreed upon was so much more generous for her. He had not, her husband informed her, even seen the first offer.

He was justifiably furious and sued the attorney, who admitted that he had not shown the first offer to his client. He pleaded negligence. The husband was paid a sum to compensate for the difference between the first and the second offer, from his attorney's insurance with the Law Society.

This is shocking behavior and may yet be another instance of an attorney who wished to keep the meter running. This fortunately is not typical. Most attorneys are straightforward and keep their clients informed as to every step in the case. You should not remain with an attorney who you feel is being less than candid with you. He is your agent and is supposed to be working in your best interests. He has every right to be paid for his efforts, but it is unconscionable for him to keep a matter going that should be settled just so he can increase his legal fees.

In fairness, some attorneys are goaded by their clients. These clients in some perverse way believe if they keep matters unpleasant enough their spouses will throw their hands up and either reconcile or settle on some grossly unfair terms.

Attorneys have a duty is to canvass the possibility of reconciliation. I canvassed this a bit too enthusiastically on a couple of occasions and had my clients reconcile only to return a few years later with a new family addition, insisting that she or he wished they had gone ahead with the divorce in the first place.

Keeping an unhappy marriage together for the sake of the children is a hollow triumph. You often end up with seriously disturbed children, who carry out the same miserable pattern in their own marriages, as they have no idea how happily married people function. I had one client inform me that the happiest day of her life was when her parents separated.

By the time that an individual seeks out an attorney, there has usually been considerable soul searching, as people do not mindlessly seek legal counsel. If one party wishes a divorce, it seems highly improbable that there will be reconciliation. I have only seen two, both women, whose husbands left them for other women and then returned and begged forgiveness. They were forgiven and, as far as I know, continued their relationship on a relatively happy basis. There were no young children in these particular cases and their marriages had been happy until the intrusion of a third party.

There are some attorneys who are so rude and obnoxious in their dealings with opposing counsel, that they instigate a veritable war. Hostile letters fly to and fro and vicious comments are muttered outside courtrooms. Distortion of facts and false accusations abound against opposing counsel.

You will, or at least should, receive all letters that are exchanged between the attorneys. You should also receive a copy of any email. Most likely your attorney's dislike of opposing counsel will be infectious and the entire atmosphere becomes toxic. Occasionally, so much animosity is generated between counsel that they become lost in their own personal battle, and the best interests of their clients end up on the back burner.

It is really unfortunate when this happens, because if the base of your problems are financial, and this is certainly the usual criteria for animosity, unless it is a custody case, then what you should want is a fair settlement at the earliest opportunity to conserve costs and bring the whole stressful situation to an end. This, of course, cannot happen when you have legal representatives who cannot speak to each other, write each other a civil letter, or comply with the Rules of Practice, so that proper negotiations can take place.

Most attorneys are well aware that financial disclosure is the order of the day. They are well aware that a client is compelled to show at least three years of income tax returns so that income can be determined. He or she is also aware that all back up information relating to finances should be produced and that demands for information made in the course of cross-examinations and discoveries must be complied with.

In spite of this, counsel who absolutely should know better, ignore such requests for months on end and when they finally do produce the requested documentation, rather than seeing it as an obligation, act as if they were presenting a great gift, which qualifies for a waterfall of appreciation. This is ridiculous and to have to go to court, time and again, to have financial disclosure given or undertakings complied with is a total waste of time and money—but unfortunately, this happens!

You can help your attorney by bringing in any requested documentation to exchange with the other side. I have had clients that I represented, and the clients of opposing counsel, who believed that producing proof of their financial position was somehow an imposition and they resented even the request. I have had the occasional captain of industry declare, "It's none of their damn business." Unfortunately, once litigation commences, it *is* their damn business, and refusing to produce documentation will do nothing but cause trouble and arouse suspicions from both opposing counsel and the presiding judge.

There is nothing worse than to have to subpoena banks just before a trial and have them send a bank manager who cites the privacy of her client and has to be questioned on the witness stand about material that he or she has refused to show you and which you are seeing for the first time.

Cooperate with your attorney and give him all requested information. If you see that he is embroiled in an ongoing battle with opposing counsel, don't be an enthusiastic audience: he may well be a showman— many litigators are— and wishes to provide you with an Academy Award Performance so you can see how vigorously he is pursuing your best interests. Even that first letter can set the tone for a battle or constructive negotiation. It was for that reason that I usually dictated letters when my clients were present. If at that time they wished me to change the tenor of my letter, then I could do so.

The occasional attorney will send incredibly nasty letters to counsel, a copy of which you will no doubt receive, to impress you with their zealous efforts on your behalf. Be sure that this will appropriately inflame opposing counsel and the battles will begin. Sometimes, if you have retained an attorney of this ilk, it may be a good idea to say to your spouse, "Our attorneys are having a great battle on our dime. Perhaps we should tell them to smarten up and that we want to settle."

The trouble is a conciliatory gesture can be construed as weakness and these warriors keep waiving their swords until the courtroom door swings open. Then, quite surprisingly, sometimes offers are made. Unfortunately, by that time both you and your attorney so thoroughly hate opposing counsel and your spouse that it takes a considerable effort to even read it.

When you are looking for an attorney, you want someone who knows the law—believe me this is rarer than you think— and is able to enunciate clearly and persuasively before a judge. However, he must also be willing, at the earliest opportunity after full financial disclosure has been made, to negotiate offers of settlement and advise you as to the appropriateness of accepting them or continuing on to litigation.

You are lucky if you can find an attorney with all of the aforesaid qualities. I once had a junior who had quick intelligence and a phenomenal knowledge of the law. She was, in fact, a walking encyclopedia when it came to current case law. Unfortunately, on one occasion, when I was called into another court, she had to represent one of our clients at a motion.

The results were abysmal. Apparently, she could not speak out or put her argument forward before a judge with any clarity. My client, a red-haired flight attendant, who was present at the motion, came storming into my office screaming, "I hired you and you sent your wimpy little lackey to court." Needless to say, I had to go to court several times to bring us back to our former position, which had been very much undermined by my junior who subsequently acquired a position with the government where litigation skills are not so necessary.

If an attorney makes a habit of constantly berating opposing counsel, being deliberately inflammatory and underhanded, he or she may acquire a reputation.

This happened to me once when I was the second attorney retained on a case with volumes of material that were impossible for me to read before the impending trial. I attempted an adjournment, but failed. Apparently attorney number one had adjourned on many occasions and the judge was having no more of it.

My client was from Hong Kong and she hated her husband with a passion that only a spurned wife can have. I was unaware at the time, but she had invited reporters from various Chinese newspapers to be present at trial. With my sparse knowledge of the file, I resigned myself to inevitable defeat and placed my client on the stand, beginning by asking the most basic questions, which frankly were all I could ask as I knew so little about the file.

Opposing counsel, with whom I had always had a friendly enough relationship, but who was known for what we in the professional call *sharp practice*, jumped to his feet to object. The judge tore a strip off him. Apparently, he was well aware of his reputation and was determined not to let him get away with a single thing. I proceeded with my paltry evidence, but on every occasion that opposing counsel objected, the judge, who I could see was going to be my new best friend, scathingly told him to sit down and be quiet. This went on until one o'clock, when the court is usually adjourned for lunch.

My client had just finished telling how her husband's father had committed suicide, so great was his shame at his son's conduct. I glanced at the unfortunate husband, who was slinking down in his seat with his head lowered. The reporters were avidly writing in the back row. Within one-half an hour the matter was settled with what I can only say was a superb result. I was as delighted as my client with the resolution, but I must admit I did have some sympathy for my friend on the other side, regardless of his reputation and his past experience with our present judge. No one wants to be put down like that in front of one's client and you don't want an attorney with an odious reputation for sleazy behavior.

Luckily, there aren't that many around.

Litigation is a tough, nerve-wracking business. I confess that during my thirty-plus years of practice, I have banged up telephone receivers, sworn, called names — really bad ones — and have been so angry with opposing counsel that it took all my willpower not to physically attack them. In turn, I have been sworn at, called vile names, had my life threatened and was pushed across an elevator by a witness who didn't wish to be subpoenaed.

The Rules of Professional Conduct tell us not only to be honest and candid with our client, but to treat the Court with courtesy and respect. We must not start actions which are motivated by spite and brought for the purpose of injury, or assist a client to do anything dishonest or to do anything which would prevent a judge from being impartial. It is forbidden to deceive the court by giving false evidence, to rely on a false affidavit, assist in any fraud or illegal conduct, misstate testimony or any law, insist a fact is true when such cannot be reasonably supported by evidence, hide what he believes the law to be, advise a witness not to appear in court, abuse or harass a witness, or to threaten a criminal charge to gain a civil advantage. Whew! This constitutes a real Magna Carta of good conduct!

An attorney, moreover, should encourage public respect for the administration of justice, not show disruptive conduct and be courteous and civil at all times. Most of us, me included, have failed to be civil and courteous at all times and have shown disruptive conduct. It's the nature of the game.

If, however, your spouse has obtained the services of an individual who is known for aggressive tactics and intemperate outbursts, I do believe that you have to retain the services of an equally strong attorney. Then, of course, there will be a Battle of the Titans and a great deal of money may be wasted and you may end up at trial. At least, however, you will have someone strong enough to stand up to the bullying tactics your spouse's attorney may be using.

I would advise you to obtain the services of an attorney who has had some experience. You really do not want a novice attorney. While he or she may work hard on your behalf, there are certain essentials that one learns from experience that are extremely important. I would attempt to obtain the services of an attorney who has been in the profession and who has specialized in the matrimonial area for at least eight years, preferably more.

One of the problems with inexperienced attorneys is that they simply do not know how to settle because they do not know what they should agree to. They are terrified that their client will turn around and sue them if they have settled inappropriately. This means they always want some judge to adjudicate. This is expensive and trying and means that you must go through days of trial or hours of motion court. You can only settle a matter if you know the law behind it. In other words, you must know what a good result would be and try to settle on those terms.

I went through a very trying six months with a junior attorney who simply did not know what he was doing. He argued everything pointlessly and we ended up in court over the most obvious matters, which could have been settled in two minutes had he any idea of what he was doing and the law upon which the issues he argued were based. Not only was he unaware of the law, but so suspicious because of his ignorance that you could not presume to tell him what the law was, or he would become defensive. These junior attorneys would profit by doing an apprenticeship under a senior attorney, or by spending some time in lower courts where they could not do quite so much harm. Whereas these juniors may not be as expensive, remember they are learning on your time—and often you get what you pay for.

Some clients believe that if they select an attorney from a large downtown law firm in a large city, then this attorney has got to be good. The offices are breathtaking and encompass several floors of an impressive high rise. The rent alone must be in the hundreds of thousands per month. No wonder these attorneys charge those breathtaking hourly fees.

Many of these senior matrimonial attorneys who work from large well established law firms are very competent, but there are some problems of which you should be aware.

The source of much of the business for these attorneys comes from the corporate section of their law firms. These are wealthy clients, whose business the law firm wishes to keep in house. They are well able to pay the huge hourly fees these matrimonial attorneys charge and the results of some of the litigation which transpires can be somewhat deceiving.

I had a client leave me as she had read in the paper that one of these downtown attorneys had obtained a judgment of some fifteen million dollars for a client. It sounded very impressive and my client wished to emulate this result. The problem was, in that case, the husband was reputed to be worth some fifty million dollars and as such, the fifteen million dollars was not in reality the equalization payment which could be expected. She did not stay with this particular firm after finding out that her case had been assigned to a junior attorney who was not in the realm of obtaining million dollar settlements!

These attorneys from large law firms have juniors. In fact, some of them have four or five juniors. There is nothing wrong with having juniors, but, as we have discussed, they are inexperienced and have several years to go before they reach the stature of being impressive litigators. Despite this, these files are handed over to juniors and they do much of the preliminary legwork. They conduct cross-examinations, appear in motions court and, in short, do all of the things that you thought Mr. Big would be doing for you.

"Oh," they explain, "you should be glad Miss Barbie Doll is doing all of this for you. You are only being charged five-hundred-dollars an hour for Miss Barbie Doll, while if you had Mr. Big, you would be paying nine-hundred-dollars an hour."

This, of course, was not what you wanted and you complain to Mr. Big. Unfortunately, when Mr. Big does take over, more often than not he does not know the file. In other words, these underlings do so much work that it is almost impossible for Mr. Big to absorb the entire file by the time you reach a trial.

There are some advantages to hiring an attorney from a prestigious law firm. Sometimes, they are treated with what appears to be more respect by the presiding judge than individuals from smaller law firms.

One problem of dealing with juniors is that you cannot really discuss settlement with them, even settlement of a relatively innocuous motion. Their authority is strictly limited to argue a motion or request an adjournment. Quite often, these juniors, lacking in confidence and experience, make up for it by being rude. This, and the flagrant misrepresentation of facts in order to ingratiate themselves with the presiding judge when arguing a motion, helps no one. The problem with telling lies is that sometimes you get caught and you do not wish your attorney, junior or otherwise, to be unveiled as an untruthful little minx.

On occasion, juniors do compensate for their restricted authority and natural shortcomings by being well prepared and quite zealous in front of a Judge. Note that I did not say aggressive, but zealous. There is a difference, but your best interests would be better served by having a legal representative with both qualities.

There are clients, however, who believe that an attorney has to be a vociferous bully to adequately represent them. Some attorneys play into this. They deliberately have loud altercations with other attorneys in front of their clients or write hostile letters ending with *govern yourself accordingly*, copies of which they send to their clients to assure them that they have avid representation.

I admit that at times I have been snappy with other attorneys. I think all of us become irritable because the whole adversarial system is irritating. But to stage hostility and send hostile letters to impress, is a pathetic way of endearing yourself to your client. Sometimes the very attorneys who do this, go out with opposing counsel for lunch and have charming and easy conversations. The other attorney, who has probably paid for lunch, then receives one of these grandstanding epistles the next day, full of vituperation, which has quite obviously been drafted to impress their lunch partner's client.

If you have retained one of these attorneys, who may very well be competent, but believes he has to show a very dark side for you to appreciate him, there is no harm in your saying, "How are you and Mr. Big ever going to negotiate a settlement when you have this hostile relationship?"

It's a valid enough comment. How indeed!

This is a problem you must look out for with your attorney and opposing counsel. On occasion, attorneys incur such a violent dislike for each other that they forget all about your case and go on a frolic of playing dirty tricks, or as the profession calls it, indulging in *sharp practice*. This means short serving on motions so that the other counsel has no time to prepare. Or even if he does stay up all night preparing, he is unable to file material. Most judges will not accept pleadings at the hearing, as they have not read them and do not wish to adjourn the matter so that they can.

Or worse, sneaking into court and getting what is known as an *ex parte order* — an order which is obtained without serving opposing counsel with notice — on the grounds that a situation poses an emergency which can only be resolved by having an immediate order. Usually, this will incite the other side, unless it is truly an emergency, so that they will immediately apply to court to have the order put aside, which may very well happen.

Again, opposing counsel, or your attorney, may serve an emergency notice to examine. As the date is not agreed to, in all probability your attorney or opposing counsel will be busy or unprepared. All of these little tricks take time and money and generate bad faith, which is a nice way of saying utter dislike and suspicion. Be assured that the animosity which flies between your attorney and your spouse's attorney will absolutely rub off on you both and all four of you will be swept along in a tempest of pure unadulterated hatred, which sends all rationality flying out the window permanently.

If you and your spouse are still speaking — at this stage you probably aren't — it is a fine idea to state the obvious. Your respective attorneys are having quite the time fighting on your dime. If your spouse's attorney is following his or her instructions and your spouse is promoting this type of behavior, then all you can do is be sure you have a strong enough counsel to withstand this type of conduct. When you get there, your attorney can vigorously bring it to the attention of the court as this is assuredly where you are heading.

# Divorce ~ A Guided Tour

Changing attorneys, even if you feel that you are not being well represented, is a daunting task. For one thing, your attorney has the right to hold onto your file until his fee has been paid. When you voice your displeasure with his or her services, you will not endear yourself to him, so when you ask that the final bill be prepared, you may be quite shocked by the amount.

Remember, you can go before an assessment or taxation officer and have your attorney's bill assessed if you believe it is genuinely exorbitant or if you are charged with services that were not rendered. There is often a time limit for this and the assessment process takes time. Getting your bill assessed may vary in difficulty depending on your State of Residence. Many State Bar Associations, however, have a fee dispute resolution procedure.

If there is enough money involved, you should be accompanied by a lawyer who is aware of the assessment or taxation process and rules. If you appear on your own to voice your displeasure, you may not be impressive. I have only experienced one taxation in my thirty-plus years of practice, which goes to show I did not charge enough! Some attorneys have their accounts assessed every month and become quite expert at it.

If you receive a bill you believe to be grossly unfair, not reflective of services rendered, and which you resent paying, my advice is go to the attorney in question and speak to him privately. Say, "I do not like your bill and I believe you've overcharged me. However, if you are willing to take (*name a lessor amount*), I will pay you immediately and you can release my file."

It is amazing how many attorneys will settle on that premise. They are not stupid, just greedy. An alternative would be offering cash for a reduction. This is tricky and can be used against either of you in the future. It also means that your attorney could be reported to the IRS for tax evasion if he does not formally bill out this amount, which effectively defeats the purpose. And it makes him look unsavory to the

Law Society or State Bar Association, if matters become even more unpleasant, even if he does put it directly into his law account pending billing and not his wallet — also unlikely.

Some attorneys send out interim bills and others, perhaps as a favor to you, wait until the end of matters to send a final bill. As a client, I believe it is more to your advantage to have interim billings. That way you know how much you are spending on your case, rather than receive a *knock out punch* at the end.

In Canada, Taxation or Assessment Officers vary in their generosity to either an attorney or client dependent on their personalities and where the taxation takes place. Attorneys are permitted to be more exorbitant, for example, in a larger city than they would be in outlying districts or small towns. In Canada, there is a time limitation as to when you must obtain a fee assessment or taxation. Each State may vary as to their respective methods. I realize that sometimes these assessments are unavoidable, especially if you have been charged an arm and a leg for a motion or trial that ended dismally.

Even if you are dismissing your attorney, try to keep it pleasant and merely state that you have been very disappointed. Specify what disappointed you and tell him or her that you believe because of opposing counsel's outrageous tactics it is necessary that you obtain a more aggressive counsel or any other reason that warrants your discontinuance of the relationship. If your relationship has become really toxic, have your new attorney deal with it. He or she will have you sign an authorization and direction to have your file released.

It is a mistake to generate bad feelings between yourself and your *about-to-be* former counsel. Attorneys hate clients who report them to the Law Society or whatever your governing body in your particular state is known as. Most of us have the occasional report and most often it is the party who your attorney does not represent who reports him.

The Law Society takes reports from an attorney's own clients much more seriously than it does from the husband or spouse represented by opposing counsel. I suggest that it is better for you to change attorneys rather than to report your present attorney to the Law Society. Once this is done, your relationship will deteriorate even further.

One client telephoned the Law Society because I did not return her telephone calls. I happened to be at trial and this particular client was notorious for wishing to have a telephonic sixty minutes for every call. I was really annoyed by her actions and our relationship went downhill from there.

On the other hand, sometimes when the opposing spouse reports you, it merely means you are doing your job. The Law Society or State Bar Association is most interested in attorneys who steal from their trust accounts or do other financial damage other than just charging too much!

Swearing and being coarse, both of which I have been accused of, are not that serious, although such is not to be encouraged. Luckily, it was the other spouse who took great exception to my conduct. My client thought it was great!

Remember, the Law Society or State Bar Association is a part of profession that monitors a solicitor's conduct and can take punitive measures if one crosses too far over the line. If you believe that your attorney has been underhanded in his dealings with you, you can, of course, make a complaint, but remember, your relationship with that specific attorney is finished. Don't believe for one minute that by reporting your attorney to the Law Society you can somehow prod him into acting more civilly and more courteously towards you. On the other hand, he will probably be so annoyed with you that any future constructive relationship is gone.

Attorneys, on occasion, threaten each other with the Law Society or with complaints to the State Bar Associations. This only occurs when attorneys have reached a high level of exasperation with each other and they believe that the conduct shown by opposing counsel is clearly unethical.

As I have already stated, an attorney is supposed to be honest, civil, and courteous to his clients. Insofar as you are concerned, may I suggest there are a few ways in which you can reciprocate?

Don't bring a conglomeration of friends with you for your first appointment. I have spent unnecessary time explaining matters of law to a sister or cousin, which were unnecessary to address or which would have been better addressed to the prospective client.

If you have problems with English, you may very well need an interpreter, who will most likely be a close family member. If you feel you need the moral support of another individual, then I suppose you must bring him or her with you. Occasionally, a client, usually a woman, will bring her best friend. Following this, and fortunately very occasionally, this best friend will advise the husband or wife or their immediate relatives exactly what transpired in the attorney's office.

Remember, everything you tell your attorney is privileged. In other words, they cannot discuss it with anyone. It is a very different matter with your friends. The attorney-client privilege is waived when strangers, not interpreters, are privy to a conversation between a client and the attorney.

I also disliked a client bringing her own cheering section to court when I argued a motion. Having a client bring four or five members of her tennis or bridge club with her is disconcerting and unsettling to both attorney and occasionally to judges, who wonder just who these people are. Men do not do this. Women sometimes do. I suggest you don't.

I also suggest that perhaps it's a good idea to leave Daddy at home. Of course, if Daddy is funding your legal action and wants to be present, there's not much you can do. Be assured, your father may then have definite ideas as to how he wishes your case to proceed and will be annoyingly intrusive. After all, he paid for your retainer and may undoubtedly, as a result, feel he should have input. Ideally, I would advise you to get your money from another source, but

if you're not working, then he may be the only bank in town —
so you and your attorney must put up with it.

Don't telephone your attorney at home unless it's
completely necessary and some dire change of circumstances
makes communication mandatory. An example could be that
your child has not been delivered back from an access visit
and you fear your spouse is in the process of leaving the
country. This does not mean that he or she is a few minutes
late on delivering the children. Incidentally, to prevent this
happening, it is sometimes necessary to obtain a court order,
which you will lodge with the Department of Transport, the
Passport Department and various airlines. That would be one
of the emergencies upon which immediate communication
could be based. Another might be an impending homicide but
that would be best dealt with by phoning the police!

Telephoning your attorney for petty reasons, either at
the office or certainly at home, is irritating for him or her and
expensive for you. Most attorneys charge for their time and
lengthy telephone conversations are docketed and expensed to
the client. For some time, I did not charge for telephone calls,
but then I started. Lengthy telephone calls, and by that I mean
any telephone calls longer than a few minutes, should be paid
for by the client. Many attorneys have legal clerks who speak
to the clients and then pass the information on to the attorney.
If the attorney then feels that the matter is an urgent one, in all
probability he will telephone you. Believe me, bringing a child
home ten minutes late or with soiled clothes, are not urgent
matters.

An occasional attorney, including me, will give a client
their home number. Some of us have very much regretted
doing it. If you are out of the country a great deal or your
spouse has been flaunting court orders and the police are
involved, for example when you go to pick up your child for
the weekend, you may want to contact your attorney, who will
bring any law enforcement officer present up to date on the
status of what is going on.

If your attorney does give you his or her phone number, do not under any circumstances abuse it. Do not telephone your attorney after eight at night, unless you have been specifically told to do so. Ask yourself, as rationally as you can, if the matter can wait until the next day and you can telephone the office. If the answer is yes, don't telephone.

Some clients are absolute geniuses when it comes to organizing and producing back up material for their case. If you can bring in a well-organized binder of copies of your IRA'S, income tax returns, bank applications for credit, mortgage statements, details of all loans and any recent appraisals of properties and/or businesses, you will save your attorney time and yourself money.

Some attorneys tell their clients to get every scrap of paper available, including anything their husbands may have in their desk or filing cabinet. The buzzword of the day is full financial disclosure and your spouse is compelled to produce proof of his worth. Despite this, some of them don't and life is much easier if you already have the documentation. Your attorney would be happy to make copies of all relevant documents and the originals can then be returned.

This often makes everyone very cross, especially your spouse, who quite justifiably believes you are snooping. It also leads to the ludicrous position of having a demand for financial disclosure from opposing counsel, when they already have copies in the file of most of the disclosure they are demanding.

I remember writing opposing counsel at one point informing him he was already aware of most of the documentation he was demanding as his client, no doubt following his instructions, had pilfered all my client's documents and had had them run off at his office. It did me no good and I still had to produce them a second time.

You do have to be honest with your attorney. He will be rightfully peeved with you if in the middle of a discovery, or worse, a trial, some documentation is revealed to show that you have more assets than you have produced on your property statements.

On the other hand, if your mother or sister is holding assets for you in their name and you are adamant that you do not wish your spouse to find out about it, and are willing to take a chance that the information will not be disclosed, then it may be best not to confide this to your attorney. It puts him or her in an awkward position where he is swearing to a document he knows to be false, although in the United States attorneys do not swear or attest to the truth of documents they prepare and file— only the client does. Attorneys, on occasion, stick their necks out for their clients, but there is a limit. Remember, if you are caught hiding your assets in this way, nothing you swear to thereafter will be believed and if this undisclosed money surfaces by means of tracing you may be facing a large award of costs against you. Think about it.

One attorney I know deliberately backdated a financial statement, in which his client showed an income that was some twenty thousand dollars less than it was the month after he had received a large increase in salary. This is underhanded stuff, especially as we were arguing the case the next week in court and the client of opposing counsel was deliberately misrepresenting his income so he would not have to pay increased support according to Child Support Guidelines.

The fact that my colleague did this surprised me, as I had known him for years to be pleasant and straightforward. I would, however, never again accept his representations at face value. It was upsetting to think he would have gotten away with this skullduggery if his client's cousin had not confided to the wife the details of his salary increase, which apparently was celebrated at a family dinner. These things do have a way of biting you in the ass, and to have an attorney conspire in this fashion is disappointing.

Critical as people may be in regard to attorneys, you do need them. When I attended a convention in San Francisco, I remember seeing the front page of a tabloid which stated, "The Sleazes are Coming," when discussing the oncoming law convention. Of course, there is the occasional sleaze and the occasional incompetent, but most attorneys wish to represent you fairly and well. They come to court prepared and they review your file before they see you, so you don't have to go over the same details time and again with them. They tell you quite candidly what to expect and what you are entitled to because they are secure in their knowledge of the law, and as such know what would be a fair result.

If your matter is heading for court, I sometimes feel it is wise to have an attorney well acquainted with the judges available and with a specific court's procedures. You may feel that you wish to retain an out of town attorney, probably from the nearest metropolitan area. That is, of course, your pre-rogative. But if there is a high flyer in your own town, one who goes to court regularly and hopefully has some social connections with the presiding judge, it may be prudent to consider retaining him or her.

On a few occasions, I traveled up north to argue several motions, as only that court had the jurisdiction to hear my client's matter. I felt awkward and uncomfortable. The other attorneys present, all local, were well aware of the presiding judge's idiosyncrasies and were able to predict the type of order he would give. I recall being rather surprised by some of the orders made, and although some were in favor of my client, I did feel that should additional appearances be necessary, I would retain a local attorney.

Judges, as I shall discuss, vary widely according to their individual propensities and some are laden with personal biases that make it quite dangerous to go before them and argue matters to the contrary. Your local attorneys will know these judges, will no doubt have mixed with them socially on occasion, and will have argued cases in front of them before. They know their thought processes and as such are one-up on a visiting attorney who knows nothing at all about the judge.

Naturally, a competent attorney who knows his material and the specific law behind the issue he is arguing should do well everywhere. A great deal, however, depends on the judge. I once had a criminal attorney say to me that his research was totally based on knowing who was sitting for each particular trial. I thought that was an interesting observation, but dismissed it. As years went by I reconsidered and was not so willing to dismiss the importance of the presiding judge. In fact, I came to the conclusion that a good or bad judge can make or break your case.

# Chapter 18
## The Trouble with Judges

He was huffing and puffing and full of hot air — and he knew very little. In fact, the joke among the members of the bar was that when he was appointed, he had to be told where to find the Courthouse. He had not, it was rumored, ever been inside a courtroom. In Canada, some appointments to the bench are politically motivated. In the United States, many judges are elected. Both of these methods contain glaring defects.

On occasion, politically endorsed appointments result in appointing judges who are quite ignorant of the law and temperamentally unsuited to act as judges, who ideally should be appointed based on merit. On the other hand, if judges are elected, then all too often there will be a bias in favor of those who helped them achieve their position. Neither of these methods of appointment is ideal and in many instances there are problems.

The judge in question had been very helpful in working for the current political party in power and his appointment appeared to be based on the result of his efforts. His practice was restricted to real estate and little else — and he did no litigation. He was uniquely unqualified to sit in judgment of anyone.

Unfortunately, he was appointed to hear a very difficult trial, where I represented one of a warring couple with considerable assets to equalize. There were assessments, difficult legal concepts of trusts, third party claims and at least a dozen witnesses, some well-known to His Honor. This, in itself, should have been a reason for him to disqualify himself.

The trial was a disaster. His conduct was rude and inappropriate and because of his abysmal grasp of law and facts, he had short-tempered outbursts. He and opposing counsel knew each other well, as they both supported the same political party. This friendship was obvious from his rulings.

By the time the trial was over, it became obvious that His Honor had no idea what to do. Months and months passed and there was no judgment.

My client, an excitable woman at the best of times, went berserk. Frantic, based upon what she observed to be the judge's bizarre conduct, she sold the matrimonial home, which opposing counsel had overlooked putting a non-depletion order against. It was a stupid thing to do and it ended up with all of us being sued, me, my secretary, my law partner and everyone remotely connected with the action.

Sure enough, approximately a year after the trial, His Honor came out with his judgment. It was incomprehensible. It was questionable as to whether he had read the written submissions given by either counsel. He found fraud on behalf of the husband but did nothing about it. It was a terrible judgment: ill-reasoned, bizarre, and definitely appealable.

There was one problem, the Court of Appeal, incensed by my client's selling of the home, demanded a large sum of money be paid into court as a condition of proceeding with the appeal; although the Court of Appeal Judge ruled that there were some *appealable aspects* to the judgment.

The money was not available, so the appeal did not proceed. The matter went on and on at the lower court level, in fact, it was still going on some ten years later. It has caused no end of grief for everyone involved and my client blamed His Honor for ruining her life — which he probably did — at least ten years of it!

Luckily, this is not typical. More often than not, most judges, if they are intelligent, have had some experience in litigation and are capable of reading the law, turn out to be competent and give well-reasoned judgments.

There is one glaring problem, however, which is a real impediment to the entire system and which results in inappropriate results that often lead to appeals and unnecessary expense to litigants.

Most judges were attorneys prior to their appointment and had special knowledge in the fields of law which were the focus of their practices — personal injury, divorce, real estate and/or criminal law.

Within their specialties, they were quite competent and expert in that area of law. Once they are appointed to judgeships, however, they must become proficient in all other areas of the law so they will be competent enough to sit in on a divorce trial, or possibly a murder trial complete with jury.

This means, of course, that when you get one of these former criminal attorneys sitting on your divorce case, they really have little idea of what they are doing. I have had some extremely well meaning judges inform me that I knew much more about matrimonial law than they did.

They were quite right — I did know much more. The fact is that they knew very little. They were excellent handling their criminal cases or matters involving whatever other areas of the law which were the focus of their practices and as judges they should have been assigned to cases involving their specific area of expertise. Unfortunately, as a practical matter the administration could argue that it would be impossible to accomplish that, although I don't see why.

I once mentioned this to a judge, who had been an extremely competent divorce attorney and a friend of mine. I heard she was sitting on a case that involved a double murder. I politely suggested, that in all probability, she might be finding it a tad demanding; and perhaps everyone would be better served to have a former criminal attorney presiding over the case.

"Oh, no," she informed me, "I'd be bored to death if I just sat on matrimonial cases."

Bored, indeed — what nerve! Judges are paid quite handsomely. You'd think they would want to preside over matters where they could apply their expertise to insure a just result.

I had the misfortune of attempting to pursue a custody action before a judge who had spent his entire professional life prosecuting criminal cases. It was painful beyond belief. Every aspect of the law had to be pointed out to him. The case took four times as long as it normally would have and the only time he showed the slightest interest in the evidence was when it appeared that the father had been indulging in criminal conduct. He deemed it to be irrelevant. Of course, he should not have been sitting. He should have been sitting on criminal cases where he would have been perfectly well qualified.

As far as our judges taking the position that they would be bored if they were restricted to hearing cases in the areas of the law to which they had limited their practices, I can only say, "tough." If they had not been appointed, they would still be pursuing their practices with the same competency that they had always pursued them. They certainly do not show competence when sitting on the bench, faced with ruling upon an entirely different area of law from their original area of expertise. This sort of nonsense leads to unnecessary appeals and unfair judgments.

You do not really wish your attorney to have to do an appeal or to hire someone else to do it. These appeals are horrendously expensive, time consuming, and are often not heard for many months or even years. The Court of Appeal Judges would really prefer not to hear matrimonial appeals. As such, many appeals are dismissed as they do not wish to set a precedent and become inundated by a swarm of bitter matrimonial litigants.

Besides, it is necessary to show that the judge is clearly wrong in law to succeed on an appeal. One judge, full of bias and limitations, has been appealed time and time again and the appeals have been successful. Sometimes, however, the litigants are sent back for a new trial, incurring more expense and more aggravation. This particular judge should not have been appointed in the first place, as she did not have an adequate background. She has her little biases, or should I say big biases, and rides her particular hobby horse over any sensible interpretation of facts and law.

Of course, once these judges are appointed, there is really little one can do. They impose years of suffering on litigants. This may be one good reason why many clients are now going the route of mediation, or even binding arbitration, where you can pick your mediator or arbitrator, knowing that he is an expert in the area, and that he will at least attempt to be impartial and fair and will impact the law on your particular problem.

Of course, quite often, everybody gets it right and some painstaking and diligent individual is appointed who is a pleasure to go in front of and who you can be assured will give your case impartial and legally competent attention.

Interestingly enough, these superb judges, are not infected with that insidious disease that prevails among certain members of the judiciary and is called by those of us who have served at the bar *judge-itis* as opposed to judicious. These particular judges feel, upon their appointments, that they have been anointed by the Divine Right of Kings and thereafter sweep around full of self-importance and pomposity, super sensitive to anything they may perceive to be undermining their judicial authority in the courtroom.

Your attorney can only bow and defer and wish by all that's holy that he or she was elsewhere. Luckily, most judges retain their humanity and can sit on the bench without making all and sundry feel like unrestrained maggots.

Just what does all this mean to you? The truth is, you don't want a bad tempered, incompetent and biased judge to hear your case. You can also do without a judge seriously affected with *judge-itis,* as he will make everyone nervous, including you as a witness; and few attorneys will be able to carry out a thorough job on your behalf. But what should you do if your judge turns out to be the judge from hell, who has been appointed to hear your motion — or worse, your trial?

Your attorney will doubtless whisper, "Bad news for you, Mr. Justice Vicious has been appointed to hear your case." If it's motions court then your attorney may ask for an adjournment.

There's always some reason to obtain an adjournment. Either it is vitally important that a reply be made to the latest affidavit which may have been short served on you, or there wasn't a chance to cross-examine on this particular affidavit which is vitally important. Or there is some vital piece of information or financial disclosure missing. Or your attorney should be in another court, although this sometimes does not go over well as every judge wishes to feel that his court is most important.

Some judges hate to give adjournments, especially when they have read the material, and you cannot blame them. Quite often, the judge who you wish to get away from, however, most likely has not read the material. If he were the type who did, you would probably wish to stick with him.

Of course, the advice I am disclosing here is inside information and your attorney may not admit that he is attempting to get away from a particular judge. But you must understand that sometimes your attorney will wish to do this.

I once had an attorney say to me, "It is professional negligence, if one is representing a man, to appear before Madam Justice Dagger Tongue."

Of course, it is even worse, when you are facing a serious trial, for which you have been preparing for months, and find that the judge who has been appointed to hear your case is well known for his perverse decisions and was a former well-known criminal attorney. Besides, he has a sexist bias, having experienced two unfortunate divorces himself and looks less than kindly at female litigants.

The problem is, if you do not go ahead, your case could be struck from the list and you may have to wait several more months. This can be serious in an atmosphere of rapidly depreciating assets or in a child custody case, where the present custody arrangement is proving to be disruptive and upsetting. It's up to your attorney as to what decision he will make.

You are not supposed to pick your judges. It's the luck of the draw. In fact, I was once or twice reprimanded for attempting to pick my judge. If, however, your attorney is convinced that the judge appointed to hear your case is absolutely the wrong judge and you can be assured of an appalling result, then you might notice a numbing feeling in your left arm which might necessitate a trip to the hospital on an emergency basis, or a debilitating case of influenza which, of course, must be attested to by a doctor's report.

All of these ailments pose difficulties and I am certainly not recommending them but they have been known to occur!

Of course, one answer is not to appear at all and your attorney will appear before the judge in question informing him that you have taken ill and cannot possibly attend the trial. This should be attested to by a medical report.

Few judges will demand a Michael Jackson scene in which you appear in your pajamas, and possibly you might get your adjournment. But if your reason for it is not good enough, then there may be an order for costs against you to cover the preparation of opposing counsel. This could be a quite nasty situation and one which, hopefully, you will not have to face.

Fortunately, most of the examples of judges you do not wish to appear in front of are rare and these judges are well known, so at times can be avoided before your actual court date. If, however, you do have the misfortune of getting one of the rare deplorable breed, then your best bet is to settle the matter before commencing your trial.

There is nothing like negotiating just outside the courtroom door. Everyone is nervous, as very few people enjoy getting into the witness box, getting sworn in and giving evidence, upon which they are cross-examined, sometimes vigorously. As a result, many things are settled at that point, and if you have the misfortune of having a judge who you do not wish to hear your case, this is the time to do it.

You could even ask this particular judge whether he will hear a pre-trial, as you have almost settled things. If he agrees, he cannot then continue to hear the case as he has already indicated his bias toward the various issues.

Hopefully, things will not have progressed to this extent. Most often, things are settled prior to trial and both sides give a little and feel that the end result is unfair, which means it most likely is not.

Custody actions are most difficult to settle, but if you are willing to concede to that joint custody badge and to have a flexible parenting plan, it is surprising how far you can go.

Difficult property questions can sometimes be settled by merely using a mid-point between the opposing appraisals. There are multitudes of ways that matters can be settled.

I have heard clients say, "I hate to settle after all the work we've done."

They aren't really thinking. The reason we can settle is *because* of the work we've done. Being prepared means you can go ahead.

When my colleague hit the ski slopes all weekend and arrived at court Monday morning to start a trial, he knew he had to settle. Being prepared gives you confidence and means that if you don't settle you can go ahead and know that you are at the top of your game.

Get an attorney who prepares and prepares you.

# APPENDIX
## Family Law

Many books have been written about divorce and property law which discuss precedents, analyze the various cases and fine-tune statutory interpretation. These books were written for attorneys and lawyers. They are written in the legal jargon taught in law schools, which quite often confuses and befuddles the average person.

When you hire an attorney and pay the big dollars for his or her hourly rate, one of the reasons is his or her ability to understand and interpret a considerable body of law which has come down from the various statutes covering your rights and obligations.

This brief outline of some of the basics of family law is to assist you in the simplest way possible to understand what occurs and what you can expect when you end your relationship. It is not all-encompassing. It merely attempts to focus on some of the more relevant aspects of family law and it also attempts to answer some of the questions I have been asked by numerous individuals who have consulted me since my retirement.

Remember, the law is constantly changing. What is the law today, may not be the law when you read this book or in many months or years from now. Your attorney will hopefully keep you informed of current changes in the law relating to your case.

## The Importance of Motions

The law is constantly changing and interpretations of the law vary with different judges, especially when certain interpretations are termed *discretionary*. When a statute gives a judge discretion, he is free to use his own interpretation of the statute, although he should always be bound by its basic premise. Most judges rely on previously decided case law and are bound by findings of the Court of Appeal, which is bound by the Supreme Court.

The judge hearing your application or motion, which is a court appearance that often occurs before a trial, will hear your attorney present your side of the case based on your sworn affidavit and financial disclosure and he will apply the current law as given to him by your attorney relating to the issues in contention.

Some courts are now insisting on having a case conference before a motion or application is brought. This is good, because it sometimes results in an agreement between the parties so that further court appearances may not be necessary, although the delay may cause frustration. It does, at least, clarify issues.

Remember, a case conference may be dispensed with if your motion is believed to be an emergency. The good thing about a case conference is that you can get the opinion of one judge before you launch further into litigation.

The motions relating to decisions which are valid and enforceable until a final trial are of great importance. They can decide such things as interim custody and access, exclusive possession or a sale of the family home, spousal and child support and restraining and non-depletion orders, in other words, orders preventing either the husband or wife from cleaning out bank accounts or transferring money to close relatives. Some of these orders, although they are not final, may very well be rubber stamped in your final judgment by a trial Judge.

Because of the importance of these motions, it is vital that you acquire an attorney who can present him or herself well in court and who can prepare material which he or she may use to present your case in as impressive a way as possible. Many cases are finally decided as the result of orders made following the hearing of these motions.

## Service of Documents

Ignoring a divorce petition or a motion, which sets a court date, can be fatal to your action. I have known clients, invariably men, who toss their papers in a corner and ignore them, or worse, a client who actually ate the first few pages of a motion in front of the process server!

It is completely necessary that you read all the documentation, see if a motion or application has been made and when it is to be heard, and if you do not have a attorney, appear yourself on that date, ask for an adjournment and seek legal counsel.

## The Importance of Attorneys

There is a saying that an individual who represents himself has a fool for a client. With only a few exceptions, I have seen most individuals who represent themselves go down in flames; but with attorneys' fees currently ascending to astronomical heights, many cannot afford legal services.

If the issues involved in the papers served upon you are important, then borrow money for a legal retainer from your parents or best friend. It is hazardous — I repeat, *hazardous* — for you to attempt to go it alone and believe that you can argue your case without benefit of legal counsel. If you do, you will be broadsided every time!

Do not ignore those letters that you get from your wife or husband's attorney attempting settlement. Although an occasional attorney will immediately start an action, probably because your estranged spouse has informed him that you are so unreasonable that recourse to the courts is an only answer, you may have a chance to attempt to negotiate a settlement before proceeding on this expensive and infuriating journey.

Many clients ignore these preliminary letters at their peril. If you and your spouse have few contentious issues and you have agreed on the basics of a separation agreement, then have your spouse's attorney draft the agreement on condition that you can then seek legal advice as to its contents and implications before signing. Better still, have your own attorney do the drafting. Your spouse's attorney cannot represent you. He or she does not have your interests at heart and you can quite often get any agreement set aside on the basis that you had no independent legal advice. This will prove to be far more expensive than obtaining your own attorney to thoroughly look over any agreement and advise you on it.

I once had a client who came to me and happily informed me that she and her husband had agreed that they would simply divide the house and their IRA'S and that he did not wish to make any claim against her pension.

I was delighted, as she had been a high-school teacher for some twenty-five years and her pension, if evaluated, would be large. I drew up the agreement according to her instructions, and naturally, refused to see her husband, writing a letter instructing him to seek an attorney for independent legal advice before signing.

Needless to say, this attorney insisted on an evaluation of this most valuable asset and when her estranged spouse learned that it was worth some four hundred and fifty thousand dollars, which would be shown on her side of the Community Property or Net Family Property Statement, the result was not nearly as favorable as she had hoped.

So much for cozy little agreements made between parties, although if you and your spouse can come to some basic agreement that you can both live with, it is certainly the least expensive and least stressful way to go.

To come to an agreement, however, you must know your rights. That is why legal advice is so important and why agreements can be put aside without it.

## Putting Aside Agreements

Agreements can be put aside if they are outrageously unfair or one party is taking serious advantage of the other because of superior financial or even mental superiority. This does not mean you can always get out of a bad deal on this premise if you are legally represented, but this premise, combined with lack of independent legal counsel, may indeed open a door.

*Undue influence* and *duress* are words used by the courts to get you out of an agreement. Undue influence is manipulation of one individual by another and is most often shown when outright lies and underhanded tactics are used. Duress is almost equal to holding a gun to the other spouse's head, but the courts will also look at financial duress. In other words, the victim may be on the verge of being foreclosed upon at the time of signing an agreement.

## Prenups

The courts dislike marriage contracts when presented to the other party on the eve of a marriage. The idea of postponing a wedding where some two hundred guests have been invited and all amenities arranged, would place sufficient pressure on a future wife to sign anything, rather than subject herself to the embarrassment of calling it all off.

One client came to me with a totally unfair agreement some five days before the marriage. The future husband was president of a well-known real estate company and worth millions. He had already been through a contested divorce and it was clearly set out that should the parties separate in the future, she was to get nothing at all.

At his request, she had discontinued her successful career and a comfortable future pension to devote herself to a life of golf and travel. Her lifestyle would be quite enough, she assured me and besides, she was confident of their future happiness.

I was not confident at all, however. I was especially dismayed at the lack of financial disclosure. I knew something of the gentleman's worth by reputation and the assets set out and attached to the agreement had an unrealistic value.

I refused to sign the certificate of independent legal advice, and she no doubt sought another attorney who would be more accommodating. Hopefully she is still enjoying a life of traveling and golfing, but if there is a future breakup, the late production of this agreement and the lack of candor on the part of the husband as to his true financial position could be used to set it aside.

Marriage contracts, also know as prenuptial agreements and separation agreements are contracts. They can be set aside in the same way as any other contract. If there is a fundamental mistake made in the contract, then the parties cannot be said to be of the same mind. Similarly, if one of the parties is in a substantial breach of the contract, he cannot then move to have it honored.

For example, a husband who refuses to honor clauses relating to wife and child support and then wishes to enforce a clause which provides for a sale of the matrimonial home, may be unsuccessful in his attempt to enforce that part of the agreement.

Gross unfairness, lack of honest financial disclosure and lack of independent legal advice are all criteria that could mean either your pre-nuptial or separation agreement could be put aside, if legally challenged. The reason I am emphasizing the importance of marriage contracts is that they are most definitely the easiest and cheapest way to resolve difficulties if your differences are not so overwhelming that they defy negotiation.

## Settlement Meetings & Mediation

Settlement meetings and mediations have now become the order of the day and the latter is quite often chosen to avoid the expense and the long wait for a trial. Besides, you can pick your mediator, but all too often you cannot pick your Judge. Also, remember, your attorney will accompany you to your Mediation Conference.

Most mediators are experts in the field and can substantially enlighten the parties as to their respective rights and obligations. Besides, you do not have to settle if your husband or wife takes an adamant and unreasonable position. You know your spouse — if he or she is bull headed, unreasonable and outraged by the marital breakup, then attempting mediation may just be a waste of time. Indeed, there are some individuals who are, and remain, so difficult that you may feel that going to court is the only answer.

Unfortunately, if your spouse has means, a trial may not end things and you may be served with a Notice of Appeal within thirty days. This means more atrocious legal fees, a long wait and a questionable ending, although more often than not, the trial judge's decision will not be disturbed; certainly not when it comes to a finding of fact. It may be disturbed, however, if your judge has made a legal error.

I have found, more often than not, that the Court of Appeal really does not wish to bother with matrimonial matters and unless the trial judge has made a blatant error in an area of law which needs definition, the Appeals Court will merely agree with the trial judge. If at all possible, you do not wish your case to go this far.

I actually had a client say to me in all seriousness, after seven years of legal wrangling with a husband who could only be called infuriating, that if she had it to do all over again she would have shot him.

"If I had," she told me, "I would have been out by now."

She half meant it!

### The Legal Circus

**W**hy some people want to keep a legal circus going on and on is something I'll never understand. During a twenty-one day trial, the husband litigated every possible issue, from joint custody to house furniture to the fate of certain money which he believed had mysteriously disappeared from joint bank accounts. As a result, he had to pay a portion of his wife's legal fees, together with his own, which were more than the total of all of his net family property. He was, nonetheless, not dissuaded from continuing his battle.

He kept filing motions to drag his wife to court. As she was a sensible woman, she did not wish to pay any more legal fees so she represented herself. There were, she informed me, when she phoned to keep me abreast of each new horror, sixty court appearances.

The judge, a reasonable and fair individual — the same judge who had sat through the trial — let it go on and on, probably wishing to circumvent an appeal. Finally, my client's job appeared to be in jeopardy. This was one of the rare cases in which I believed a judge to be much too patient, albeit well meaning.

Another couple, a dentist and his wife, went the same route. Both self-represented after exhausting their money and attorneys, they haunted the halls of the Supreme Court in Toronto for months on end. In fact, the husband brought his dentistry practice to an end so that he could concentrate exclusively on his self-promoted litigation. It did not end well, I am told.

These things never do.

I often wonder what is behind this destructive urge to litigate against all rational odds so that money, which could be used so much more constructively, ends up going to attorneys in these litigious marathons.

One of my favorite clients, who I knew as well as any brother, had a case that lasted for some nine years. His wife retained a large downtown law firm and proceeded to exhaust the entire matrimonial department, who kept passing her on to every new reluctant junior counsel. She was determined to prove that her husband was worth millions and had assured her attorneys of this fact.

His business, which catered to the public, was assessed by our valuator as being worth next to nothing because of the huge debts involving its purchase and subsequent renovations. Apparently, she could not grasp the notion that they were not living on the profits of this business, but on debts run up on a monthly basis.

Unfortunately, she convinced three successive attorneys from the same firm that there was indeed a mountain of money ripe for the plucking and she finally owed them so much money — well over one hundred thousand dollars — that they refused to even entertain sensible offers of settlement; they did not wish to settle until their legal fees were paid. The husband's net worth was much less than the legal fees.

The trial was a disaster for the wife. They sent the most junior member of the matrimonial department—I suspect the only attorney who could be cajoled into attending. She knew next to nothing about the file, which consisted of some twenty boxes of documentation. This couple had enjoyed an exceptionally hot sexual life prior to separation and kept seeing each other periodically throughout the nine years. I sometimes wonder whether individuals who pursue litigation to this extent really want to keep a connection with the other party, regardless of how toxic it may be at times.

From a practical point of view, if you owe your attorney that much money, he will try to get it back from the spoils of litigation and it will become increasingly more difficult to settle anything.

In this particular case, the husband made a reasonable offer to settle which would have been more than appropriate except for the huge legal bill owed by the wife to the law firm in question. Indeed, at one point in the middle of this nine-year marathon, the parties, no doubt after a session of lovemaking, decided on a settlement.

A member of the firm, who had been appointed to a judgeship a few months later, went to the wife's home and talked her out of it. In other words, the firm simply was unwilling to absorb the loss of that much in legal fees and if they were even paid one-half of what they were owed, the wife's share of the settlement would be zero.

Nobody benefited from any of this, as my client could not collect the costs awarded to him against the wife. In fact, he felt so sorry for her that he gave her twenty thousand dollars.

What a waste of time and money!

## Evaluating Assets & Determining the Separation Date

Some clients have a simplistic or a totally wrong view of what happens after a breakup. I have had clients tell me that they don't want their spouse's pension or business, as if that meant literally going in with an axe and chopping up business and pension equally and taking their share as of the time of the breakup.

Unless you are a government employee who has a special scheme, meaning that a pension can be divided within the plan or you actually own shares of a spouse's company, this is simply not the way it's done. What happens is that each spouse's property is evaluated and the spouse who has less than his or her equal share gets an amount to equal things up — which can be satisfied by a money payout or a property transfer.

For example, a pension is evaluated by a pension evaluator, who will take into consideration the value of the pension at the time of marriage and the increase in value from that date forward. Appropriate discounts are made for projected taxes at the time the pension is to be received.

The date of your retirement makes a difference to the value of your pension. The earlier you intend to retire, the more valuable your pension. It's surprising how many individuals intend to work forever when it comes to evaluating their pension.

Where a business is concerned, much depends upon whether the spouse is a majority or minority shareholder and if it is a private or public company. The value of the spouse's shares in a private company should be professionally evaluated. This can be an expensive proposition, but it is well worth the effort. Then the value of the Community Property can more accurately be determined to include both the value of the spouses shares of the company and the worth of the pension.

The value of each spouse's net family property or Community Property is calculated as of the date of separation. This in itself can be a focus of argument. Sometimes a couple discusses separation and yet continues to live under the same roof, often for the sake of the children. At times, they simply have no other place to reside and the money for a future home is tied up in the present matrimonial property. If you do not physically separate from your spouse, a court may very well find that you are still continuing to live together and order you to divide your community property at the time of actual physical separation or at the time of trial.

Clients often believe that they are physically separated when they stop having sex. This is not so. The courts are well aware that some individuals live together without having any sex at all. To find your date of separation, the court looks at a number of things including whether the wife, if she does not work outside the home, prepares meals for the other spouse and does his laundry.

Most women say to me indignantly, "Of course he eats with the children. What am I supposed to do, tell him to watch the rest of us eat?"

In addition, the court will consider whether the parties continue to attend social functions together. Since children's marriages, teachers' appointments, children's school concerts and the weddings of mutual friends are often mutually attended, one or the other spouse could very well argue that they were not separated at all and that the date of establishing their Net Family Property or Community Property did not arrive until the divorce petition was served.

This can be quite important if one of the spouse's assets

is increasing rapidly because of a rapidly ascending stock market.

In one of my court cases, the husband's stock portfolio dropped drastically immediately after the separation, but at the date of separation it was quite impressive. The trial judge felt that this was not a case where it would be unfair for the wife to share in the higher value. Naturally, the furious husband fought it tooth and nail, accusing the wife of timing the separation according to the vacillations of the stock market. If true, that could have landed her a top job with a Wall Street Brokerage!

Legally, the courts speak of a *triggering event*, which is the date that the spouses separate and there is no reasonable prospect that they will live together again. If you believe that your spouse has an asset which is solid in value at the date which you choose to separate, by all means see your attorney and have a letter drafted clearly establishing that even though you are still living under the same roof, you have ceased cohabiting as husband and wife and wish to make full financial disclosure to affect an equal division of property. If feasible, your attorney could apply to the court for an early division of property. This is only done on rare occasions, as usually the marital home is still being occupied.

I wrote such a letter for a client who was a stock promoter. When no reply was received, he had me issue a divorce petition to document the low price of his corporate shares at a given time. Unfortunately, the shares did not go up in value as he had predicted. In fact, they went down, so it was all for naught. He instructed me to withdraw the petition. It all goes to show how important the date of separation can be.

The *triggering event* can be as traumatic and definite as the husband coming home unexpectedly and finding the wife in bed with the pool man, which did happen to one of my clients or the husband telling his wife that the marriage is finished.

Incidentally, gentlemen, if you wish to terminate the marriage in that manner, it is unwise to inform your wife that you have not loved her for years or worse still, that you never ever loved her. I don't know why men do this, but somehow they believe that this will ease the wife's pain. Of course, it doesn't. It only makes it worse, especially when she finds out that you've been taking your secretary with you on all those out of town business trips that have become so frequent.

All right, you want to break up but why be so nasty about it? And cool it with the secretary, at least until you have something agreed upon with your wife. Trying to negotiate with a jealous wife is like trying to disentangle a boa constrictor from your neck.

At lot of my clients tell their wives that they are moving out to, "get their heads together." I suppose that is as good as anything. I usually advise husbands not to move out at all until a settlement is reached.

There are times, however, when there is a real chance that things will get physical and then I suggest that the husbands run like rabbits. Even holding your wife's arm so that she doesn't claw your eyes out could be twisted into a spousal assault and you could be led away in cuffs.

## Estimating The Net Value of Your Family Property

Upon breaking up, you have a right to an equal share of what is known as Community Property or to have your property divided in a *fair and equitable manner* according to *Equitable Distribution laws* depending upon the State in which you reside. Community Property is generally defined as all property acquired during the marriage, less debts with the exceptions of gifts and inheritances. Separate property, which does not go into the communal pot, is generally defined as all property acquired before marriage, after separation or property received by gift or inheritance.

There are no set rules under the Equitable Distribution laws and the court looks at a variety of factors including the relative earning contributions of spouses and the value of one spouse staying home and raising children. The non-Community Property states, which greatly outnumber the community property states, examine more carefully your unique situation and rely more strongly on the discretion of the presiding judge.

What does your family property consist of? Just about everything: your bank accounts, IRA'S, pensions, corporate shares, cars, furniture, absolutely anything you can think of that's in your name. Of course, anything that is in both names merely shows a fifty percent share on each side of your net family property. Most matrimonial homes are in both names, so such would be the case. You would be shown as joint owners of the appraised value.

Deductible from your Net Family property value would be your debts, which most likely are credit card and bank loans, but occasionally spouses attempt to deduct gambling debts and those related to escort services.

The individual who attempted the latter was not my client, but actually had the nerve to attempt to do this during a trial. Needless to say there are certain debts which will not be allowed by the courts, but most debts are.

## Before Marriage Deduction

At the date of marriage, most people, especially if it is a first marriage, have little to deduct. A five-year-old car with two hundred thousand miles on it and a diamond you'd need a microscope to see dangling on a gold chain, purchased in the Bahamas, are certainly not worth bringing into play, although I have known the occasional client who has insisted upon it. There are a few concerns involved in your before marriage property, the value of which, if proven, can be deducted.

For one thing, you have to prove that the property on which the deduction is based was really in existence. Secondly, you have to prove its value at that time.

What kind of nut really keeps proof of things like that? The kind of nut you wouldn't want to marry, that's who!

"But she'll admit that I had thirty thousand dollars in a bank account," insisted my client's husband. "We used it for the honeymoon."

Of course, he couldn't prove it. They had moved several times and she had to subsidize his assortment of businesses, which all went down in flames. Besides, she made three times his salary and had in reality supported the family for twenty years.

"I'll admit no such thing," snapped my client, "let him prove it."

He couldn't, but it set the tone for a very nasty and prolonged bout of litigation.

## **The Importance of Prenups**

The above example is what prenups are meant to avoid. A good prenup does not fit the criteria of Arnie Becker in L.A. Law who said, "I never saw a prenup I couldn't break."

A good prenup is one in which each party has their own attorney, has plenty of time to negotiate and is straightforward about the assets they wish to deduct. If you don't want to fit in under the Arnie Becker criteria, then present your prenup several months before the wedding and before any invitations are sent out. Make your prospective spouse see his or her own attorney and have a certificate of independent legal advice signed. Be scrupulously honest in giving your actual net worth.

Some of my clients have quite cheerfully confided in me after the prenup had been negotiated and executed by both parties and hopefully placed in a safety deposit box, never to be seen again unless a marriage break up occurs, that they had not been entirely candid about the value of his or her property. In fact, they were worth three times more than they had disclosed.

How stupid can you get? For one thing, if the marriage breaks up, you wish to have the advantage of deducting *all* your net worth as of the date of marriage.

That was the whole idea behind the prenup in any event, wasn't it? So why in the world would anyone underplay their wealth? The answer, "I don't want her to know how much I'm really worth," doesn't cut it. The courts demand full financial disclosure and the utmost good faith in negotiating these contracts to an even greater degree, believe it or not, than the separation agreement. They will put your contract aside in a heartbeat if it can be shown that you were less than candid.

The fairer an agreement appears to be, the less likely it is that it will be put aside. Even if you do not have a prenup, the courts will permit you to deduct what was yours on the date of the marriage, provided you can prove your deductions. Your prenup makes it easier because everything has already been itemized and agreed to.

Most successful prenups stick pretty much to the structure of the law of the state where you reside. For example, in California, there is usually an equal sharing of assets once a marriage takes place. Most pre-nups follow this, but exclude certain assets and properties.

Many women freak out when presented with a prenup. They scream that it's not romantic and their future spouse doesn't really love them or he would not be insisting on such a thing. Most of my male clients inform the hysterical one—if they are a partner or a shareholder in a private company— that their family or partners insist that their corporate or business assets be exempt from being part of their Community Property or of being involved in any Equitable Distribution. Their business associates simply do not want the disruption of the company in the case of death or separation.

This is a sensible explanation, and should suffice. If she still refuses to sign and pouts and fusses, I advise you to reassess your situation. I know you love her, and she's dynamite in the sack, but do you really want to take on a life partner with mind like a cash register? If your company is poised to grow by leaps and bounds and she is not to share in any part of its growth, if there is a break up, she can usually benefit from spousal support unless you wish that waived as well. I suggest that this could be seen as somewhat harsh, or as the courts say, *draconian*.

In other words, if you're making five hundred thousand dollars per year, it's surprising how generous the courts will be to her and those three great kids you intend to have. If the marriage lasts for a decent amount of time and she has experienced a financial disadvantage by withdrawing from her employment in order to parent your kids, the court expects you to take care of her. Considering age and length of marriage, this caring could go on for many, many years. In fact, if your marriage lasts long enough, it could be a lifetime obligation.

After twenty years of marriage, no court is going to allow you to live in a penthouse with your new lovely, while your ex-wife grubs along in a second rate townhouse and the kids attend an around the corner school where two recent shootings occurred. An occasional client has wished he or she had an irrevocable waiver of spousal support should a break up occur. Unless you are both highly paid professionals, this waiver may not be accepted by the courts, unless her assets are such that support may not be necessary.

## **Lump Sum Payout**

Some of my clients who were going through a break up of a first marriage, and who were successful professional men, gave their wives a lump sum, which in reality consisted of one-half of the matrimonial home, to get rid of spousal support. Writing that check on a monthly basis drives some men mad. Of course, they are also angry to have to forfeit one-half of the matrimonial home which, after all, is the only asset you can dispose of in Canada without paying the tax man some capital gains, unlike in the United States, where they deduct their mortgage interest and do pay capital gains on their homes.

Sometimes, it's a very good thing to forfeit that house and clearly set out that you are giving your wife a lump sum in place of ongoing spousal support. If she has a boyfriend, she'll jump at this offer immediately. Beware, however, of the lady who is not used to balancing her bankbook, and who blows that whole lump sum and then comes whimpering to the court to reinstate spousal support. What's even more horrible is, she may get a judge who feels sorry for her under the circumstances, puts the agreement aside and initiates monthly support. Nothing makes a guy madder than this. And do you blame him?

In their marriage contracts, two of my more wealthy clients specifically deducted some very valuable assets and also exempted certain assets from any future division. Both, however, wanted a specific clause built into the contract wherein their future wives would get an increased amount of family property, depending on how long the marriage lasted and the number of children. Their future brides agreed.

I admit I was a bit uneasy. Both clients had considerable assets and I was uncomfortable as to how these agreements would look to a judge hearing a divorce. I suggest it is very likely that he would attempt to compensate these women. Even if he did not put the agreements aside, they would probably benefit in some other way, probably by increased support, not touched upon in the agreement

As far as I know, both marriages are still continuing and all conditions as to the production of children have been fulfilled. I was informed that one of the wives works very actively in the business, but fortunately she's being paid a salary for her efforts. If not, this could be quite dangerous, as she could make a claim and be seen as a part owner by imposition of a trust. Life can be very complicated when you've got the big bucks, but it sure beats the alternative!

## **Inherited Money**

**O**ften a prenup will exclude not only company assets, but also inherited money which is in any event usually excluded through state legislation.

"But is it too late for all that? We didn't have a prenup and I just inherited all of my father's estate worth over a million dollars. Do I have to share?"

Suzanne L. Hillier

The good news is, no, you don't. This is even if you have no prenup whatsoever. Community Property States and Canadian Provinces allow you to keep your inherited money all for yourself. After all, if your dad or mom wanted their money to be shared with your spouse, they would have set this out in their will. They did not do so.

So to be doubly sure that you are the only one to benefit, and if you want to preserve this money for your exclusive use, regardless of how this may affect your spouse, who may very well resent it, may I suggest the following:

• Keep that money entirely in your name. Do not intermingle it with other funds. If you do, you may lose your exclusion.

• Do not pay off the mortgage on your matrimonial home with this money. If you do, it will be presumed by the court that you wished to benefit both you and your spouse and your exemption will be lost.

• Do not place this money in a joint account or pay off joint debts with it. If you do, it will be quite sensibly presumed that you meant to benefit your spouse and you will lose your exemption.

There is such a thing as tracing in Family Law and what you do with your inherited assets or gifts from Mom and Dad or Uncle Bill can be traced. I had a case where my client's husband lost his exemption, simply because he had placed the money in a jointly owned stock portfolio. Another client placed his money in a joint account before excluding it by depositing the funds into a bank account in his name. He lost the trace because of this.

My little blonde client, who was a cashier, had a husband with family money. He placed some two hundred thousand dollars of inherited money in a joint bank certificate. I thought we were home free and my client could have a hundred thousand dollars from her husband, who fought for every cent, which resulted in a six-day trial. The judge, however, let the husband deduct his one hundred thousand dollars as exempt (inherited) property, so that in the general

264

thrust of things, she really only benefited by fifty thousand dollars.

Judges do not like other individuals benefiting from inherited properties, but they do adhere to these strict tracing rules. So if you do have an inheritance, keep that money separate, even labeling it as *inherited funds* in your bank account. Remember, if you use it for family purposes, it could be argued that they are not your inherited funds but, in reality, family money.

I had a client who wished to deduct a diamond necklace from his Net Family Property, as he had gifted it to his wife from inherited funds. He would, of course, have one-half the benefit in any event, as she would have to show the jewelry as part of her net family property. We decided not to attempt it. Even if it could scrupulously be done, I thought it would look bad and, in any event, he had kept the rest of the money separate.

"Of course, I used my inheritance to pay off our mortgage and our debts," protested one of my clients. "What was I supposed to do, sit on my money when we were paying on a mortgage and a line of credit?"

"No," I replied, "Of course not. You're a nice guy and you were doing the decent thing. But that money is gone and you can't take it out of your little basket now we are dividing things up."

Suck it up, sweetie. Sometimes nice guys do finish last, but perhaps they sleep better at night!

## Your Pre-Separation Lifestyle

One of my clients protested, "But she never did a damn thing. If she wasn't getting her hair done, she was taking golf lessons and she ended up sleeping with the pro at the golf club. And here I was, working my butt off ten, twelve hours a day and sometimes weekends to give us all the goodies. Now she's getting half and I'm going to have to pay her to *re-establish herself* as you put it. She says she wants to go to university and she's never read a book in her life."

---

Suzanne L. Hillier

I didn't blame him for being mad. He's right. It's all very unfair. But the courts are not going to go into people's finances and working habits during a marriage. The way individuals wish to conduct their lives financially during the time they live together is their business. The courts are not going to waste hours of time listening to a meticulous rendering of how one person did everything and the other nothing. In fact, the courts presume that each person makes a vital contribution to the family unit in some way or another, and, as such, is entitled to one half of everything as of the date of separation.

A woman who withdraws from the workforce and remains at home, whether bringing up a family or playing bridge and golfing every afternoon is, the law usually states, seen to be economically disadvantaged by the marriage break-up. It is the duty of her former husband to pay her an amount which will allow her live in comfort, perhaps indefinitely. This is especially the case if the marriage has been long-standing and it would be impractical for her to attempt to re-establish herself.

The wife who has pursued her own career and who has been both a breadwinner and mother does not fare nearly as well. But whoever said that life was fair?

## Discretionary Rulings

I had a client whose wife worked for a large American-based technology company and had hundreds of thousands of dollars worth of shares as of the valuation date. She also had options, which turned out to be extremely valuable. My client had reasonable employment and had contributed to the matrimonial home, although not as much as the wife.

There was absolutely no financial bad faith, but the parties fought over everything and my client fell into a relationship with a co-worker shortly after the birth of the child of the marriage.

The new spouse was a gorgeous blond who was also a brilliant accountant. Unfortunately, I let her sit in as an

266

observer and financial expert throughout the trial. The judge, obviously disapproving, curled her mouth in contempt during all of my client's evidence and completely eliminated any equalization payment.

It was all grossly unfair and the case was appealed. Unfortunately, it was settled at a pre-trial at the Court of Appeal level, but I would like to think that the decision would have been reversed, had the appeal continued.

It all goes to show that you are, in reality, at the mercy of the judge. Unequal division is ultimately within the discretion of the judge hearing the case. In other words, get the wrong judge, who believes you are a real bastard for dumping your wife and a new baby for a beautiful blonde — and you're chopped liver!

## Kitchen Table Agreements

Courts are allowed to consider written agreements that are not formal domestic contracts, in other words they are not duly witnessed and afforded the amenities of contract law. I do not believe that these informal contracts can be relied upon and have had, what are known as *kitchen table contracts* put aside.

The wives usually complain that they have been induced or threatened to sign some paper, which they did not agree with, understand, or which was unfair in any event. In one case the couple had their children sign as witnesses.

The presiding judge was not impressed. If you and your wife really want an agreement to have some teeth, then get a neighbor to witness it or better yet, your accountant or financial advisor and then have it formalized by an attorney.

I know what you're saying — you don't want to involve an attorney because they are so expensive and they always cause additional problems. Maybe so, but how much are we talking about? Maybe it's worth it in the long run.

## Rotten Behavior

Although I did say that judges do not like poking into the private way you manage your finances during the time you are living together, they will look hard at your situation if your husband has spent twenty years of the marriage lying in a comatose state on the sofa with a gin bottle by his side, while you carried out two jobs, brought up the four children and were the exclusive mainstay of the family.

There have been cases like this and in that situation, the court was sufficiently shocked, believed the situation to be grossly unfair, and cut the husband off his equalization payment. Again, remember, this has to be really an extreme abdication of a spouse's responsibilities. Taking too many vacations, changing jobs too frequently, and earning much less than your spouse usually just doesn't cut it.

My client made ninety-five thousand dollars per year while her husband deliberately made twenty-five thousand dollars so that he could continue to collect a disability pension. She believed it despicable that they should share equally in the net family property and that he should obtain one-half of her quite generous government pension. I believed it was despicable as well, but nothing could be done.

One bright spot was the fact that a judge, hearing the husband's application for spousal support, refused to give him any. In gratifying bursts of sexism, I found many male judges just do not wish to give a husband spousal support, as they do not consider it to be *manly*.

This is not said up front, but that is the gist of the remarks made at court. This is unfair and I have been quite annoyed by it when I have represented men who have put their wives through nursing programs or university and then are adamantly denied spousal support, although they make only one-quarter of their newly educated wives' income.

The wives sometimes drop these guys as their new status has made them feel superior. Interestingly enough, female judges are much more inclined to benefit men than their male counterparts. Don't ask me why. Perhaps it's because they feel the need more than the men to at least look impartial and not biased in favor of their own sex.

Female judges are often better than the male Judges, as they try harder to understand the issues, and surprisingly, are more influenced by the law. Unfortunately, if you get the occasional bad one, they are total horrors, showing maddening bias and seizing on irrelevant trivia with an unworthy relish.

Luckily these are few and far between, but beware when one is sitting.

## Avoiding a Dubious Judge

If your attorney comes from the area where your case is being heard, he will have knowledge of the judge, either personally or by reputation. You can also get a strong inkling of the judge's thinking merely by sitting in the courtroom during a motions court day, especially if some of the cases are similar to yours.

Usually adjournments are addressed before the motion list proceeds, or your attorney's office has telephoned the day before so the judge will not bother to read the material. At times, an adjournment may be contested, but it is always prudent to attempt to obtain one if you have a judge whose thinking is well known and who is not predisposed in your favor.

Reasons for an adjournment could well be that your attorney states that he wishes to examine on an affidavit, that certain bits of financial disclosure have not been forthcoming or that your motion is so long that you will need to be given a special appointment.

Obviously, your attorney will not say, "Your Honor, we know you always rule in favor of women, as you quite obviously had a great relationship with your mother. As such, because I am representing Mr. Brown, I am going to try to see that someone less biased and more reasonable hears this case."

There was a judge who I loved to see when I represented a woman. He was generous to the extreme, so generous that he awarded my fabulously beautiful, blonde client huge monthly support on an interim motion, which I have explained, is a court appearance your attorney makes sometimes several months before a trial.

The matter settled within weeks.

Again, I do recall being present when the same judge gave one of his magnanimous awards against an individual of modest means, who cried out, "Do you want me to live in a f…ing tent?"

## Appealing a Bad Interim Order

Remember, it is usually a real waste of time and money to appeal an interim order as the Court of Appeal does not want to be bothered with such things and will merely tell you to wait until trial, which can be months or even years away. In the meanwhile, a precedent will have been set and your trial judge may not wish to vary it.

In any event, if the order is interim and not final, in Canada you have to get special leave to appeal. This leave is based on whether the matter is of public importance and there is other case law going against the ruling. Don't waste your time. It's better to stick it out under the same roof until the trial, if you have to, provided that you do not end up killing each other and damaging your children who will witness the animosity between you.

## The Importance of Following Interim Orders

I cannot emphasize too strongly how important it is for you to follow court orders after the date of the breakup.

My client's wife had inherited five acres of land. He had almost single handedly constructed a large bungalow on the property, pouring the foundation, working along with the construction workers, completing the roofing and painting entirely on his own. In fact, his efforts were so dedicated that he infuriated his wife, who took care of horses at a neighboring stable, and she assaulted him with a two by four lying by the semi-completed home.

Things went from bad to worse and the case eventually landed in court. The husband won all issues. The judge disbelieved all of the wife's witnesses and made a ruling that he was entitled to one-half the proceeds from the sale of the home. However, something happened within a month of separation.

There had been an application to the court for child custody and support. The result was that custody of the child, whose maternal grandparents seemed to be the surrogate parents in any event, was given to the wife and the sum of five hundred dollars per month was awarded as child support. My client, unfortunately, did not pay it for various reasons.

Interestingly, that amount would be in excess of that recommended by the current Child Support Guidelines, as he was not steadily employed and his income came from occasional carpentry work. After the breakup, he met and commenced living with a single mother and had another child.

The wife, obviously wishing to start anew, walked away from her horses and became a firefighter. Their relationship was acrimonious, to say the least. They fought over everything from her wish not to sell the home, but to proceed to court, to his wish to have access to his son.

At one point, he fell from a ladder and because of his back injury, did not work for several months. His new common-law wife detested wife number one and I suspected used her best efforts to see that he did not pay the child support, as ordered. Suffice it to say when we went to court, there were arrears of child support owing.

Ideally, an application would have been made to the court long before trial to vary my client's child support payments, but he did not bother to do so, partly because of lack of funds for legal fees, and partly because he insisted he would pay any arrears out of his one-half of the matrimonial home after a judgment.

As a result of his non-payment of child support, the judge ordered that although he was entitled to one-half of the home, it was not to be sold for a ten-year period. He verified the order as to child support and charged the husband's one-half of the home with any arrears that had accumulated and might accumulate in the future.

The husband went mad upon hearing the judgment. "There must be an appeal," he shouted. There was no way, he insisted, he could get on with his life if he had to wait for ten years for his equity from the home.

Not being paid for a trial sometimes causes attorneys to do strange things. Stupidly, I funded the appeal. The situation at Appeal Court was worse. He had still not paid any support pursuant to the court order, as he insisted he could not afford it.

Suffice it to say, the Court of Appeal awarded the wife the entire home, considering the husband's one-half equity to be lump sum child support. The entire situation was a horror for everyone, including me. There is nothing like not being paid to make you wonder why you ever became an attorney!

This case is a horrendous example of what happens when court orders are disobeyed between the date of separation and a trial. I cannot impress upon you too strongly the importance of conforming to child support or any other interim orders. Going into court when you owe child support, or when you have sold assets against a court order or have otherwise defied the court's authority, is like wearing a red sign on your forehead that says: "Finish me off."

My client should have begged or borrowed money to comply with that court order, regardless of how unfair he regarded the amount or how disabled he was because of his back injury—or he should have kept me aware of the situation so I could have attempted to vary the amount. Although his new spouse detested the old one, she should have tried to cough up the money to help him. Instead, I suspected she dissuaded him continually from even attempting to comply with the child support order.

Even borrowing the money is better than not complying with a court order. Being in contempt, sours the judge before you even start your case. He or she will then make an order taking into account the amount owed and will consider a lump sum to your spouse, especially if you are self-employed and your wages cannot be garnished.

Ignoring interim orders is one way for your wife or husband to get an unequal division of net family property and it is a really stupid thing to do, regardless of how unfair you believe the order to be.

Ignoring court orders is the kiss of death for any future trip before a judge. Besides, as well as making you look bad, there are multitudes of ways that money can eventually be collected, like seizing bank accounts, garnishing wages, even seizing passports and driver licenses in some States or Provinces until arrears are paid.

The lesson? Don't ignore those court orders. Respect for them can only hold you in good stead at your trial. Those who do ignore them do so at their peril.

## Those Kitchen Table Agreements (again!)

**I** have mentioned the kitchen table agreement, which I have had some luck in putting aside, especially if there has been a history of abuse or if there is unequal bargaining power, i.e., the husband is a CEO of a successful company and the wife did not complete high school. Usually, these written bits of paper and IOU's that the occasional spouse wishes the other to sign, carry little weight.

Ignore completely any spoken agreements made, such as when your wife has assured you throughout the marriage that she has no interest whatsoever in your business or your husband has informed you that he would never claim against the matrimonial home, which you inherited from your parents. Believe me, your wife will want to have your business appraised and will be after you for the cost of the appraisal, no less. She will demand that you include its value as part of your net family property. Similarly, the spouse who assured you that he would be making no claim toward your inherited matrimonial home will suddenly remember the fact that he put the recreation room in downstairs and renovated both kitchen and bathroom during his vacation.

Surely, his attorney will remind you, he would not have done that if he felt he had no right to the home.

In the province where I practiced law, the section of the Family Law Act relating to an unequal division of assets suggested that a court should consider a written agreement between the spouses that is not a domestic contract. This section, however, is far from satisfactory. While a court may indeed consider such a situation, they seldom act on it.

As originally stated, the above very limited overview is anything but all encompassing. It merely touches on certain areas which have been the focus of concern to many of my clients. These areas, hopefully, may also prove of interest to you.

Your attorney or lawyer will clarify legal difficulties relevant to your particular situation. Hopefully my information will, however, direct and help you in your search for answers.

# Author's Note

So what is your overall goal? If you are a man — to receive your fair amount of the net family property; to not have your business ruined, but to be able to get on with your life without feeling impoverished; to have the ability to pay the reasonable support agreed to, knowing that it can be varied should you experience a drastic change of circumstances.

If you are a woman — to get your fair share of net family property, knowing that your former spouse has honestly declared all his assets; to receive sufficient support for your re-establishment or if such is impossible, sufficient support to live out your life in an independent and comfortable way.

Then, if there are children involved, you want them happy and well-adjusted. You do not want them to hate their father or mother. This will scar them forever. Remember, once they are in their teens, their interest in both of you will be very much elsewhere.

Allowing your child love your estranged spouse is one of the best gifts you can ever give. If you deliberately undermine this, you have damaged your child forever, and believe me, it will come back to haunt you.

My hope is that this book will have proven to be of practical benefit. The prospect of ending a marriage is a daunting one; made even more so by the lack of knowledge the ordinary person has about the process. It has been my goal in writing this book, to guide you through some of the more obvious errors individuals make and some of the better choices, you, as reader, may make.

If this book has proven to be useful to you, then I am both grateful and happy. In life, we all wish to have a sense of accomplishment in one way or another. If, by reading this book, you have in some way been enlightened as to the legal process, and have made or will make better and more thoughtful choices than you would have otherwise made, that to me is a substantial reward.

In fact, if I have helped any of you, which has been my goal, it will mean that all those years of practicing law may have been worthwhile.

To any of you now contemplating, commencing, or going through a divorce, I can only wish you the very best and hope that in some small way my years of experience, and the experiences of my clients, will help guide you forward in the most positive way possible.

# Acknowledgements

**M**y gratitude to Mike Foley and Liz Joyce for their editing services. I must acknowledge Joan Scott, for her painstaking retyping and organizational skills, as well as Laura Moore for her interest and transcription of my work on this project. And, of course, Ron Sharrow, fellow attorney and author for his creative cover design, ingenuity and publishing knowledge which he so generously shared.

# About The Author

**Suzanne L. Hillier** is a graduate of McGill University and did post- graduate studies at Columbia University. She earned post-graduate degrees in English (MA) Law (LLB) from the University of Toronto. In addition to her certifications as a high school teacher and matrimonial mediator, she engaged in the practice of divorce law for over 30 years in partnership with her daughter, Ava, a personal injury lawyer, in Brampton, Ontario, Canada.

She was a highly regarded trial lawyer credited with several reported high court decisions.

Although currently retired, she retains her interest in matrimonial law, still attending seminars and maintaining relationships with past clients.

The mother of 3, the grandmother of 6, and the great grandmother of 2, she divides her time between Rancho Mirage, California and Caledon, Ontario.